FIGHTER PILOT

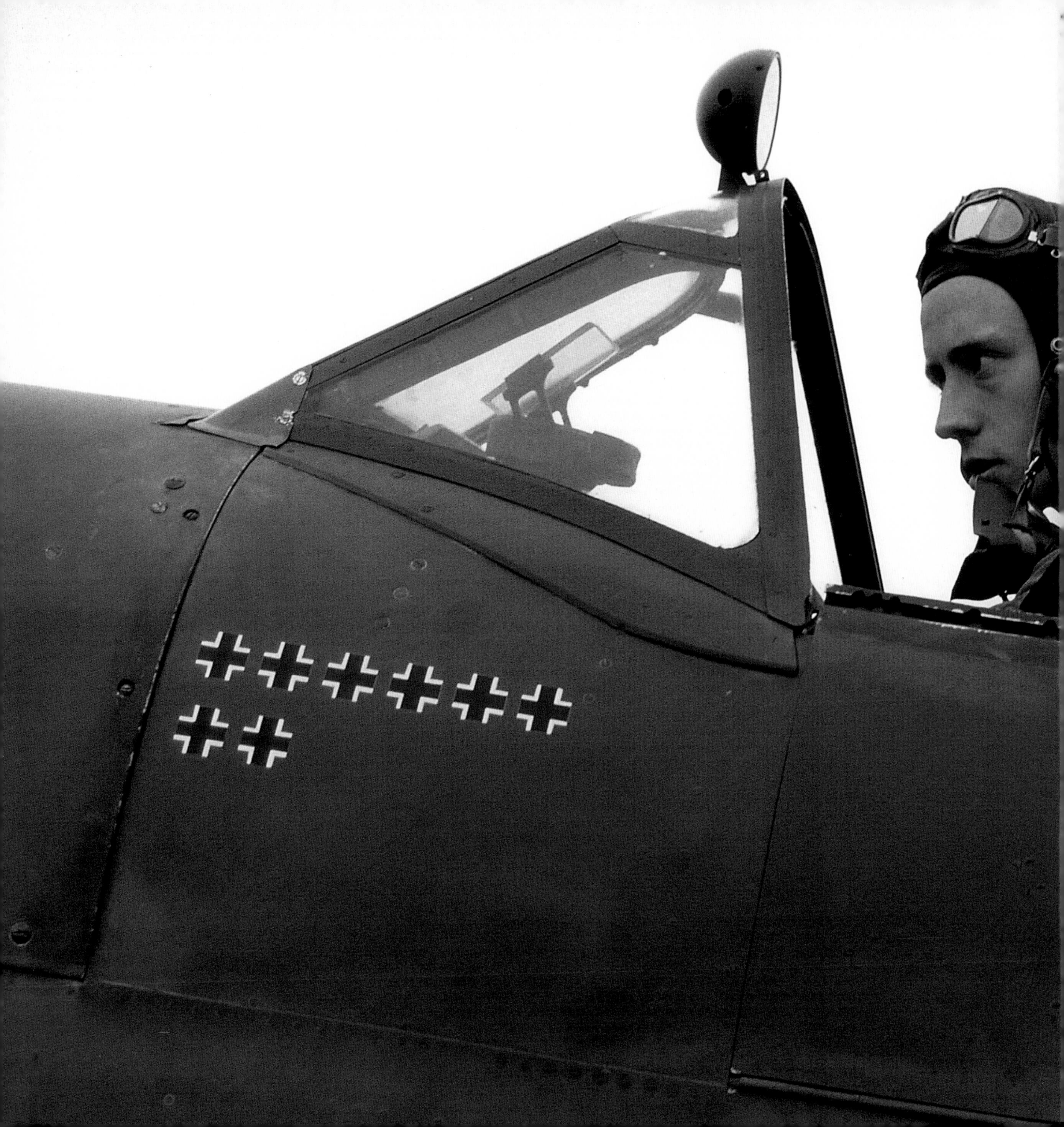

FIGHTER PILOT

A HISTORY AND A CELEBRATION

PHILIP KAPLAN

BARNES
&NOBLE
BOOKS
NEW YORK

This edition published by Barnes & Noble, Inc., by arrangement
with Aurum Press, London.

1999 Barnes & Noble Books

M 10 9 8 7 6 5 4 3 2 1

ISBN 0-7607-1397-9

Printed and bound in Singapore by Imago

CONTENTS

The fighter pilot is a figure unique in the long history of warfare: a man (or, nowadays, a woman) who fights single-handedly against an individual opponent and whose success or failure—life or death—depend almost entirely upon his own skills and wits. His only precursors (and they are probably mythological) are the heroes of Homeric Greece and the medieval knights of Arthurian legend.

It is hardly suprising, then, that the fighter pilot has developed his own ethos, has been enshrined by popular mythology and become the subject of hero-worship. The list begins with legendary airmen of World War I: the Frenchmen, Charles Nungesser and George Guynemeyer; the British Commonwealth's William Bishop, Albert Ball and Edward Mannock; the Americans, Edward Rickenbacker, Frank Luke and Raoul Lufbery; and the Germans, Ernst Udet, Oswald Böelcke and Manfred von Richthofen. It continues with the aces of World War II: J.E. Johnson and A.G. Malan of the British Commonwealth; Richard Bong, David McCampbell and Francis Gabreski of the United States; Günther Rall, Erich Hartmann and Adolf Galland of Germany; Hiroyoshi Nishizawa, Saburo Sakai and Tetsuzo Iwamoto of Japan; Ivan Kojedub, Lily Litvak and Alexander Pokryshkin of the Soviet Union; Stanislaw Skalski and Witold Urbanowicz of Poland; Josef Frantisek and Frantisek Perina of Czechoslovakia; and Marcel Albert and Pierre Clostermann of France. In the post-war years, further Americans have been added to the list: James Jabara, Joseph McConnell, Junior, and Manuel Fernandez in Korea; Steve Ritchie and Robin Olds in Vietnam; and Mark Fox, Rhory Draeger and Anthony Schiavi in the Gulf War.

Many characteristics distinguished these pilots from their earthbound comrades. To be effective, they needed exceptional marksmanship, superior eyesight, courage, decisiveness, cunning, raw aggression and daring, brains, nerve and stamina. But one thing was, and remains, more important than all the others put together: the fighter pilot must have desire. He must want to be in a fighter cockpit, facing an enemy in aerial combat. That, more than anything else, continues to be the fighter pilot's most important characteristic. Without that single-minded determination, a pilot may be a competent flyer of an airplane, but he will never be a true fighter pilot.

From the beginning, the fighter pilot has operated in a one-to-one relationship with a machine that has represented the pinnacle of technology and, like their pilots, the planes themselves have become legendary: Camel, Spad, Spitfire, Hurricane, Hellcat, Corsair, Mustang, Thunderbolt, Me 109, Fw 190, Zero, MiG, Sabre, Phantom, Tomcat and Eagle, these are the names that will be remembered as long as men and women study the history of warfare.

Of course, the planes have changed. The first fighters were built of sticks, fabric and wire. By the beginning of World War II, greatly improved and more sophisticated airframe and systems design afforded the fighter pilot new levels of safety, comfort and efficiency. Today, there are fighters fabricated from exotic alloys and composite materials. They can cruise at speeds that exceed Mach 1, and be controlled by Direct Voice Input (DVI) pilot commands.

As technology has advanced, so the job of the fighter pilot has expanded and became infinitely more complex. In World War II, the physical exertion coupled with the mental and emotional expenditure of a few minutes of air fighting could bring the pilot near to exhaustion. Today, spectacular advances in computerization and electronics both simplify and complicate the fighter pilot's task and the demands made upon him—the skills and intelligence required and the sheer scope of the workload would be utterly incomprehensible to his World War I counterpart. But, in the final analysis, the job is still the same: to out-think, out-fly and out-fight another fighter pilot in a contest that pits one young man or woman against another amid what W.B. Yeats described as "That lonely tumult in the clouds".

INTRODUCTION

Left: Delicate and insect-like, a flight of DeHavilland Tiger Moths over Cambridgeshire in 1997. With a top speed of 110 mph, the fabric-covered Tiger Moth was flown as a basic trainer by most Royal Air Force and British Commonwealth Air Training Plan pilots of World War II. Below: F-16 Fighting Falcons on a Gulf War mission in 1991. The versatile F-16 was effectively employed in fighter sweeps, bombing and ground-attack roles during Operation Desert Storm.

SPIDERMAN

...the first World War...took me from school at sixteen, it destroyed all hope of University training or apprenticeship to a trade, it deprived me of the only carefree years, and washed me up, inequipped for any serious career, with a Military Cross, a Royal handshake, a six-hundred-pound gratuity, and— I almost forgot to say— my life. There were men older than I whose education was complete. To them the War was a setback, disastrous but not irremediable. There were others, older still, who had positions to which they could return. But we very young men had no place, actual or prospective, in a peaceful world. We walked off the playing-fields into the lines. Our preoccupation was the next patrol, our horizon the next leave. We were trained with one object— to kill. We had one hope— to live. When it was over we had to start again.
—from *Sagittarius Rising* by Cecil Lewis

HE CAME FROM JAVA, the son of a wealthy Dutch coffee planter. The family returned to the Netherlands in 1897 when he was six so that he could be educated there. Little Antony Fokker was reputed to be spoilt, cocky, arrogant and selfish, as well as extremely bright and inventive.

He became interested in aviation at an automobile and airplane exhibition in Brussels, but was not encouraged by his father. Hermann Fokker told the boy that he would never buy him an airplane, believing, as did so many in the early part of the century, that one must have a death wish to get involved with flying machines.

For all his protestations, Hermann Fokker kept his son, now enrolled in an aeronautical engineering school, well-financed through the boy's first attempts to build a successful flying machine. The elder Fokker provided more than 180,000 marks to keep his son afloat in his continuing failures, and he was astonished when, early in World War I, young Antony was able to repay his father every cent, with interest.

In the years leading to up to that War, Antony Fokker followed the principles of automatic stability that he had developed as a child building experimental model airplanes, and concentrated on the design and construction of a series of planes that he called *Spinne* (Spider). These were a simple blend of skids with wheels attached, tilted fabric-covered wings, and welded tubes, wires and turnbuckles... all improvised into forms and shapes from his wild imagination. He dedicated himself to becoming known for his flying machines by selling them when he could, giving flying lessons in them, and performing for crowds at weekends. He tried, without success, to interest the German Army and Navy in his planes. He made a meagre living but was mostly in debt and in grave danger. On one occasion a bracing wire parted when his aircraft was at 2400 feet. He rode the disintegrating machine down into the trees and survived with only the slightest injuries,

although his passenger died. And so it went, flying for promoters, taking great risks, and cheating death.

When the War did come, it came as a surprise to Fokker, as did a sudden turn in his fortunes. He was, he thought, just a businessman, and neutral about the conflict. He wanted only to make and sell his airplanes and was not concerned about who bought them. Virtually overnight every machine he had built was snapped up by the very same German Army and Navy that had coolly dismissed his earlier proposals.

Germany's military men, who now had an inkling of the combat potential of the airplane, called on Fokker to outdo the French in their efforts to make a plane serve as a flying gun platform. A Moraine-Saulnier monoplane was forced down behind the German lines in April 1915. The craft had a Lewis gun mounted in line with the propeller, and they noted the rather crude steel deflector plates on the propeller blades. To the Germans, this French idea was interesting, but they considered it a poor solution to the problem of firing a machine gun through the arc of a propeller. They gave the problem to Fokker, who solved it in two days with a rod-and-cam device which interrupted the firing each time a propeller blade passed in front of the gun muzzle. The Germans were duly impressed, but remained indecisive, and it took three trial flights by the great ace Leutnant Oswald Böelcke to convince the German Air Corps of Fokker's genius.

Orders poured in for Fokker's gun-synchronizing device and for his current monoplane which, when equipped with the device, proved devastating. It was more than a year before the first Allied fighter plane appeared in action with a gun-interrupter gear. By his mid-twenties Antony Fokker had become a millionaire, but he still lived in a modest German boarding house with his dog and a pet monkey.

Throughout the War he continued to visit the front to consult the pilots who flew his planes. He got on well with them and relied on their advice

Mark Twain said, "Courage is the mastery of fear, resistance to fear, not the absence of fear." At times the nearness of death brings an inexplicable exhilaration which starts the adrenaline flowing and results in instant action. The plane becomes an integral part of the pilot's body, it is strapped to his butt, and they become a single fighting machine.
—from *Double Nickel– Double Trouble* by R.M. Littlefield

Left: The wreck of a US-built Bristol Scout which crashed at McCook Field, Dayton, Ohio in 1918. Below: Antony Fokker in 1914 with his model M 16 aircraft.

and opinions in his efforts to design new and improved fighters.

Fokker's main problem in trying to compete with the latest Allied aircraft designs was inadequate power. The finest German aero-engine of the day was the water-cooled 160 hp in-line Mercedes, but the entire factory output of the Mercedes engine was committed to the Albatros company. Fokker could obtain none for his own firm. This shortage inspired him to develop a better fighter that did not rely on increased power (speed), but rather on improved manoeuvrability and rate of climb. The Fokker Triplane featured three wings, a clean line and very few wires and struts. Manfred von Richthofen, Germany's leading ace, was mightily impressed: "It climbs like a monkey and manoeuvres like the devil." It was so manoeuvrable that most of his opponents never realized how slow it was, nor how limited its range. The Triplane had twin Spandau machine guns and an amazing rate of climb —ten minutes to 13,000 feet, a ceiling of nearly 20,000 feet, cantilevered wooden wings, cable-operated ailerons, balanced controls and a landing speed of 30 mph. Its main fault was its seeming determination to groundloop. Apart from that, it was strong and very difficult to shoot down.

However, the German Army wanted speed more than any attribute offered by Fokker's Triplane and orders for the radical craft were limited. Fokker still needed the Mercedes engine to develop the plane that he and the German Army knew was required. In meetings with von Richthofen's technical officer, Fokker proposed a contest among the leading aircraft makers to build a new plane, which the best German fighter pilots would evaluate. His condition was that each manufacturer should be able to use the Mercedes engine to power his entry. The trials were held in January 1918, and initially Fokker's design was a disaster. Von Richthofen flew it and clearly identified its severe problems. Undeterred, Fokker quickly corrected the problems, and von Richthofen was amazed at the improvement. The

German Air Corps implored Fokker to move immediately into mass production of his winning entry, which was, in fact, a redesigned two-wing version of his Triplane. He was asked to name his price to build 400 machines. He asked for ten million marks, and got it. He even had the satisfaction of watching Albatros and AEG, his primary competitors, ordered to build his design and to pay him a royalty on each plane they produced. Thus was born the famous Fokker D-VII.

Nearly 1000 D-VIIs had been built by the time of the Armistice, the first of them going to Baron von Richthofen's unit, JG-1. He was to die later in one of Fokker's Triplanes. Another World War I airman who flew the D-VII subsequently became famous in the next conflict: Reichsmarshall Hermann Göring of the German Air Force.

The first true fighter pilot was French Air Service Lieutenant Roland Garros who, on 1st April 1915, claimed the initial fighter victory of World War I. Garros was *en route* in his Morane-Saulnier to drop two 155mm bombs on a German railway station when he encountered an enemy two-seater. He emptied three Hotchkiss gun strip magazines into the craft and sent it down in flames.

On an early morning patrol in June 1917, the German fighter pilot Ernst Udet, at this point a raw twenty-one-year-old, spotted a French Spad VII approaching him from the west. Udet was relatively inexperienced in terms of flying time and combat sorties flown, but he was already credited with having downed six enemy aircraft. When the two planes engaged, Udet was able to make out the word *Vieux* on the fuselage of his opponent's machine. It was common knowledge among airmen on the Western front that the great French ace, Capitaine Georges Guynemeyer, flew a Spad with *Vieux Charles* painted on it, and Udet was now certain he knew the identity of the man he was fighting. Guynemeyer's score at that point was

Left: *The NCO Pilot, Royal Flying Corps, Flight-Sergeant W. G. Bennett* by Sir William Orpen

MARSHALL ISLANDS

F-1 Camel

32

In Flanders fields the poppies blow / between the crosses, row on row, that mark our place; and in the sky / the larks still bravely fly / scarce heard amid the guns below.

We are the dead, short days ago / we lived, felt dawn, saw sunset glow, / loved and were loved, and now we lie / in Flanders fields.

Take up our quarrel with the foe / to you from failing hands we throw / the torch: be yours to hold it high / if ye break faith with us who die we shall not sleep, though poppies grow in Flanders fields.
—*In Flanders Fields*
by John McCrea

thirty kills. Udet quickly considered the odds against him. In addition to Guynemeyer's skill and fearsome reputation, his was a vastly superior aircraft to the Albatros that Udet was flying. The Spad was faster, climbed better, and was stronger and better able to take the stresses imposed by aerial combat.

Udet tried every trick he knew to no avail. His fate seemed sealed. Nothing worked until, finally, his luck improved for one brief moment and the Spad crossed through his sights. He tried to fire and found that both his guns were jammed. He beat furiously on the gun breeches, trying to free the jams without success. He saw that Guynemeyer was observing his predicament. Seconds passed and then, astonishingly, the Frenchman waved and departed westward toward his own lines. Udet was confused. He knew, without any doubt, that Guynemeyer could have killed him easily in the few terrifying moments of their encounter, but had clearly elected to show mercy to his hapless, helpless enemy. There may be another explanation for the Frenchman's apparent act of chivalry in sparing the life of a still-combatant enemy pilot. Maybe Guynemeyer's guns were also jammed, maybe his ammunition was already expended, or perhaps he feared the German might, in desperation, decide to ram his plane. It seems probable, though, that Guynemeyer's act was that of a gentleman who hoped that he would be accorded a similar treatment if he were to one day find himself in Udet's situation.

Most historians agree that airmen in World War I behaved in a chivalrous manner. War correspondents remarked on the "knightly" behaviour of the pilots on both sides. Willie Fry, a fighter pilot, wrote of the contrasting horror of the Battle of the Somme, and of Passchendaele: "The public at home, and to a certain extent the ground troops in France, could not understand that, from the first, fighting in the air was conducted on chivalrous lines and not with the hate largely generated by propaganda, justifiably in

Left: High-scoring Billy Bishop, a Canadian Major in the Royal Flying Corps, with his Nieuport 17 in 1917. Below: The 95th Pursuit Squadron, RFC, and their Nieuport 28s.

Spin! I suppose nobody reading this to-day who is at all familiar with flying thinks anything of spinning. In 1916, to spin was a highly dangerous manoeuvre. A few experts did it. Rumour had it that once in a spin you could never get out again. Some machines would spin easier to the left than to the right; but a spin in either direction was liable to end fatally. The expression "in a flat spin," invented in those days, denoted that whoever was in it had reached the absolute limit of anger, nerves, fright, or whatever it might be. So spinning was the one thing the young pilot fought shy of, the one or two things he hoped he might never do—the other was, catch fire in the air. Now that I have done both, I assure you there is no comparison. Spinning is a mild stunt. It makes you a bit giddy if you go on long enough. It's a useful way of shamming dead when a Hun is on your tail; but fire in the air! That's a holy terror!
—from *Sagittarius Rising* by Cecil Lewis

13

OUT FOR VICTORY.

order to keep up the tempo of the war effort." This is not to argue that a chivalrous or gentlemanly approach to air fighting was dominant in the Great War; only that there is evidence that such acts and such behaviour did occur then.

A World War II commander of JG27, German Air Force (1942–43), Eduard Neumann recalled: "It may be a little difficult for most people to understand today that the British flyers always enjoyed our respect and sympathy. This is more conceivable if one knows that in all German pilots' messes in peace time the old veterans of World War I always spoke of the British pilots, of air combat with them, and of the British fairness in the most positive way."

In *Sagittarius Rising*, the remarkable memoir of his career as a fighter pilot in "the war to end wars", Cecil Lewis brought a wonderful clarity and colour to his subject. Born in 1898, he joined the Royal Flying Corps, earning his wings at Gosport in February 1916 while still only seventeen years old. At eighteen, he was posted to France with No. 56 Squadron, RFC.

"The squadron was to be equipped with the SE-5, the last word in fighting-scouts, turned out by the Royal Aircraft Factory. It was fitted with a 140 hp Hispano Suiza engine and two guns: one Vickers, synchronized, and firing through the propeller by means of the new Constantinesco gear; and one Lewis gun, clamped on to the top plane and firing over the propeller. To change drums, the Lewis could be pulled down on a quadrant mounting, and in this position it could, if necessary, be fired straight upwards. The machine (for 1917) was quite fast. It would do about a hundred and twenty [mph] on the level and climb ten thousand feet in twelve minutes. It could be looped and rolled and dived vertically without breaking up. Altogether it was a first-class fighting-scout (probably the most successful designed during the war), and was relied upon to re-establish the Allied air supremacy lost during the winter.

"I always regarded instruction as a come-down, a confession that the pilot was finished, no use at the front, and condemned to flip young aspirants round and round the aerodrome day after day on obsolete types of machines. Of course it was unreasonable, for competent instructors were most valuable to the rapidly expanding Force. Although their qualities were not necessarily those of successful active service pilots, they were equally important. A good instructor was, and still is, a pretty rare bird. It needs some guts to turn a machine over to a half-fledged pupil in the air and let him get into difficulties and find his way out of them. Instruction demands, besides, an ability to communicate oneself to another person (the secret of all good teaching), and not so simple as it sounds. Add to this great patience, the quality of inspiring confidence, and an extremely steady flying ability in the man himself, and it will be obvious that nobody need look down his nose at an instructor. All this I know now; then, the idea of flying an uninteresting machine condemned the thing out of hand, for flying itself, handling the latest and fastest types, trick flying, exhibitionism if you like, was all I cared about. Unconsciously quoting Shaw (with whom I was then unfamiliar), I thought, 'Those who can, do; those who can't, teach,' and prayed that I might not be posted to a Training Squadron.

"The squadron sets out eleven strong on the evening patrol. Eleven chocolate-coloured, lean, noisy bullets, lifting, swaying, turning, rising into formation—two fours and a three—circling and climbing away steadily towards the lines. They are off to deal with Richthofen and his circus of Red Albatrosses.

"The May evening is heavy with threatening masses of cumulus cloud, majestic skyscapes, solid-looking as snow mountains, fraught with caves and valleys, rifts and ravines—strange and secret pathways in the chartless continents of the sky. Below, the land becomes an ordnance map, dim

MORE
AEROPLANES
ARE
NEEDED

WOMEN
COME AND
HELP!
FREE TRAINING
AND
MAINTENANCE ALLOWANCES

Apply at Once

ISSUED BY THE MINISTRY OF MUNITIONS.

110344 W.E 5600/6518. 10500. 5. 18. DPCºLᵗᵈ E3117.

When the bloom is off the garden, / and I'm fighting in the sky, / when the lawns and flower beds harden, / and when weak birds starve and die, / the death-roll will grow longer, eyes will be moist and red; and the more I kill, the longer / shall I miss friends who are dead.
—*War* by Pilot-Officer A.N.C. Weir, formerly with No. 145 Squadron, RAF

Above: The uniform of a Royal Flying Corps officer, displayed at the Tangmere Military Aviation Museum in Sussex, England.

Left: The popular and highly successful Nieuport 24. The similar Nieuport 23 was the mount of the French fighter ace Charles Nungesser who achieved most of his forty-five air victories in the agile, reliable little fighter.

Below: Captain Eddie Rickenbacker was the most successful American World War I fighter pilot with twenty-six victories in his excellent Spad S-13.

green and yellow, and across it go the Lines, drawn anyhow, as a child might scrawl with a double pencil. The grim dividing Lines! From the air robbed of all significance.

"Steadily the body of scouts rises higher and higher, threading its way between the cloud precipices. Sometimes, below, the streets of a village, the corner of a wood, a few dark figures moving, glides into view like a slide into a lantern and then is hidden again.

"But the fighting pilot's eyes are not on the ground, but roving endlessly through the lower and higher reaches of the sky, peering anxiously through fur-goggles to spot those black slow-moving specks against land or cloud which mean full throttle, tense muscles, held breath, and the headlong plunge with screaming wires—a Hun in the sights, and the tracers flashing.

"A red light curls up from the leader's cockpit and falls away. Action! He alters direction slightly, and the patrol, shifting throttle and rudder, keep close like a pack of hounds on the scent. He has seen, and they see soon, six scouts three thousand feet below. Black crosses! It seems interminable till the eleven come within diving distance. The pilots nurse their engines, hard-minded and set, test their guns and watch their indicators. At last the leader sways sideways, as a signal that each should take his man, and suddenly drops.

"Machines fall scattering, the earth races up, the enemy patrol, startled, wheels and breaks. Each his man! The chocolate thunderbolts take sights, steady their screaming planes, and fire. A burst, fifty rounds—it is over. They have overshot, and the enemy, hit or missed, is lost for the moment. The pilot steadies his stampeding mount, pulls her out with a firm hand, twisting his head right and left, trying to follow his man, to sight another, to back up a friend in danger, to note another in flames.

"But the squadron plunging into action has not seen, far off, approaching from the east, the rescue flight of Red Albatrosses patrolling above the body

of machines on which they had dived, to guard their tails and second them in the battle. These, seeing the maze of wheeling machines, plunge down to join them. The British scouts, engaging and disengaging like flies circling at midday in a summer room, soon find the newcomers upon them. Then, as if attracted by some mysterious power, as vultures will draw to a corpse in the desert, other bodies of machines swoop down from the peaks of the cloud mountains. More enemy scouts, and, by good fortune, a flight of Naval Triplanes.

"But, nevertheless, the enemy, double in number, greater in power and fighting with skill and courage, gradually overpower the British, whose machines scatter, driven down beneath the scarlet German fighters.

"It would be impossible to describe the action of such a battle. A pilot, in the seconds between his own engagements, might see a Hun diving vertically, an SE5 on his tail, on the tail of the SE another Hun, and above him again another British scout. These four, plunging headlong at two hundred miles an hour, guns crackling, tracers

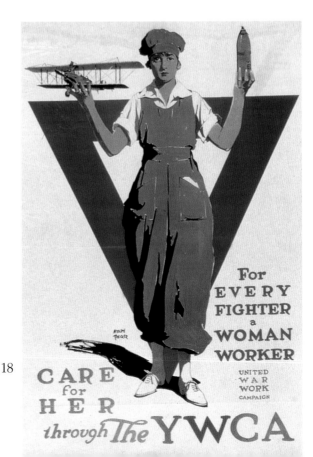

For EVERY FIGHTER a WOMAN WORKER

CARE for HER through The YWCA

UNITED WAR WORK CAMPAIGN

Above left: An F-4 Phantom of 71 Fighter Wing, "Richthofen", Jagdstaffel 712, German Air Force, at Schleswig-Jagel in April 1998. The "Richthofen" fighter squadron is named after the "Red Baron", Manfred von Richthofen of World War I fame. Above: An F-4 drawn by Hauptmann Mike Herrling, pilot of the Phantom above. Left: The D-VII was Antony Fokker's most effective fighter. It helped establish the reputation of the great airman Ernst Udet.

streaming, suddenly break up. The lowest Hun plunges flaming to his death, if death has not taken him already. His victor seems to stagger, suddenly pulls out in a great leap, as a trout leaps on the end of a line, and then, turning over on his belly, swoops and spins in a dizzy falling spiral with the earth to end it. The third German zooms veering, and the last of that meteoric quartet follows bursting. But such a glimpse, lasting perhaps ten seconds, is broken by the sharp rattle of another attack. Two machines approach head-on at breakneck speed, firing at each other, tracers whistling through each other's planes, each slipping sideways on his rudder to trick the other's gun fire. Who will hold longest? Two hundred yards, a hundred, fifty, and then, neither hit, with one accord they fling their machines sideways, bank and circle, each striving to bring his gun on to the other's tail, each glaring through goggle eyes, calculating, straining, wheeling, grim, bent only on death or dying.

"But, from above, this strange tormented circling is seen by another Hun. He drops. His gun speaks. The British machine, distracted by the sudden unseen enemy, pulls up, takes a burst through the engine, tank and body, and falls bottom uppermost down through the clouds and the deep unending desolation of the twilight sky.

"The game of noughts and crosses, starting at fifteen thousand feet above the clouds, drops in altitude engagement by engagement. Friends and foes are scattered. A last SE, pressed by two Huns, plunges and wheels, gun-jammed, like a snipe over marshes, darts lower, finds refuge in the ground mist, and disappears.

"Now lowering clouds darken the evening. Below, flashes of gunfire stab the veil of the gathering dusk. The fight is over! The battlefield shows no sign. In the pellucid sky, serene cloud mountains mass and move unceasingly. Here where guns rattled and death plucked the spirits of the valiant, this thing is now as if it had never been! The sky is busy with night, passive, superb, unheeding."

...I hardly remember a time when I was not air-minded. At prep. school I was already making gliders out of half-sheets of paper, curving the plane surfaces, improvising rudders and ailerons, and spending hours launching them across the room from chairs and tables.
—from *Sagittarius Rising* by Cecil Lewis

Above: Captain Albert Ball, brilliant ace of No. 56 Squadron, Royal Flying Corps, in World War I, with forty-four aerial victories. He was killed on 7th May 1917. Ball was posthumously awarded the Victoria Cross. Left: A woodcut by artist Robert Dance, *The SE 5a*. The Sopwith Camel and the SE 5a were the two best British fighters of the War.

21

NO MORE
MR NICE GUY

I should of course join the Air Force. "In the first place," I said, "I shall get paid and have good food. Secondly, I have none of your sentiments about killing, much as I admire them. In a fighter plane, I believe, we have found a way to return to war as it ought to be, war which is individual combat between two people, in which one either kills or is killed. It's exciting, it's individual, and it's disinterested. I shan't be sitting behind a long-range gun working out how to kill people sixty miles away. I shan't get maimed: either I shall get killed or I shall get a few pleasant putty medals and enjoy being stared at in a night club."
—from *The Last Enemy* by Richard Hillary

There is no working middle course in wartime.
—Sir Winston Churchill

Right: Royal Air Force fighter pilots in their crew room between World War II sorties.

"ETHICS IN WAR? The object of war is to kill and wound as many of the enemy as one can and to destroy all his supplies and communications in as short a time as possible. However, at the time I was there, it was an unwritten gentlemen's agreement between the fighter pilots of the Luftwaffe and the US Army Air Force not to shoot an airman in a parachute."
—Lieutenant-Colonel Robert M. Littlefield, USAF (Ret), formerly with the 55th Fighter Group, 8 USAAF

"I never thought about 'ethics' in regard to air combat. I had decided that even if the opportunity arose I would never shoot at a man in his parachute. Why I thought that way, I am not sure. It just didn't seem the right thing to do."
—Wing-Commander Douglas "Duke" Warren, RCAF (Ret), formerly with No. 66 and No. 165 Squadrons, RAF

"Fighting in the war does not know mercy. In case I don't kill the enemy, he will kill me. Fortunately, a fighter pilot never becomes a subject of bad conscience. He just defends his life, the lives of his comrades and the justice against cruel tyranny."
—Generalmajor Frantisek Fajtl, formerly with No. 313 (Czech) Squadron, RAF

"Ethics went out the window. The principles of right or good behaviour—the rules and standards of conduct certainly did not—could not apply to the combat fighter pilot's profession. This is where the beast came out, self protection ruled—get that SOB before he gets you."
—Captain Jack Ilfrey, USAF (Ret), formerly with the 20th Fighter Group, 8 USAAF

"If I saw them and could get to them, I tried my very best to get 'em. That was why I was there."
—Colonel George L. Hollowell, USMC (Ret), formerly with VMF-224

22

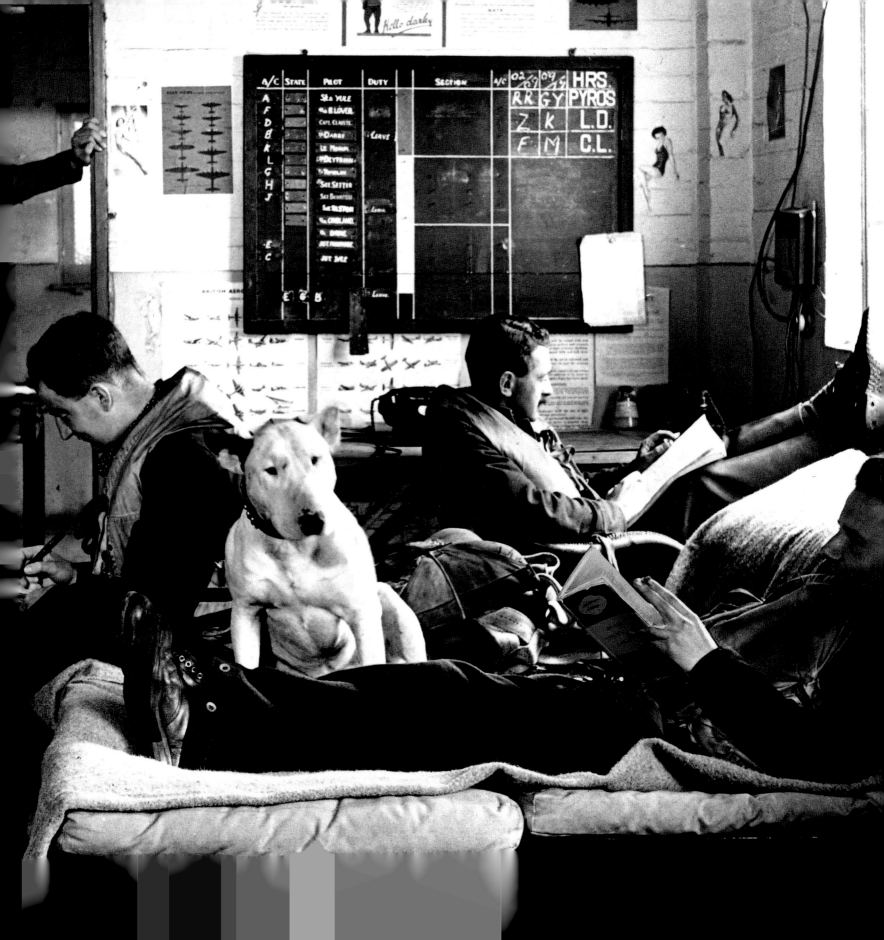

At age thirteen, Kazuo Tsunoda fell in love with his niece. With little money, however, he resolved to improve his financial condition and ask her to marry him when he was twenty. He later applied for and was accepted in the Juvenile Flying Soldier programme of the Japanese Navy and became an NCO fighter pilot. He served aboard the carrier *Soryu* in 1939, and fought over the Solomons for ten months with 582 Ku. An ace with at least nine victories, Tsunoda returned to Japan later in the War to marry the woman he loved for so long, but his family objected as the woman had since married and been divorced. Returning to combat, he fought the rest of the War over Iwo Jima, the Philippines and Okinawa. He survived many missions escorting Tokko (suicide attack units).

"I think wars bring out the best and the worst in people. The days of the open cockpits and pilots with blowing scarves, waving at the enemy as they were shot down, as we were led to believe [occurred] in World War I, were over. World War II didn't have the same closeness to the enemy. Of course, today's aerial warfare is even more remote, where you never see the enemy, and push a button which fires a missile to destroy the target.

"We did hear of cases where German pilots allegedly fired at Allied airmen who had bailed out and were floating in parachutes. I recall one of the pilots on my squadron (a very nice guy) who claimed that if he saw a German airman floating in a rubber dinghy after being shot down, he would attack him from the air. His rationale was that total war pulled no punches. Personally, I would not have done that, but I guess there are two sides to every coin."
—Flight-Lieutenant Charles M. "Ack" Lawson, RAF (Ret), formerly with No. 165 Squadron

"My own personal experience shows that there definitely was a spirit of 'camaraderie of the knights of the air', at least in the European theatre.

"On 29th January 1945, I shot down Oberleutnant Waldemar Balasus in his Me 109G-14 'Blue 32'. After a ten-minute running battle, he was hit and bellied in at high speed on the snow-covered ground. He slid nearly a half mile, and when I passed over the wreckage at 30 feet the pilot was climbing out of the cockpit with one foot on the wing root and one foot still in the seat, and he rendered a snappy salute as I flew by. I was gone too quickly to return the salute but acknowledged it by rocking my wings. Incidentally, this pilot survived the war but died in 1989, just two years before I found out his name. Some German friends finally located his forty-nine-year-old son in 1996 and I received a picture of the man I shot down from his son, who works in a Hamburg bank."
—Major Walter J. Konantz, USAF (Ret), formerly with the 55th Fighter Group, 8 USAAF

"Not much change in ethics [from World War I]. There was still fairness on both sides, as our great teachers from World War I would have never allowed any other way! Sad exceptions were happening on both sides [but] the number was small!"
—Feldwebel Horst W. Petzschler, German Air Force (Ret), formerly with X/JG51 "Mölders"

Erich Hartmann, the German World War II ace of aces, recalled an incident that occurred when he was stationed in western France. A young German Air Force Leutnant had shot and killed a parachuting RAF pilot who had bailed out of his crippled Spitfire. When the German's squadron commander learned of the incident, he wanted to shoot the Leutnant, but others in the squadron convinced the commander to transfer the young man out of the squadron instead.

There are many examples of airmen who were fired on while descending by parachute. Likewise, there are many instances on record of pilots who refused to take advantage of the opportunity to kill a foe coming down by parachute or in an otherwise defenceless position.

"By the rules of war it was justifiable to kill a pilot who could fight again. But few of us could bring ourselves to shoot a helpless man in cold blood."
—from *Duel of Eagles* by Peter Townsend, formerly with Nos. 43 and 85 Squadrons, RAF

"This is perhaps a convenient opportunity to say a word about the ethics of shooting at aircraft crews who have bailed out in parachutes. Germans descending over England are prospective prisoners-of-war and, as such, should be immune. On the other hand, British pilots descending over England are still potential combatants. Much indignation was caused by the fact that German pilots sometimes

Above left: US Marine Corps pilot Jack Bolt flew Corsairs with Gregory Boyington's famous "Black Sheep" squadron. Above: US Navy World War II Hellcat pilot E.R. Hanks. Below: A Navy Grumman F6F-5 Hellcat near the Grumman plant on Long Island, New York.

fired on our descending airmen (although, in my opinion, they were perfectly entitled to do so), but I am glad to say that in many cases they refrained."
—from the post-Battle report of Air Chief Marshal Sir Hugh C.T. Dowding, Commander-in-Chief, RAF Fighter Command, during the Battle of Britain

"My habit of attacking Huns dangling from their parachutes led to many arguments in the mess. Some officers, of the Eton and Sandhurst type, thought it was 'unsportsmanlike' to do it. Never having been to a public school, I was unhampered by such considerations of form. I just pointed out that there was a bloody war on, and that I intended to avenge my pals."
— Ira "Taffy" Jones, World War I fighter pilot

In September 1940, Squadron-Leader John Kent commanded No. 303 (Polish) Squadron, RAF. On the 23rd, Kent downed a German fighter over the English Channel: "The 109 dived straight into the sea, while he, apparently unhurt, drifted down in his parachute. I circled round him a couple of times and felt it might be kinder to shoot him as he had one hell of a long swim, but I could not bring myself to do it. Without waiting for him to hit the water I turned for home. The Poles were fed up with me when I admitted that I could not bring myself to shoot the chap in the parachute and they reminded me of events earlier in the month when we were told that one or two pilots of No. 1 Squadron had bailed out and had then been shot by German fighters. At the time the Poles asked me if it was true that this was happening. I had to tell them that, as far as I knew, it was, at which they asked: 'Oh, can we?' I explained that, distasteful as it was, the Germans were within their rights in shooting our pilots over this country and that, if one of us shot down a German aircraft over France and the pilot bailed out, then we were quite entitled to shoot him. But this was not so over England as, aside from

Left: *Hawker Harts, 57 Squadron, RAF* by Frank Wootton. The Hart was used in the 1930s for Army Co-operation, as a fighter and light bomber. It led to the development of the Hurricane fighter.

The RAF seemed to have a different social feeling from the other services. Those who cared about such things noted a preponderance of 'minor public school' men; they called them the Brylcreem Boys in semi-affectionate recognition of the fact that no 'gentleman' would use such cheap hair cream. None of this mattered. What was significant was the character of a man who wanted to fly fighter planes. He needed to be competitive and scornful, eager for a chance to prove himself; he needed also a rarer combination of qualities: he had both to be young and alert, yet attach no great importance to his life. This was the requirement that came before patriotism, political belief or even skill in flying. It was not like being in the infantry where, even during the slaughters of the Western Front in 1914–18, you had a better than even chance of surviving. If you flew more than a certain number of missions in 1940–1 you were not likely to come back. This did not mean that all the pilots were reckless, willing to risk their lives for the sake of the chase and *continued*

LT. LINDSAY

anything else, he would be out of the war and might even be a very useful source of information for us. They thought about this for a bit and then said: 'Yes, we understand—but what if he is over the Channel?', to which I jokingly replied: 'Well, you can't let the poor bugger drown, can you?' This remark was quite seriously thrown in my teeth when they heard about the 109 pilot I had just shot down. There was no doubt about it, the Poles were playing the game for keeps far more than we were."

Captain Richard E. Turner, Commanding Officer of the 356th Fighter Squadron, 354th Fighter Group, 8 USAAF, described an incident in combat on 16th March 1944: "A few seconds later I saw ahead of me the parachuting pilot of the 109 I had shot down a few minutes before. Pointing the plane at him, I flipped the gun switch to 'camera only' to get a picture, but the thought crossed my mind that this circuit had been known to foul up and fire the guns, so I restrained my desire to get a confirming picture of my victim. Instead, I turned aside, passing within 30 feet of him. I suppose when he saw me point straight at him, he fully expected to be gunned down, for he had drawn himself up and crossed his arms in front of his face as if to ward off the bullets, and when he saw me turn aside without firing, and waggling my wings as I passed, he started waving his arms and grinning like a Cheshire cat. I thought as I climbed that, since he had provided me with my tenth victory, he deserved a break. I just hoped he'd live to spread the word that Americans didn't shoot helpless pilots in parachutes. Maybe the Germans would follow suit."

Though a civilian, the celebrated aviator Charles Lindbergh, spent part of World War II flying with US Marine Corps and Navy fighter squadrons in the Pacific theater of operations. On 24th May 1944, Lindbergh was flying with three Marine pilots off the coast of New Ireland on a reconnaissance and strafing mission. He wrote of the incident: "Out to the coast line—four [F4U] Corsairs abreast, racing over the water—I am the closest one to land. The trees pass, a streak of green; the beach a band of yellow on my left. Is it a post a mile ahead in the water, or a man standing? It moves toward the shore. It is a man.

"All Japanese or unfriendly natives on New Ireland—everything is a target—no restrictions—shoot whatever you see. I line up my sight. A mile takes ten seconds at our speed. At 1000 yards my .50 calibers are deadly. I know just where they strike. I cannot miss.

"Now he is out of the water, but he does not run. The beach is wide. He cannot make the cover of the trees. He is centered in my sight. My finger tightens on the trigger. A touch, and he will crumple on the coral sand.

"But he disdains to run. He strides across the beach. Each step carries dignity and courage in its timing. He is not an ordinary man. The shot is too easy. His bearing, his stride, his dignity—there is something in them that has formed a bond between us. His life is worth more than the pressure of a trigger. I do not want to see him crumple on the beach. I release the trigger.

"I ease back on the stick. He reaches the tree line, merges with the streak of green on my left. I am glad I have not killed him. I would never have forgotten him writhing on the beach. I will always remember his figure striding over the sand, the fearless dignity of his steps. I had his life balanced on a muscle's twitch. I gave it back to him, and thank God that I did so. I shall never know who he was—Jap or native. But I realize that the life of this unknown stranger—probably an enemy—is worth a thousand times more to me than his death. I should never quite have forgiven myself if I had shot him—naked, courageous,

defenceless, yet so unmistakably a man."

Captain Eddie Rickenbacker, the American ace of the 94th Aero Squadron in World War I, made this entry in his diary on 10th March 1918: "Resolved today that hereafter I will never shoot at a Hun who is at a disadvantage, regardless of what he would do if he were in my position." Of that perspective he later wrote: "Just what influenced me to adopt that principle and even to enter it into my diary I have forgotten. That was very early in my fighting days and I had then had but few combats in the air. But with American fliers the war has always been more or less a sporting proposition and the desire for fair play prevents a sportsman from looking at the matter in any other light, even though it be a case of life or death. However that may be, I do not recall a single violation of this principle by any American aviator that I should care to call my friend."

By the beginning of World War II, the large numbers of airmen and aircraft involved, the airspeeds, the technical sophistication and the armaments, had all changed dramatically from those of the Great War, and these changes inevitably influenced the conduct of all the participants.

"I shot an Me 109F down on 25th March 1945. The pilot bailed out from a vertical dive at about 7000 feet. I felt quite elated that his parachute opened, and was quite contented with having destroyed the enemy aircraft. However, had my CO been on this mission, he would probably have had fits about me not attacking the pilot on the parachute. F.W. Lister, DSO, DFC and bar, had no time whatever for live Germans—or anyone else who might be enemy killers. Our work was air-to-ground—so we were killing German soldiers every day. Soldiers versus airmen? Not much difference to most of us."
—Flying-Officer E.A.W. Smith, RAF (Ret), formerly

kill above the clouds; nor did it mean that they had to be more patriotically motivated. It meant only that they had to have, at heart, some indifference to dying. The public were encouraged by Churchill's speeches to believe this indifference was heroic; the pilots themselves did not see it as such. Far from subscribing to the myth, they tried to subvert it. They cultivated understatement in a private slang; they came close to callousness: they claimed to feel nothing.
—from *The Fatal Englishman* by Sebastian Faulks

Battle, n. A method of untying with the teeth a political knot that would not yield to the tongue.
—from *The Devil's Dictionary* by Ambrose Bierce

Above left: US Navy pilot Lieutenant-Commander Elvin Lindsay of VF-19 flew F6F Hellcats in the Pacific during World War II. He later became skipper of VBF-19, flying F4U-4 Corsairs until the war ended. Left: High-achieving Spitfire pilots of No. 54 Squadron, RAF, New Zealanders Colin Gray and Al Deere at Hornchurch, their Essex, England airfield. In World War II Group-Captain Deere destroyed twenty-two enemy aircraft.

Above: The remains of the control tower at Kings Cliffe in Northamptonshire, World War II home of the 20th Fighter Group, 8 USAAF, Right: The flying goggles of RAF Flying-Officer Richard H.A. "Dickie" Lee who flew with No. 85 Squadron in the Battle of Britain.

with No. 127 Squadron

Pilot-Officer Richard Hillary of No. 603 Squadron, RAF, fought in the Battle of Britain, was badly burnt and became one of Archibald McIndoe's plastic surgery 'guinea pigs'. Hillary wrote a book, *The Last Enemy*, one of the finest books to come out of World War II. In it he recalled: "The voice of the controller came unhurried over the loud-speaker, telling us to take off, and in a few seconds we were running for our machines.

"I climbed into the cockpit of my plane and felt an empty sensation of suspense in the pit of my stomach. For one second time seemed to stand still and I stared blankly in front of me. I knew that that morning I was to kill for the first time. That I might be killed or in any way injured did not occur to me. Later, when we were losing pilots regularly, I did consider it in an abstract way when on the ground; but once in the air, never. I knew it could not happen to me. I suppose every pilot knows that, knows it cannot happen to him; even when he is taking off for the last time, when he will not return, he knows that he cannot be killed.

"I wondered idly what he was like, this man I would kill. Was he young, was he fat, would he die with the Führer's name on his lips, or would he die alone, in that last moment conscious of himself as a man? I would never know. Then I was being strapped in, my mind automatically checking the controls, and we were off."

No. 152 Squadron, RAF Pilot-Officer Roger Hall flew Spitfires in the Battle of Britain. In his book, *Clouds of Fear,* he remembered: "I watched the Hurricane turn over on its back and fall away. The pilot himself was on fire as he fell away from the machine. As the Hurricane went into a shallow dive, he released his parachute but, as it opened, its shrouds caught fire. The pilot, who had now succeeded in extinguishing the flames on himself, was desperately trying to climb up the shroud lines before they burnt through. I witnessed this scene with an hypnotic sort of detachment, not feeling myself able to leave it as I circled above. I was thankful to see the flames go out and the parachute behave in a normal manner. I felt a great surge of relief well up inside me, but it was to prove short-lived.

"Two 109s appeared below me coming from the north and travelling very fast towards the south as though they were intent upon getting home safely to France.

"I disregarded the pilot hanging from the parachute and diverted my attention to the 109s, which appeared to be climbing slowly. I felt I should get my first confirmed aircraft now and turned on my back to dive on them. When I was in the dive I laid my sights well in front of the forward 109 with lots of deflection, for I was coming down upon them vertically. The leading 109 was firing and I looked to see what he was firing at but could see no other aircraft near him. Then I saw it all in a fraction of a second, but a fraction that seemed an eternity.

"He was firing at the pilot at the end of the parachute and he couldn't possibly miss.

"I saw the tracers and the cannon shells pierce the centre of his body, which folded before the impact like a jack-knife closing, like a blade of grass which bends toward the blade of the advancing scythe. I was too far away to interfere and now was too late to be of any assistance. If to see red is usually a metaphorical expression, it became a reality to me at that moment, for the red I could see was that of the pilot's blood as it gushed from all the quarters of his body.

"I expected to see the lower part of his body fall away to reveal the entrails dangling in mid-air but by some miracle his body held together. His hands, but a second before clinging to the safety of the shroud lines, were now relaxed and hung limp at his sides. His whole body was limp also, like a man just hanged, the head resting across

31st October 1942
...I admit I'm sticking my neck out but I'd rather take my chances in the air than in the infantry, armored divisions, tank corps or the navy! Of course it's dangerous but name me a war job that isn't. Anyway I'm one of those that believe that if a guy is supposed to lose his life in this war it will happen no matter what or where and vice versa.
—Donald R. Emerson

Above: 1st Lieutenant Jack Raphael flew P-47s and P-51s with the 336th Fighter Squadron, 4th Fighter Group, 8 USAAF at Debden, Essex, during World War II. With 1016 victories to its credit, the 4th Fighter Group became the highest-scoring US fighter group in the European Theater of Operations in World War II.

one shoulder, bloody, scarlet with blood, the hot, rich blood of youth which had traversed and coursed through his veins for perhaps not more than nineteen or twenty years. It had now completely covered and dyed red an English face which looked down on but no longer saw its native soil."

Again Richard Hillary remembers in *The Last Enemy*: "My first emotion was one of satisfaction, satisfaction at a job adequately done, at the final logical conclusion of months of specialized training. And then I had a feeling of the essential rightness of it all. He was dead and I was alive; it could so easily have been the other way round; and that would somehow have been right too. I realized in that moment just how lucky a fighter pilot is. He has none of the personalized emotions of the soldier, handed a rifle and bayonet and told to charge. He does not even have to share the dangerous emotions of the bomber pilot who night after night must experience that childhood longing for smashing things. The fighter pilot's emotions are those of the duellist—cool, precise, impersonal. He is privileged to kill well. For if one must either kill or be killed, as now one must, it should, I feel, be done with dignity. Death should be given the setting it deserves; it should never be a pettiness; and for the fighter pilot it never can be."

"We were told that some Americans had been shot as they descended by parachute, but I have no personal knowledge of that happening. We were also told that if our planes were damaged in combat to the point that we had to abandon them, we would not be fired on if we dropped our landing gear. Again, I have no personal knowledge as to whether this was true or not."
—2nd Lieutenant Robert N. Jensen, USAF (Ret), formerly with the 55th Fighter Group, 8 USAAF

"A good fighter pilot must have one outstanding trait—aggressiveness. Without that he's of no use to

his squadron or the Air Force."
—Major John T. Godfrey, formerly with the 4th Fighter Group, 8 USAAF

From a conversation with General Adolf Galland, of the German Air Force, here are his thoughts on chivalry in the air during World War II:
"In summer and autumn of 1940 I shot down twenty-one Spitfires, three Blenheims and one Hurricane. The battle was tough but it never violated the unwritten laws of chivalry. We knew that our conflict with the enemy was a life and death struggle. We stuck with the rules of a fair fight, foremost being to spare the life of a defenceless opponent. The German Air Sea Rescue people therefore picked up any RAF or American pilot they found floating in the Channel as well as the German airmen.

"To shoot at a pilot parachuting would have seemed to us an act of unspeakable barbarism. I remember the circumstances when Göring mentioned this subject during the Battle of Britain. Only Mölders was present when this conversation took place near the Reichsmarshall's train in France. Experience had proved, he told us, that especially with technically highly developed arms such as tanks and fighter aircraft, the men who controlled these machines were more important than the machines themselves. The aircraft which we shot down could easily be replaced by the English, but not the pilots. As in our own case it was very difficult, particularly as the war drew on. Successful fighter pilots who could survive this war would be valuable not only because of their experience and knowledge but also because of their rarity. Göring wanted to know if we ever had thought about this. *'Jawohl, Herr Reichsmarshall!'* He looked me straight in the eyes and said, 'What would you think of an order directing you to shoot down pilots who were bailing out?' 'I should regard it as murder, *Herr Reichsmarshall*,' I told him, 'and I should do

everything in my power to disobey such an order.' 'That is just the reply I had expected from you, Galland.' In World War I similar thoughts had cropped up, but were just as strongly rejected by the fighter pilots."

"I always associated the German pilot in his aircraft as just 'the aircraft trying to shoot me down'. However, the beast in me was always there, making every effort to stay alive. I can remember saying to myself 'Ha ha, you SOB, I gotcha.' The after feelings were various—remorse, guilt, elation, joy... victorious. I think my worst experience along this line was the day my flight of four P-38s got jumped in North Africa. I saw my wingman firing at one, while two enemy aircraft were coming in on him. It was like they were right in front of my eyes, but out of my range. I did my damnedest to get over to help him, but saw him hit the silk, and I suddenly had to fight for my life. I got two Fws, but lost the other three in my flight. A most awful feeling of helplessness. There was a bond between us that most people can never attain in a lifetime... somewhat akin to love of your fellow man, I guess. Then there were the feelings in reverse, when my flight leader literally saved my life when I was badly shot up. I find all this hard to explain."
—Captain Jack Ilfrey, USAF (Ret), formerly with the 20th Fighter Group, 8 USAAF

Unteroffizier Karl Missy and the crew of a Heinkel He 111 bomber, No. 3232 of 2nd Gruppe, KG 26, the Lion Geschwader, were not operating from their permanent field at Westerland on 2nd February 1940. They had been sent to Schleswig, north of Hamburg, for their next mission, and take-off was set for dawn the following day. The crew of the Heinkel was made up of Missy, a gunner, pilot Hermann Wilms, observer Peter Leushake, and flight mechanic Johann Meyer, all of them Unteroffiziere.

They were awakened the next morning at 2 a.m.

Top left: Captain William F. Tanner, a 353rd Fighter Group pilot based at Raydon, Suffolk in World War II downed an Fw 190 on 5th December 1944 to become an ace. Bottom left: Lieutenant Urban Drew. a Mustang pilot with the 361st Fighter Group at Bottisham, Cambridgeshire. On 7th October 1944 Drew became the first Allied pilot to destroy two Me 262 jet fighters in aerial combat.

This time I had the feeling I had killed a man, but there was no time for remorse. If it were he this time, it could be me the next. In the mounting frenzy of battle, our hearts beat faster and our efforts became more frantic. But within, fatigue was deadening feeling, numbing the spirit. Both life and death had lost their importance. Desire sharpened to a single savage purpose—to grab the enemy and claw him down from the sky.
—Group-Captain Peter Townsend, formerly with Nos. 43 and 85 Squadrons, RAF

Every mind has its share of Dr. Jekyll and Mr. Hyde. When you are in combat the beast comes out. It's kill or be killed. But when removed from this pressure, the mind heals its innermost scars by helping, by giving, until, once again you are a human being.
—Captain Jack Ilfrey, formerly with the 20th Fighter Group, 8 USAAF

Some of your questions about fighter pilots have a bearing on the people I have met in my civilian life and in general I believe I liked the fighter pilots I met a lot better than many of the civilians.
—Colonel Walker M. Mahurin, 56th Fighter Group, 8 USAAF

to the sounds of a snowplough and a hundred soldiers busily clearing three feet of snow from the runway. Missy and his fellow crew members went out to help with the clearing. When the runway had been cleared, the crew of No. 3232 went to briefing where the bomber crews received orders to take off in pairs at three-minute intervals and steer west. It was expected that, after about two and a half hours flying, one or two of the Heinkels would sight an enemy convoy reported to be steaming south, off the north-east coast of England. They were to attack and shadow the convoy and report its position. The other bombers were then to close in and expand the attack.

In the early hours of that morning, Flight-Lieutenant Peter Townsend and the rest of No. 43 Squadron's (RAF) B Flight were dozing fitfully in the cold and discomfort of their dispersal at Acklington, Northumberland. They were awakened and sent out to their Hurricane fighters which were dispersed on the far side of the

airfield. The wind was blowing fiercely and, as usual, some of the starter batteries had gone flat and some engines had to be cranked by hand. This could at best scrape the skin off your knuckles, or break your wrist through a kick-back, or at worst decapitate you if you slipped forward into the propeller. The Merlins started one by one, and the pilots of B Flight taxied their fighters back to their dispersal hut, where the duty corporal reported by telephone to the sector headquarters, "Blue and Green Sections, B Flight, 43 Squadron at readiness."

At 9.03 a.m., the duty operator at Danby Beacon radar station was looking at blips indicating unidentified aircraft about 60 miles out to sea and approaching the English coast at an altitude of 1000 feet. The plots were passed immediately to Fighter Command and relayed simultaneously to 13 Group and to the Acklington Sector. In minutes the telephone in 43 Squadron dispersal rang ordering a scramble of Blue Section to Angels One.

34

Townsend, flanked by Jim Hallowes and Tiger Folkes, was climbing out, vectored to one-eight-zero with throttles wide open. They kept low over the water, Hallowes to Townsend's left, Folkes to his right. They searched the cloud base, and then the Heinkel appeared, above and to their right. They banked into a climbing right turn and Townsend had his thumb on the firing button. It was at that instant that the observer in the bomber, Peter Leushake, spotted the Hurricanes and yelled, "*Achtung, Jaeger.*"

Peter Townsend fired at the Heinkel. He saw only a big enemy bomber, and had no thought of the four men it carried. In that instant Peter Leushake died and Johann Meyer lay mortally wounded, his stomach punctured by bullets from Townsend's guns. Townsend closed quickly on the bomber, passing it as it entered the cloud cover and became a vague black shape uncomfortably close above him. Then he, Folkes and the Heinkel tumbled out of the cloud almost on top of one another. The bomber turned towards the shore, trailing a tail of black smoke.

Karl Missy was badly wounded in the back and legs, but kept firing his machine gun as Wilms struggled with the disabled bomber. By bare inches it crossed the cliffs at Whitby and flew low over several houses. A young girl looked up in alarm as the German bomber seemed to cross directly in front of her window. At his house in Love Lane, Special Constable Arthur Barratt was having a cup of tea when the stricken plane passed overhead at less than 200 feet "with three of our fighters round him like flies round a honey pot". He roared off in his car toward Sneaton Castle, where he expected the bomber to come down.

Throughout the action, Karl Missy remained at his gun, crumpled in his small swivel seat in the rear upper gun position. Wilms continued to guide the plane towards what he hoped would yet be a safe touch down. The ground below was

"you buy 'em
we'll fly 'em!

F.Wilkinsons

DEFENSE
BONDS
STAMPS

THE MORE BONDS YOU BUY - THE MORE PLANES WILL FLY

35

Below: Czech Air Force Colonel Antonin Vendl at his La-5 fighter. In World War II he flew 260 operational hours with the RAF and with the Russians. Right: Flight-Lieutenant Peter Townsend (left) and Squadron-Leader Caesar Hull (right). Both were members of No. 85 Squadron, RAF, during the Battle of Britain. Townsend's flight of three Hawker Hurricanes downed the first German aircraft, a Heinkel He 111 bomber, to fall on English soil in World War II. Far right: 56th Fighter Group aces Robert S. Johnson, Hubert "Hub" Zemke and Walker M. "Bud" Mahurin.

covered with snow, just as it had been at their Schleswig base. Thoughts of becoming a prisoner of the English began to form in his mind, and then quite suddenly the big bomber slammed into a line of telegraph poles and their wires, and seemed to float towards a barn just beyond them. Wilms tried desperately to haul the plane over the roof... to no avail. It was down and slithering across the snowpack.

Circling a few hundred feet above the scene, Flight-Lieutenant Townsend watched snow and mud flying up in the wake of the bomber as it sluiced on towards a line of trees, where the right wing snapped off, whipping the plane around to where it came to rest, a few yards from Bannial Flat Farm.

Constable Barratt and some farm hands rushed on to the wing of the Heinkel, the first enemy aircraft to fall on British soil since 1918, and saw Wilms trying to burn the aircraft's papers "with two of his mates leaning against him and groaning". The German pilot appeared to finish

the job before Barratt could drag him out. The pilot then emerged as Barratt and the farm folk struggled to assist the rest of the crew.

As a small crowd gathered, edging ever closer to the broken bomber, the pilot Wilms raised his hands and shouted at them, "*Boom! Boom!*", at which they backed away. The farm hands used five fire extinguishers and several shovelsful of snow to put out the fire in the wreck and, despite Wilms' efforts, some of the valuable German papers in the plane were recovered by RAF Intelligence officers.

A Mrs Smales called several times to Karl Missy, urging him to come out of the aircraft, but when he tried to leave he found that his legs had been shattered. They were useless so, using his arms, he lowered himself into the 'bath' below his position, to where Johann Meyer lay huddled. Meyer had massive stomach wounds and was screaming with pain as Missy tried to release him. Instead, Missy collapsed on top of Meyer, blood pouring freely from his own wounds. He called to

The greater issues were beyond us. We sat in a tiny cockpit, throttle lever in one hand, stick in the other. At the end of our right thumb was the firing button, and in each wing were four guns. We aimed through an optical gunsight, a red bead in the middle of a red ring. Our one concern was to boot out the enemy.
—Group Captain Peter Townsend, Nos. 43 and 85 Squadrons, RAF

There was no sportsmanship in the Pacific.
—Lieutenant-Colonel John F. Bolt, USMC (Ret)

Wilms, "Hermann, come and help Johann." He then managed to haul himself out and on to the wing, where he slid on to the ground. There he watched as Wilms dragged the body of Leushake out from the shattered nose of the plane. Wilms then returned to drag Meyer from the wreck. A young boy moved in to assist Meyer, who was trying to crawl in the snow. The boy then tried to help Karl Missy, who cried out in agony.

Missy and Meyer were carried into Mrs Smales' house, where she made them tea, gave them hot water bottles, and wrapped them in blankets. They were also given cigarettes. When a local doctor arrived, he injected Meyer with morphine, cut off Missy's boots, and put his legs in splints. He had suffered a broken left leg and a mutilated right one. Meyer and Missy were taken to hospital by ambulance. There Meyer died. That night Karl Missy's right leg was amputated; his other leg was put in a plaster cast.

Missy spoke no English then; his head nurse

spoke no German, but the care he received from her gave him hope. The next day, in his pain and misery, Karl Missy had a visitor—Peter Townsend. "Sister Oldfield met me in the corridor and told me that Missy was very ill and that they didn't know whether he would pull through, so I should only stay two minutes. Then she opened the door of Missy's ward and I entered, walking straight up to his bed. I held out my hand and, turning towards me, he clasped it with both of his until it hurt. But it was the way he looked at me that I can never forget. We had no common tongue, so could only communicate as the animals do, by touch, by expression and by invisible means. As he took my hand Missy had in his eyes the look of a dying animal. If he had died I would have been his killer. He said nothing and only looked at me with a pitiful, frightened and infinitely sad expression in which I thought I could recognize a glimmer of human gratitude. Indeed Missy felt no bitterness. He sank back on the pillows and I held out the bag of oranges and the tin of fifty Players I had brought for him. They seemed poor compensation. Then I left Karl Missy and went back to Acklington and the war.

"I called on Karl Missy one day in the summer of 1968, in the tidy little house where he was born and where his father had started him off in the plumbing trade. The old man had brought Karl up to be honest and hard-working like himself, and a first-class tradesman. It was from this house, where I now sat talking to Karl Missy, that he had set out on the road which would lead him into a gun battle with me.

"He reminded me of what I had said (his pilot, Hermann Wilms had interpreted) when I saw him in Whitby Hospital the next day. 'Sorry for having shot you down. English and German airmen should only try to compete with each other in peacetime.'

"Looking at him now and listening to his story, I

realized how futile it was to have tried to kill a man like Missy—a good, solid type, the kind the world needs. It was a pity that he had to leave his plumbing and go off to fight for Adolf Hitler. But now that affair is settled, Karl Missy and I can look each other straight in the face, depite the harm I have done to him. That is a small victory for humanity."

Five foot 6 inch Zdzislaw Krasnodebski of No. 303 (Polish) Squadron, RAF, learned to fly as one of the first pupils of the new Polish Flying School in 1925. On 6th September 1940, 303's Hurricanes lifted from London's RAF Northolt airfield under orders to attack a formation of German bombers that was approaching the capital.

On intercepting the enemy bombers, Squadron-Leader Krasnodebski manoeuvred to open fire on one of them and was himself hit at that moment. The glass covering the instruments of his cockpit panel shattered and the fuel tank immediately in front of it poured aviation spirit into the cockpit. The fuel instantly ignited, forcing Krasnodebski to abandon the airplane as quickly as he could. Pulling the hood back, he rapidly undid the harness and seat belt, disconnected the radio lead and the oxygen mask, and jumped from the burning Hurricane.

Wishing to avoid becoming a slowly descending, defenceless target for the Me 109s in the area, Krasnodebski delayed opening his parachute until he thought it reasonably safe to do so. At that point he could not find the parachute handle and wasted precious seconds searching for it as the earth seemed to rush up to meet him. He finally located the handle, deployed the parachute, and found that he was floating down in complete silence. He then became aware of the tremendous pain in his badly burnt hands and legs. Fortunately for him, the speed of his brief fall, caused by the delay in opening his parachute, extinguished the flames of his clothing and helped

to preserve the integrity of the parachute and the shroud lines.

As he descended toward a landing in a farm field, several members of the local Home Guard emerged from the bushes and moved towards the spot where the Pole was likely to land. They raised their rifles and Krasnodebski thought his time had come.

It was his yellow Mae West that saved him. The British home defence troops recognized it, if not the unfamiliar Polish uniform, and refrained from shooting him. He landed yelling 'Polish Officer, Polish Officer' to the Home Guard men. They took him straight to a hospital for burn treatment.

Flight-Lieutenant Findlay Boyd of No. 602 "City of Glasgow" Auxiliary Squadron, RAF, was thought to be one of the best pilots in his squadron. His no-nonsense approach to his work as a fighter pilot in the Battle of Britain, and, in particular, his attitude to air fighting, earned him considerable respect from many but left others perplexed. For

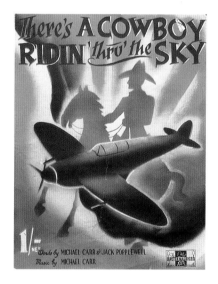

War is a continuation of policy by other means.
—Karl von Clausewitz

Boyd, shooting down an enemy pilot produced exhilaration, and if the foe bailed out, Boyd would try to shoot him as he dangled in his parachute. If the enemy pilot safely reached the sea, he would try to shoot him there. Boyd saw it as the only logical option. He believed that no German airman should be allowed to get back to his base to take off again and shoot at more RAF airmen.

It was the evening of 15th August 1940 and the pilots of No. 54 Squadron, RAF, sprawled in near exhaustion on the grass of RAF Manston in Kent. Colin Gray said: "I've had enough today. I reckon the Huns have too. I'm just dying for a beer, a good meal and bed." Al Deere shared his fellow New Zealander's wants, but just then they were ordered up and the pilots of Deere's flight ran for their Spitfires. The nine Merlins roared into life and in seconds were lifting from Manston's grass surface. The controller called: "Hello, Hornet Leader, seventy plus, Angels twenty heading Dungeness–Dover. You are to engage fighters."

Squadron-Leader James Leathart of No. 54 Squadron took his pilots up to 25,000 feet and they bounced the Me 109s. Al Deere concentrated on a Messerschmitt that he was chasing southward in a gentle dive towards France. Suddenly it was Deere being chased by two 109s and in an instant the instrument panel in his Spitfire exploded, the engine screamed as it was hit and his windscreen was quickly filmed with black oil. The 109s turned for France and the New Zealander for England. The crippled Spitfire floated across the Kentish cliffs and Deere managed about 1500 feet of altitude as he got ready to leave the doomed plane.

He jettisoned the canopy and rolled the plane on to its back to drop out. On the way, his parachute pack caught on something as the Spitfire began to dive upside down. He freed himself and his parachute opened in time to save him but it also deposited him within 100 yards of where his plane, *Kiwi II*, had impacted and exploded.

He lay there collecting his parachute and his thoughts, when two airmen arrived introducing themselves as ambulance personnel on their way to Kenley. "We thought we might help."

"Excellent service," thought Deere.

In a few hours he was in treatment at the East Grinstead Cottage Hospital burn unit, where the pioneering plastic surgery techniques of Archie McIndoe were being perfected. McIndoe's famed "guinea pigs", the horrendously burnt and battered Battle of Britain pilots whose wounds he treated, would forever be grateful for the many healing miracles he achieved. Al Deere's injuries were relatively minor, and in the night he checked himself out of East Grinstead and caught a train back to base.

"The obscure future date on which I should at last go into action had always been remote in my mind, imperfectly realized, even, I suspect, deliberately shut out. Now, suddenly, with a brief order, it had become startlingly clear and close at hand. For months after, with a few brief moments of respite, I was to live hypnotized not so much by the dread of death—for death, like the sun, is a thing you cannot look at steadily for long—as by the menace of the unforeseen. Friends, mess companions, would go out on patrol and never come back.

As the months went by it seemed only a matter of time until your turn came. You sat down to dinner faced by the empty chairs of men you had laughed and joked with at lunch. They were gone. The next day new men would laugh and joke from those chairs. Some might be lucky and stick it for a bit, some chairs would be empty again very soon. And so it would go on. And always, miraculously, you were still there. Until tomorrow.... In such an atmosphere you grew fatalistic, and as time went by and left you unscathed, like a batsman who has played himself in, you began to take liberties with the bowling. You took unnecessary risks, you volunteered for dangerous jobs, you provoked enemy aircraft to attack you. You were invulnerable: nothing could touch you. Then, when one of the old hands, as seemingly invulnerable as yourself, went West, you suddenly got cold feet. It wasn't possible to be sure—even of yourself. At this stage it required utmost courage to go on—a sort of plodding fatalism, a determination, a cold-blooded effort of will. And always alone!"
—from *Sagittarius Rising* by Cecil Lewis, No. 56 Squadron, RFC

"In the Navy's Pre-Flight School, one-half of the time was devoted to body contact athletics. Football was rough enough. We also played basketball with ten men on a side, and the referee was there for the sole purpose of breaking up fist fights. We played water polo at the deep end of the pool, and the instructor cracked the knuckles of anyone caught hanging on to the side. Push ball was another form of mayhem that was designed to inflict bodily harm on the other guy. In hand-to-hand combat we learned how to knife fight, break a man's neck, go for the jugular, break an arm, dislocate a shoulder, apply a knee to the groin, and so on.

"Physical fitness training where competition was stretched one step further to combativeness was re-emphasized at each phase of the flight training program, which lasted about ten months at that time [1942].

"I think it's fair to say that we came out of the cadet programme with a certain killer instinct and an aggressive approach to survival. When it came time for me to go into combat with the Japanese, the issue was uncomplicated. They were out to kill me and I was determined to do unto them before they did unto me."
—Commander William E. Copeland, USN (Ret), formerly with VF-19

All wars are boyish, and are fought by boys.
—from *Battlepieces and Aspects of the War* by Herman Melville

War may make a fool of man, but it by no means degrades him; on the contrary, it tends to exalt him, and its net effects are much like those of motherhood on women.
—from *Minority Report* by H.L. Mencken

Above: Generalleutnant Adolf Galland of JG 26 and JG 27, achieved a score of 104 victories and became *General der Jagdflieger*, Commander of the German Air Force Fighter Arm in World War II. Far left: Pilots on a US fighter station in World War II England.

COLONEL Bert McDowell, Junior, USAF (Ret), was a member of the 55th Fighter Group, 8 USAAF, based at Wormingford, Essex, England. There he flew fifty-five missions before falling to German ground fire while strafing an airfield: "I believe I had natural flying ability in that I took to flying easily and had no trouble going through pilot training. I believe those flyers who had this natural flying ability had the edge on those who did not, those who got shot down more than they should have. The fighter pilots in my squadron, for the most part, had it; there were only a few who did not and normally they did not last very long."

As one who flew Mirages and F-16s in the Israeli Air Force, Colonel Gidi Livni (Ret) believes that flying ability is not the most important feature of the successful fighter pilot: "I knew some pilots who lacked this gift of nature, yet scored more than ten kills. Often, agility, aggressiveness and a 'hunting sense' are more important than the ability to fly the aircraft smoothly with co-ordination."

Captain Alan J. Leahy, RN (Ret), flew the Hawker Sea Fury with No. 801 Squadron, Royal Navy, in HMS *Glory* during the Korean War: "Natural pilots found it easier to achieve high scores in air-to-air and air-to-ground exercises as they were less likely to fly with skid, slip or excessive negative or positive G forces on the aircraft. If the aircraft is not in balanced flight, the weapon will not go where the sight is pointing."

"Natural-born flyers... birds only!"
—Captain William O'Brien, USAF (Ret), formerly with the 357th Fighter Group, 8 USAAF

"I doubt that I had any 'natural flying ability', and I do not know of anyone else that I felt had any natural ability other than good co-ordination, eyesight and quick responses."
—2nd Lieutenant Robert N. Jensen, USAF (Ret),

formerly with the 55th Fighter Group, 8 USAAF

"Many fighter pilots were not natural-born flyers. [Werner]Mölders had some problems at the beginning of his pilot's career. [Hans-Joachim] Marseilles, on the other hand, was to my knowledge, a natural-born flyer."
—Generalleutnant a. D. Günther Rall, German Air Force (Ret)

"Every [RAF] fighter pilot had about two hundred hours of flying logged before joining a squadron. That was gained through Elementary Flying Training, where you first learned to fly; Service Flying, where you gained experience in all aspects of flying such as instrument flying, night flying, advanced aerobatics, formation flying and navigation, where you finally earned your wings. After that you spent time in an Advanced Flying Unit, which helped you prepare for combat duty, and finally, you were posted to an Operational Training Unit where you first flew Spitfires and were trained in actual aerial warfare and low-flying techniques. Of course, every trainee didn't get that far, as you could be 'washed out' at any time if your performance was unsatisfactory or if your instructor believed that you were not cut out to be a pilot.

"To be a fighter pilot you had to be trained on single-engine aircraft (such as a Harvard), be of a certain size and age, desire to fly fighters, and be recommended for the role by your Service Training flying instructor.

"Did we have natural flying ability? I didn't think so! World War II required so many pilots that all of them couldn't be naturals, but I do think that the intensive training helped immensely in sorting out the boys who could handle the task. Some were instinctively better than others and became the leaders on the squadrons, but I never knew anybody on our squadron who lacked ability or guts."
—Flight-Lieutenant Charles M. "Ack" Lawson, RAF (Ret), formerly with No. 165 Squadron

NATURAL-BORN FLYER

Far left: He was "Gentle" to his fellow 4th Fighter Group pilots at Debden, Essex, England during World War II. Major Don Gentile of Piqua, Ohio, was called "a one-man air force" by General Dwight D. Eisenhower. Gentile was credited with 27.8 kills by the end of his combat career. He died on 28th January 1951 while on a routine training flight in a T-33 jet which crashed near Andrews AFB, Maryland. Above: Leo Nomis, who flew with No. 71 (Eagle) Squadron, RAF in World War II, is the son of a World War I Lafayette Escadrille pilot. Nomis later flew Me 109s with the Israeli Air Force.

"It was important to have that skill. Being a soaring pilot helped a lot to begin with."
—Feldwebel Horst W. Petzschler, German Air Force (Ret), formerly with X/JG51 "Mölders"

"I became a natural-born flyer through instinct. Both of my parents were somewhat adventurous. My father was a World War I fighter pilot and instructor... never went overseas. After the war, he joined the Texas National Guard. My first ride in an airplane, as a very young kid, was strapped on my mother's lap in a Jenny while my father flew it. He [also] did some motorcycle, speedboat and auto racing, while I tagged along, revelling in the thrill of it all. I did some of the same as a teenager, so you can see where it all came from. Even though some of us were considered to be natural-born flyers, we still had to learn to be masters of our aircraft."
—Captain Jack Ilfrey, USAF (Ret), formerly with the 20th Fighter Group, 8 USAAF

"Can't fly, but can shoot— / He still can be a bit of a brute. / Can fly but can't shoot— / For him the Huns don't give a hoot."
—from *Tee Emm*, a World War II magazine of the RAF, July 1942

"The general consensus was, if we could get four or five missions under our belts, we'd be in pretty good shape. We had pretty good instructors. They worked for the German air force."
—Captain William O'Brien, USAF (Ret), formerly with the 357th Fighter Group, 8 USAAF

"Natural flying ability was very important. I started flying lessons at age fifteen, owned my own airplane at age eighteen, and had a private pilot's license and 250 hours of flying time before I entered the aviation cadet programme. I knew many fighter pilots with better than average ability and most did well in combat. This is not to say that the best went to fighters and the worst to bombers and transports, although there is some truth to this assumption. Some misfits occasionally slipped into the fighter groups. The sole purpose of some of these 'fighter pilots' was to survive the war, not necessarily to win it. I knew one pilot in my squadron who finished his tour of 270 combat hours (about sixty-five missions) and openly bragged that he had never fired his guns."
—Major Walter J. Konantz, USAF (Ret), formerly with the 55th Fighter Group, 8 USAAF

"I don't know how one would determine a natural-born flyer. Certainly some pilots were better than others, just as some men drive cars better or paint houses better."
—Flight-Lieutenant Douglas "Duke" Warren, RCAF (Ret), formerly with No. 66 and No. 165 Squadrons, RAF

"As the pilot of a Martin B-26 Marauder bomber, I never saw a good dogfight. When enemy fighters got through our fighter cover they flashed past the formation so fast we saw only fleeting glimpses of them—and even that was too much. Our tail gunners saw a few skirmishes but no sustained engagements. When I finally did see one, it was from the ground.

"While flying my thirty-fifth mission, with the 344th Bomb Group to attack bridges across the Seine River near Paris on 28 May 1944, I was shot down by German flak. The following day I contacted members of the Resistance. They took good care of me and for five days I was hidden in a small tavern where I ate well and was treated royally as the guest of a fine couple, Carlos and Maria. They spoke excellent English, having spent many years in New York City where Carlos had led a rhumba band at the Waldorf-Astoria, and were glad to aid an American.

"On Thursday, 2nd June, I was moved to an apartment on the top floor of a building on the rue I don't recall any pilots I would consider to be naturally born with pilot ability. Once a pilot got to the point where both he and the aircraft were one, he would have the ability to become a superior pilot because he didn't have to think about driving his aircraft and, instead, could think about missions, victories, escort, weather and all the other requisite things. One doesn't get to be a champion acrobatic pilot unless he practices hour after hour at his trade. It is almost like any other sport, one has to have the desire to excell and the energy to spend the time and effort to do so before he achieves success. I knew some pilots during the wars that I thought were really good during training, but that was mostly because they wanted to be. Another factor was that one had to be good if he wanted to survive.
—Colonel Walker M. Mahurin, USAF (Ret), formerly with the 56th Fighter Group, 8 USAAF

Right: Former Israeli Air Force Colonel Gidi Livni in the cockpit of his F-16 fighter. Below: Canadian CF-18 Hornet pilots at the Cold Lake Air Force Base, Alberta, Canada. Cold Lake is the home of Maple Flag, an annual exercise in which élite aircrew from various Air Forces are invited to participate and measure their skill and proficiency in air combat competition. The lessons learned there, and at Red Flag, the US equivalent, are invaluable to today's fighter pilots.

de Chantier in Versailles. There I was the guest of Charles and Delise. From their windows I could see the Eiffel Tower in the distance to the north-east. Less than 4 miles to the east I could see German aircraft taking off from Villacoublay aerodrome. At first there was only moderate activity, but on D-Day things really picked up, reaching a peak which was sustained for several days.

"Flights began arriving at dawn to refuel and fly shuttle runs to the invasion beachhead throughout the day. Often they returned individually, badly battered and damaged. Just before dark, they would refuel and fly to the more remote fields of eastern France to escape the night-bombing RAF. I was always amazed to witness their mass departures because they were so unorthodox compared with American techniques.

"Their take-off procedure seemed to consist solely of a left climbing turn at maximum climb after gear-up. There was no regular interval between take-offs. Each plane departed when it was ready, started the left climbing turn and merged with the swirl of snarling aircraft.

"The first big mission departure I saw was on D-Day, before I learned of the Normandy landing a hundred miles or so to the west. It was about seven o'clock in the morning, and when I heard the sound of so many engines I pulled a chair over to the window and waited for something to happen. The revving of the engines continued, then suddenly a red-nosed Me 109 with red wing tips leapt up in a very steep angle, starting a left climbing turn. Others followed immediately, and with each new launch the stack grew higher and higher, forming one great, ever enlarging corkscrew-shaped spiral. When the last plane was airborne there must have been at least fifty fighters involved, and the whole shebang just seemed to collapse as the leader nosed his plane down, accelerating as the others tagged along in a sort of indiscriminate mass, behind, alongside, underneath and above him. Without an apparent

pattern, they looked like a swarm of bees—either there was no precision or the utmost precision possible.

"I couldn't tell which was the case, but they never flew it any other way. I watched them many times and never saw them have any trouble, but I couldn't figure out how they could keep everyone in sight.

"That morning they headed westwards, and I wondered why such a large flight was in the area. It was far and away the largest I had seen, for most of the previous flights had been only small patrols.

"About two hours later, I heard several aircraft coming in from the west and looked out the living room window. The red nosed Messerschmitt slanted hurriedly in, knifing down for a landing. There was a sense of urgency about it because he made no attempt to set up a preliminary pattern but maintained airspeed all the way through a long, straight-in approach. Before he touched down, out of sight behind the trees ringing the field, others flew in from the same direction. Several trailed smoke, one badly. Then another group came in, milling about over the field as they set up a landing priority. Some were Focke-Wulf Fw 190s. There must have been nearly a hundred fighters altogether. I remember counting more than sixty, and I missed several flights.

"Throughout the next half hour they continued to straggle in, revving their engines, jazzing them like kids in hot rods. The jazzing bit made me cringe. In B-26s we wanted power all the way in.

"A neighbour on a nearby balcony excitedly called Delise over and told her about the invasion. Delise came running inside, calling me by the name on my forged identity card which said I was a forty-two-year-old merchant from Deurdan.

" 'Albert, Albert. Le débarquement. Le débarquement est ici.' She was so excited I couldn't get much information from her. We turned on the radio, but the German-controlled French station had nothing so I switched to the Yankee Doodle network. They were playing music—Glenn Miller.

Within six or seven months of its operational début, the Fw 190 was causing widespread consternation among RAF fighter squadrons based in the south of England. The [Kurt] Tank-designed fighter could out-perform the contemporary Spitfire on every count with the exception of the turning circle. I recall clearly the excitement with which I first examined the Focke-Wulf fighter; the impression of elegant lethality that its functional yet pleasing lines exuded. To me it represented the very quintessence of aeronautical pulchritude from any angle. It was not, to my eye, *more* beautiful than the Spitfire, but its beauty took a different form—the contrast being such as that between blonde and brunettte! It sat high on the ground, the oleo legs of its undercarriage appearing extraordinarily long, and it was immediately obvious that, despite the superlative job of cowling done by the Focke-Wulf designers, the big BMW 801D air-cooled radial engine was pretty obtrusive. Nonetheless, I was pleasantly surprised to find, after clambering into the somewhat narrow cockpit, that the forward view was still rather better than was offered by the Bf 109, the Spitfire or the Mustang. The semi-reclining seat—ideal for *continued*

47

high G manoeuvres—proved relatively comfortable and the controls fell easily to hand, although the flight instruments were not, in my opinion, quite so well arranged as those of the contemporary Bf 109G. Decidedly the most impressive feature of the German fighter was its beautifully light ailerons and its extremely high rate of roll. Incredible aileron turns were possible that would have torn the wings from a Bf 109 and badly strained the arm muscles of any Spitfire pilot trying to follow. Just as the Spitfire Mk IX was probably the most outstanding British fighter to give service in WW II, its Teutonic counterpart is undoubtedly deserving of the same recognition for Germany. Both were supreme in their time and class; both were durable and technically superb, and if each had not been there to counter the other, then the balance of air power could have been dramatically altered at a crucial period in the fortunes of both combatants.
—from *Wings of the Luftwaffe* by Captain Eric Brown

Right: RAF Hurricane pilots during the Battle of Britain. Many RAF pilots who flew in the Battle had only average flying skills and very little experience and flying hours in their aircraft.

After a pause and the phrase of the song which identified the station, the announcer gave the latest report on the invasion, with a detailed analysis of the whole story. Then I knew where the Jerries had been and why their numbers had increased after take-off. The Luftwaffe was probably being diverted from all over Europe to Normandy. It was tremendous news, and to me it was a real boost. I kept listening to the radio all day and telling Delise what was happening. The French radio stations told us nothing, but all morning cryptic messages were transmitted over both AFRS and the BBC. The BBC's were delightful.

" 'Pierre, there is a red, red rose in the icebox for you.'

" 'Marcel, your interest will be due on the 12th.'

"I often tuned in to the BBC after that to catch those messages and to get the news at dictation speed, which gave me a chance to take notes.

"Later, one of our own teams went into action. Charles learned that the marshalling yard was full of German tanks which were supposed to depart for Normandy that night. I wrote a note to an English agent who had contacted me, and he got the message off by portable radio units at about eight o'clock in the evening. Just before midnight it got results, for the RAF started a raid which lasted until one a.m. The marshalling yard was closer to our apartment than I had thought, and for the entire raid there were flashes from exploding bombs, crumbling buildings, the thudding WHAM of anti-aircraft batteries and the almost constant rocking of our building on its foundation. We finally went to bed about three a.m.

"The next morning I was still sleepy and stayed in bed, dozing until something awakened me. It was an unfamiliar sound, a sort of popping. Then came sounds I recognized—racing aircraft engines. I jumped out of bed and ran over to the window, dragging the sheet with me. Coming straight toward me at not more than 50 feet above the roof

was an American P-51 Mustang, going flat out. Close behind it were five Fw 190s, sort of bunched together, flying like the bees again, and all of them were taking pot shots with their 20mm cannon at the poor old Yankee boy.

"I saw all this simultaneously, before the planes flashed by just over the rooftop. They were coming from the airfield towards the apartment, headed north-west. I could even see the pilot, tensely hunched over the controls. He was wearing helmet and goggles and his chute straps showed plainly against the darker colour of his A2 jacket; a patch of white scarf was visible at his throat. The checquered yellow, or maybe chequered yellow and white, nose of his plane was clear and distinct. The aircraft was unpainted, bright aluminum, and its marking—black letters and the national insignia—stood out. It had a bubble canopy, the first one I'd ever seen.

"As they passed overhead, I whirled and ran through the apartment, across the living room to the window at the balcony on the other side of the building. The fighters actually dipped lower going away, for our building stood on the side of a slope, and the terrain fell away toward the centre of Versailles. They were soon out of sight, and I was sure the P-51 jockey was a goner. I turned away from the window and for the first time realized Delise was standing by my side and that I was wearing only a pair of shorts.

" 'She looked at me and said, *'Albert, l'Américain?'*

" 'I think so, Delise, yes.'

" *'Ahh... pas bon,'*

"I went back into the bedroom and put on my pants and uppers. Then, suddenly, Delise opened the door, shouting.

" *'Albert, ici, ici!'*

"I followed her quickly into the living room and on to the tiny balcony. A couple of minutes had passed, with the battle unexpectedly continuing, but the tide had changed. Coming toward us from the south-west, still at rooftop level, were the six

fighters, but leading the pack was a lonesome Fw 190, frantically trying to escape the P-51 pilot who was relentlessly hosing him with .50 caliber slugs in short, accurate bursts. Behind were the other four Jerries, holding their fire for fear of hitting the first Fw 190. Not more than 300 yards separated the first plane from the last.

"I began to really sweat out the American, though, because the Jerry was playing it cosy by heading straight for an anti-aircraft battery in a patch of woods. Sure enough, it opened fire. The Fw waggled his wing and the ground fire stopped, but the P-51 did the same thing and they didn't shoot at him either. Its pilot continued firing, and the law of averages caught up with the German plane. It exploded in a great, angry, red and black and orange burst.

"The Mustang pilot flew through the debris, but he was again the hunted and being shot at, so he banked toward Villacoublay a mile or so away. As he started a low pass over the field, all the ack-ack in the base opened up, even on their own planes. The three on the left, nearest Paris, turned left to avoid the flak, but the other one was too far to the right and had to turn to the right to stay clear. The Mustang turned also, heading for the lone Fw which apparently lost sight of him momentarily. Within thirty seconds the Yank was sitting on his tail, taking pot shots at the Luftwaffe again. The two planes were now heading toward me, almost on the same track they had flown on their first pass over the house earlier. The other three were completing a wider turn and were grouped some distance behind, and even though no physical change had occurred, they didn't seem to have the pouncing snarl or the look of the hunter so apparent in their first low-level pass. They straggled, trying to catch up, but they were too far back to save their buddy.

"Again I raced through the apartment to the other window. As the two planes came over, the thunder of their engines was punctuated by the

short, ammo-saving bursts of the .50 calibers. Scraping over the rooftops, twisting and yawing, they crossed the city, and finally the Fw 190 began to trail smoke. It nosed down into the horizon to merge with the red flame and black smoke-cloud of impact just west of town. (We learned later that the pilot got out alive but was badly injured.)

"The Yank racked the 51 around in a steep chandelle, right off the deck, almost reversing course. Two of the other 190s flashed past and pulled up also, but the third was a little further back and turned north, away from the tiger who continued his turn, diving a little now. With the height advantage for the first time, the Yank began firing on a dead pigeon. Smoke immediately trailed from the Fw, but the 51 pilot had to turn away as the other two planes closed in on him. The distressed Fw 190 limped away, trying to get back to Villacoublay, but crashed north of town several miles from the base. Now only two Germans were left, and the American had put a little distance between their planes and his.

"By this time I was absolutely going nuts. It was all I could do to keep from shouting in English. Everybody else was excited, too. People had come out on the rooftops of nearby apartments, and the balconies were full of men and women silently cheering for the crazy, lone American. I knew he would have a rough time from here on out. The last two wouldn't give him any breaks. On the other hand, they were wary, which might be in his favour. They flew out of sight on the deck south-west of the city. It was quiet for a minute or two and the rooftop audience became restless, frustrated.

"Then they returned, still on the deck, and the Yank was miraculously in the middle. They made a long pass across town while the Mustang closed to a range from which he couldn't miss—I figured he was very low on ammunition. The 190 was trying to outrun him this time, but when he saw his nemesis so close behind, the pilot pulled up frantically. The .50s cut loose in a brief, shattering

Far left: German Air Force Tornado pilot Peter Grosserhode of 511 Squadron, AG 51 based at Schleswig-Jagel. Left above: Hauptmann Mike Herrling and, left below: Flight-Lieutenant Gary Dunlop, Phantom pilots with 71 "Richthofen" Fighter Wing based at Wittmund, all highly-skilled and gifted airmen of many years military flying experience. Sadly, Flight-Lieutenant Dunlop, on an exchange with the German Air Force from the RAF in 1998, was killed in a tragic accident while on a training exercise in a Phantom near Goose Bay, Labrador, a few weeks after our interview.

blast. The 190 nosed straight up and its engine died. As the prop windmilled almost to a stop, the plane began to stall about 1000 to 1500 feet off the deck, and the pilot bailed out, opening his parachute immediately. At first its slow, billowing trail made me think it would never open, but it blossomed full and white only a few feet above the trees between me and the Eiffel Tower, standing very tiny in the distance.

"Now the odds were even-up, and what had seemed an eternity to me had really happened in just a few minutes. I began to worry about other German fighters getting airborne to aid their shot-up air patrol, but they were either engaged elsewhere or were unable to fuel up, fearing attack from other aircraft.

"In the distance I could see the last two planes in another long, low arc. The American had started a gradual swing to the west, but he was not about to leave the deck. The Jerry was still behind him, but his guns were silent now, indicating he might also be low on ammunition. When they disappeared over the rim of the rolling hills west of the city the Mustang was taking evasive action, and I was sure the dogfight was almost over. The Jerry had the advantage and was sure to hold it. A moment later, a black, blotchy mushroom of smoke billowed upwards.

"I knew then that one hell of a good pilot had bought the farm. He had given it everything he had and reduced the odds from five to one to even before the end, and I wondered what he had thought when only that one Fw remained. Just a few pilots had ever shot down five German aircraft in one day.

"I noted the time and tried to fix the approximate location of the action and also made a mental note of the aircraft markings, determined to confirm the four victories if I ever got back to England. I just couldn't forget the way the man had flown, dreaming up tactics as he went along, playing it by ear, only to have his luck run out a little too soon.

"The spectators on the rooftops felt as I did. They stood up slowly, stretched, gestured with their hands and went back inside. They seemed to feel a personal loss, almost as if they had been with the pilot themselves, pushing him on to victory with their will alone. They had prayed for his survival, now they prayed for his soul.

"Delise said nothing but went into the kitchen and returned with two glasses and a bottle of Armagnac. She filled the glasses, raised hers and said, 'Le pilote Américain.' Her voice was soft and her eyes brimmed.

"I nodded and we drank.

"I had a couple more—alone.

"I sat there thinking about the pilot and the action-packed few minutes just passed. Suddenly, after three weeks of almost no war at all, it was back with me again and then suddenly gone. All I could do was sit there and think.

"Twenty minutes later, Charles, Delise's husband, came home. He was very excited and laughed as he asked if we'd seen the fight.

" 'Did you the American kill those Germans?'

" 'Yes.' I said, 'We saw. He got four of them. Four out of five.'

He looked at me and grinned, taking another sip of brandy, and suddenly I wanted to hit him, he looked so smug.

" 'Non. No, no! He got five. He got them all. I see... everything. Especially the last. It was magnificent.'

"He said this in a mixture of French and English, the way we always conversed. I wasn't sure I understood. He launched into a stream of French I couldn't understand, but it didn't make any difference because I could tell that he was certain the Yank had gotten all five. We had several more brandies before Charles calmed down enough to explain what had happened.

" 'Charles, how do you know he got them all?'

" 'Because I saw. Especially the second, third and fifth, you know? The last was near me. I was at the garden. I have to rake—to hoe, you see? The last one he did not even shoot—much. They came near, so fast. There is this little hill, with woods. The planes almost skim the ground. The American goes zip, like so, around the hill once, and the German follows, but in a greater circle. It is like the cat and mouse. The the second time the American plane slows—abruptly—its wheels drop out, you know? The German goes in, towards the American, now so much slower, and they are almost sideways, but he loses control of his machine. Only a kilometre or so from where I was standing he crashes in the woods. I jump up and down and wave my hoe and everybody does the same, but then the Germans come and we hide our smiles and I come home fast.'

"I thought about what must have happened. The American pilot was out of ammunition and had dropped his flaps and gear—everything—chopped his throttle, to slow down, forcing the German to turn in, risking a stall to make the German stall. The German didn't have much choice. If he didn't make one last try he would have wound up in front of the Mustang anyway—so he had made the try.

"Everybody I saw for the next few days talked about the dogfight. Coming so soon after D-Day, it gave all of us, me especially, a tremendous boost in morale.

"The plans to get me out of France by a night pick-up from a wheatfield didn't materialize, and it was early September before I reached London. I reported the dogfight during my debriefing, but by that time I had forgotten a key factor—the aircraft marking, including the squadron code.

"Years later, I spent several days in the Air Force Historical section at Maxwell Field, Alabama, trying to learn the name of the pilot by reading all operational reports submitted by Mustang pilots for the period. (Now, I do not even remember the exact date.) I narrowed it down to twenty-one pilots. Several were killed on the missions involved and others had been killed later in Germany. One noted 'confused fighting at house top level in the

Right: Lieutenant Saburo Sakai (third from left) at Chino Airport, California in May 1992. Below right: Most of the Japanese suicide pilots of World War II were not natural-born flyers. This is a staged version of a Kamikaze ceremony for the US Strategic Bombing Survey Motion Picture Project in November 1945 at Chofu, Japan.

"Men, welcome to the 4th Fighter Group. You have been assigned here after completing your training in the 3rd Air Force. There you were required to comply with a myriad of rules, regulations, and orders, governing your conduct in the air and on the ground. These requirements were designed to promote safety for you and your fellow flyers during your training period. Now you are trained combat Fighter Pilots assigned to a top Fighter Group, in the 8th Air Force. We have the same rules, but we are capable and aggressive, and you must be also. To this end, whenever you leave the base on a flight, do not return to land until you have broken those rules. BUT DON'T GET CAUGHT, or you will never fly with this group again! Secondly, if anyone 'Prangs a Kite' while stunting, he's out!"
—Colonel Don Blakeslee, formerly Group Commander, 4th Fighter Group, 8 USAAF

Paris area' but claimed no victories.

"As of now, the identity of the American pilot has never been verified, and it's too bad. But there's one thing I know. Even if I never find out who he was—it was the best damned dogfight I'll ever see!"
—1st Lieutenant Henry C. Woodrum, formerly with the 344th Bomb Group (M), 9 USAAF

Two of Japan's greatest fighter pilots of World War II were Lieutenants Hiroyoshi Nishizawa and Toshio Ohta. Nothing mattered more to them than their function as fighter pilots. Their skills, their determination and their intensity made them extraordinarily dangerous to the Allied fliers who faced them in combat. Unfazed when they found themselves on the wrong end of the odds, or in an engagement with aircraft of superior performance to that of their Zeroes, they prevailed repeatedly.

Physically, Nishizawa was the antithesis of the image of a fighter pilot. He weighed only 140 lb, was pale and gaunt, and looked extremely malnourished, with his ribs showing prominently through his skin. He was chronically ill with tropical skin diseases and suffered from malaria.

Quiet and reserved, he impressed most of his fellow pilots as being cold and unfriendly, a loner who would often go an entire day without saying a word to anyone. But no Japanese fighter pilot commanded and deserved the admiration and respect of his peers more than Nishizawa. Few, if any of them, were more dedicated and committed to the fight than he, and none was to match his score. Referred to as 'the Devil' by those who flew with him in combat, Nishizawa came into his own when the fight was on. The famous Japanese World War II ace Lieutenant Saburo Sakai recalls how Nishizawa seemed to become one with his plane; how the seeming genius of his gentle touch at the controls made his fighter respond almost magically, in ways Sakai had never seen before. His aerobatics were at once brilliant, spectacular, breathtaking and totally unpredictable. He flew

like a bird—better than a bird. He finished with a total of eighty-seven victories.

Friendly, amiable and gregarious, Toshio Ohta was an exact opposite to Nishizawa in personality, but no less intense in the air. He enjoyed a good joke, was quick to join with his friends in a good time, and even quicker to come to the aid of a fellow pilot who needed help in the air or on the ground.

Like Nishizawa, his superb flying skills and his brilliance in combat brought Ohta considerable recognition in their Wing at Lae, New Guinea, and throughout the Japanese air forces. Ohta's final score was thirty-four.

"I can't remember the time when airplanes were not part of my life and can't remember ever wanting anything so much as to fly one. Once I had started I had to keep flying.

"But it was not until I was seventeen that I finally got into an airplane. At that time I felt I had come to the place where I belonged in the world. The air to me was what being on the ground was to other people. When I felt nervous it pulled me together. Things could get too much for me on the ground, they never got that way in the air. Flying came into my mind like fresh air into smoked up lungs and was food in my hungry mouth and strength in my weak arms. I felt that way the first time I got into an airplane. I wasn't nervous when I first soloed. There was excitement in me, but it was the nice kind you get when you're going home after a long, long unhappy time away."
—Major Don S. Gentile, formerly with the 4th Fighter Group, 8 USAAF

In World War I, he was known by his men as *der Rittmeister*. Today, he is the stuff of legend, one of the world's first fighter pilots and certainly among the greatest of all time, the man everyone knows as 'the Red Baron', Manfred Freiherr von Richthofen.

That eighty Allied aircraft fell to his guns is

certainly remarkable. Also of interest is the judgement, made during his pilot training in 1915, that he was 'lacking in natural aptitude'.

In time, von Richthofen met Oswald Böelcke, the father of the German fighter arm, and eventually became his protégé. Richthofen's career took off in the summer of 1916 when Böelcke selected him for the new Jagdstaffel 2, and he joined their first offensive patrol in mid-September. Flying an Albatross DII, he downed an FE2b over Cambrai that day, and that night he celebrated by ordering a silver trophy cup from Berlin, to commemorate the kill. It was the first of many such cups.

On 28th October, the great Böelcke, having been credited with forty aerial victories, was killed in a mid-air collision. Manfred von Richthofen succeeded him as Germany's leading ace, averaging one kill a week.

On 23rd November 1916, von Richthofen shot down the top Royal Flying Corps ace of the time, Major Lanoe Hawker, 'the English Böelcke'. His victories mounted quickly, and on 16th January 1917 he was awarded the *Ordre Pour le Merite* (colloquially known as The Blue Max) and was given his first command, that of Jasta 11.

In December 1916, von Richthofen began to paint parts of his plane a bright scarlet to show the other side whom they were up against when they encountered him. He felt that the red paint might intimidate some of his opponents, and he was right. His score continued to build, to sixty by September 1917, to seventy in March 1918, to eighty by 20th April 1918. On the 21st, however, his luck ran out.

Flying from their airfield at Bertrangles, the Sopwith Camels of No. 209 Squadron, RFC, led by Captain Arthur Royal Brown, engaged von Richthofen's fighters over the Somme valley. The German's red Triplane came through Brown's sight and the Canadian's twin Vickers guns brought a quick finish to the spectacular life and career of the Red Baron.

IN HIS AUTOBIOGRAPHY, Captain Eddie Rickenbacker, the American World War I ace, wrote that after the War the Universal Studios producer Carl Laemmle made frantic efforts to contract Rickenbacker to perform in a motion picture about his wartime adventures. Universal offered Rickenbacker a reported $100,000. Laemmle's assistant, Irving Thalberg, badgered the flyer on a cross-country rail journey, trying to wear down the veteran airman's resistance to signing. Finally, Rickenbacker had had enough, and threatened a lawsuit against the producer for personal harassment. Said Captain Rickenbacker: "I could just see myself up there on the screen, making movie love to some heroine. I was fully aware of my potential influence upon the youth of America, and I intended to continue to do my best to inspire them by both deeds and words. Depicting myself in the movies, I felt, would degrade both my own stature and the uniform I so proudly wore."

Ever since World War I, the motion picture industry's films on military aviation themes have tended to stray wildly from reality.

Even today, when studio committees consider the potential merits of an aerial epic the truth seems to take a lower priority than, say, the likely profit from the sale of toys and other by-products related to the picture. Authenticity is often side-stepped with arguments such as "We'll do it all with models (nowadays *effects*)", "It'll be cheaper and the audience will never know the difference", or "The script calls for our hero to be a skirt-chaser... never mind that the real guy was and is happily married. That won't play in Poughkeepsie. Action in the air, action on the ground. That's the ticket".

Most producers, it would seem, hire a "technical adviser" (if they even bother) to give an artificial credibility to their film. In general, they seem disinclined to listen to the poor soul whose name and credentials they proudly list in their credits,

much less actually take his advice. The resulting film is almost always an embarrassment.

One such was Universal's 1942 production *Eagle Squadron*. Produced by Walter Wanger, this was the first major American film on the air war made after the attack on Pearl Harbor and the United States' entry into the war. Unfortunately, the movie trivializes the activities of the first three American fighter squadrons in the European war. Several members of the Eagle Squadrons (American fighter pilots who had volunteered to serve with the RAF), along with many prominent English guests, were invited to the London première in July 1942. As USAF Colonel Lee Gover, former RAF Eagle and USAAF 4th Fighter Group pilot, recalled: "The film was so far-fetched from actual combat... it was really embarrassing." Most of the American pilots in the theatre that evening wanted to walk out *en masse*, but felt that, as invited guests, it would be impolite. However, some could stomach no more of the film after the first half hour, and quietly departed by a side door. Another Eagle, Bill Geiger recalled: "That movie upset everybody, and Squadron-Leader [Chesley] Peterson in particular. We had been told that it would be a documentary, like the *March of Time* of those days. We all felt that we had been double-crossed. Pete was so bitter about it that he never responded to any requests for information for publicity about the Eagles from that day forward." After the release of *Eagle Squadron*, even the popular correspondent Quentin Reynolds, who had been well liked and regarded by the Eagles—whom he frequently entertained in his London flat, and who had delivered the opening narration in the film—was refused access to Peterson's airfield. "We were just another RAF squadron trying to do our best. We deserved, and wanted, no special attention, because of our American background, which overshadowed the British (and the Commonwealth) squadrons who were doing the same job and with whom we had to fly," said Gover.

THE MEDIA VERSION

In an era of swashbuckling, hard-drinking, carousing fighter pilots, Don stood out like a symbol of virtue. His only vice was an occasional cigar. The majority of us lived from day to day; Don was just the opposite. Every payday most of his month's pay was sent home to be banked in his account. Don had been born of immigrant parents, and maybe for this reason an ambition boiled inside of him to prove his capabilities to the world. The hard shell about him was very seldom broken. To deviate from his appointed task seemed to him a weakness. Sometimes I was able to observe, through an occasional crack in this shell, a different Don, one who could suffer spells of depression and who knew his human limitations. These cracks didn't show very often though, and like a turtle sensing danger, Don would retreat once more into his armor. In the air, however, it was different...
—Major John T. Godfrey on Don Gentile, from *The Look of Eagles*

Left: Kenneth More and Muriel Pavlow in the 1957 Rank Film production, *Reach For The Sky*, a film biography of RAF World War II fighter pilot Douglas Bader.

It is easy for the press to idealize pilots and air crews during wars. This must have started during WWI and was exagerrated by books and stories such as *G-8 and His Battle Aces,* or *Battling the Flying Circus.* In any circumstances where heroes are made and medals are awarded the characters tend to be exaggerated by the media. Of course, there were a lot of flamboyant characters who wanted to create the image of "hot-shot charlies". There were also a lot of pilots who would tend to magnify their exploits, not only in front of their fellow pilots, but also in front of members of the press. Any story becomes better with a lot of embellishment. Even today, when I get around some of my fellow aces, I am amazed at the stories they tell. Quite often I have been involved with the circumstances of these stories and they don't resemble what I have known to be the facts. In most of these cases, the stories are really great, but not exactly true. It pays to advertise!

—Colonel Walker M. Mahurin, USAF (Ret), formerly with the 56th Fighter Group, 8 USAAF

"When they had the showing at the premiere in London, they made a big deal about it, getting a lot of Eagles, as many as they could at the time, in to see it, and I don't know of anybody that stayed through the picture. I'd say the bulk of us got up after about the first thirty minutes, and walked out. The English were madder than hell at us... the protocol people, because there was supposed to be a lot of public relations and anyway, you didn't walk out on the King, for God's sake. So, it was just a farce. Typical Hollywood. It was insulting at the time because here were the people being bombed all the time, and fighting the damned war, and then they come in with a thing that's obviously so phoney even a little kid would know it."
—Major-General Carroll W. McColpin, USAF (Ret)

Generally, television has not shown itself to be more earnest than the movies in pursuit of authenticity where stories of fighter pilots are concerned. The 1988 UK production *Piece of Cake*, based on Derek Robinson's excellent 1983 novel of the same title, is a case in point. Many Royal Air Force fighter pilots who were operational on squadrons in Britain in the early years of World War II, have stated that they were appalled by the representations made in the TV production. They saw little similarity between the real pilots they knew, and were themselves at that time, and those portrayed in the multi-part epic. It is also the case that no Spitfires were operating in France in the period before the Battle of Britain, contrary to the way *Piece of Cake* represented events. On the plus side, the aerial sequences were flown and filmed with a wonderful graphic power, and the fighter planes were worked hard and well by consumate professionals. So-called "creative licence" often comes into play, even in big-budget productions, and limitations, or directorial whims, tend to dictate a fudge here and a larger compromise there. The actual events and people represented become unrecognisably distorted. Those who lived the events reshaped on film, and all who care about accurate representation of history, can only wince.

War movies, and especially air war movies, have not found great favour with film critics over the years. Once America had entered World War II, and Hollywood had a full year of war movie-making under its belt, Bosley Crowther summed up the product to date: "By and large, the general quality of motion pictures this past year has reflected the confusion and uncertainty which the war has exposed in Hollywood. Producers have plunged willy-nilly into purely escapist pictures or have made the war out to seem illusory by dodging it into old routines." Film historian Clyde Jeavons has suggested that it was not the nature of these early films so much to inform the public, as "to stimulate... to wrap the war up in attractive packaging and sell it to the people". James H. Farmer wrote in his fine book on aviation films, *Celluloid Wings*, "Within such a context, death for the Allies, if not the enemy, was often antiseptic and painless. The protagonists were naively heroic and unashamedly patriotic. Such story lines were usually entertaining and professionally smooth but generally were far removed from the harsher reality." Crowther did feel that: "the one encouraging trend has been the growing one towards actuality films [documentaries], indicated mainly in the short product and more recently in the films of the OWI [Office of War Information]. Still very much on the periphery of screen entertainment, these films at least are foretelling a more thoughtful and realistic fashion in screen fare. This is the brightest prospect for films in the months—or years—ahead."

Yet another aspect of air war entertainment was the multi-episode serial, produced for both film and radio in the war years. In these brief potboilers, all pretence of reality went out of the window; pulp-fiction adventure and fantasy were all. Such efforts as *Flight Lieutenant*, *Captain*

When "at readiness" during the Battle of Britain, an RAF fighter pilot had a drill that he had to do. He had to go out to his plane and open the side hatch, pull back the cockpit hood and pull out the straps to make them ready for collecting and fastening when the time came. He had to check all the instruments, "dope" the engine to be sure it was ready to start (it had already been warmed up), polish the hood and the mirror, test the R/T and the oxygen system and, if all was well, sign the form 700 showing he accepted the aircraft for the next flight. All this took about ten minutes and after that all he had to do was go back to dispersal and wait.

Above: Group-Captain Alan C. Deere, formerly with No. 54 Squadron, RAF, photographed in 1989. Deere was one of the most famous Battle of Britain pilots.

Below: World War II pilots of the 8 USAAF 79th Fighter Squadron, 20th Fighter Group, ride out to their aircraft at Kings Cliffe, Northamptonshire, England. Bicycles and the ubiquitous jeep were basic transport on the fighter and bomber stations of the Eighth and Ninth US Army Air Forces in wartime Britain.

Fortune favors the bold.
—Virgil, *Aeneid, X*

Midnight, Sky Raiders, Smilin' Jack, Hop Harrigan and *Adventures of the Flying Cadets* were avidly followed by teenage and pre-teen would-be fighter pilots who, years later, remember being inspired by these serials. They count them among the influences which led them to follow their dream and become real fighter pilots.

"The fighter pilot was a very indvidual person, often not shown [correctly] on TV, [or in the] press; Hollywood often gave the wrong picture and so did the UFA in Potsdam on our side. Too much propaganda, not enough truth."
—Feldwebel Horst W. Petzschler, German Air Force (Ret), formerly with X/JG51 "Mölders"

Early in 1943, Colonel Robert L. Scott had a hit on his hands. Scott, one of the highest-scoring American fighter aces, had gained prominence as commander of General Claire Chennault's 23rd Fighter Group, descendants of the Flying Tigers,

in China. Now, at the age of thirty-four, he was back in the States dictating his virtually guaranteed best-seller, *God Is My Copilot,* to stenographers at Scribner's, the New York publishing house. So hot was this still-unpublished book that Scott was offered, and accepted, the then staggering sum of $100,000 for the screen rights by Warner Brothers. Before accepting the Warners offer, Scott cleared the movie deal with General Henry H. 'Hap' Arnold in Washington, who told him: "You make it authentic and you make it faithful to the Air Force and you make them pay you." Clearly, Arnold believed strongly in the value of showing the American public what the Army Air Forces were doing around the world. His agenda included the ultimate creation of a separate and independent United States Air Force, and he knew the importance of effectively promoting his service.

In Hollywood, Warners assigned Hal Wallis to produce the movie version of Scott's book, and he brought in the writer Steve Fisher to do the

screenplay, working with Scott. Fisher wrote the first draft and met Scott. "When Steve showed it to me it began to take on all these things... malaria [which Scott never contracted] and a Japanese pilot called Tokyo Joe, which had nothing to do with the book." James Farmer stated in *Celluloid Wings*: "Scott, a happily married man of many years, most strongly objected to the script's equally fictitious love affair." "I loved my wife and I never wanted anything like that in the movie!" said Scott, and after his many protests the China-based love interest was deleted.

After several months delay, *God Is My Copilot* finally began filming in August 1944. When it was released early in 1945, the movie-going public seemed to like the film; the critics did not. Bosley Crowther: "Obviously Warner Brothers took the title of Colonel Robert L. Scott's war book... much more literally than the author did. For their rip-roaring film... is heavily and often embarrassingly larded with piety. For Colonel Scott's popular, vivid story of his career in the Far East has been turned by the Warners into another, rather cheaply theatrical war film." James Farmer: "Sadly much of the Peter Milne dialogue degenerates into 1942 vintage pulp fiction that pleased neither Scott nor critics—'Okay you Yankee Doodle Dandies, come and get us. I'm going to drop one of you right in Chennault's lap. Where are you gangsters? Come up and get a load of that scrap metal you sold us.' "

Scott recalled his feelings about the film: "Chennault had evidently sent a letter to Arnold and had used the phrase, 'I am being made to look over-sympathetic in the role projected by Raymond Massey.' So I got orders to report to the Pentagon to view that film with all the staff. And, man, I had to sit there and see that corny film in which so little is true. They made me have that malaria attack which never did happen... and here I sat in the Pentagon with every general and most of the admirals watching *Copilot*, embarrassed as hell. When it was all over they applauded. Arnold stood

up and said, 'I see no oversimplification or over-sympathetic performance. I think it's a good picture.' And I wanted to say, 'General, what are you talking about? It never did happen like that!' And with 'Big Mike' sitting back in that P-43 saying, 'Fear can sabotage the strongest heart...' well, it's amazing how they make a movie!"

RAF Group-Captain Al Deere commented on the 1968 Guy Hamilton/Harry Saltzman production of *Battle of Britain* filmed mainly in Spain and at Duxford in Cambridgeshire: "I think they did it quite well, but the air battle was fought in the air, and nothing was going on on the ground... they had to try and make something there... into a film. For example, we never got off the airfield [during the actual battle]. There were no girlfriends or pubs or things... we just didn't get off the airfield. How could we? We were so short of pilots! So they [the filmmakers], in order to make a story, had to have a girlfriend, driving up and meeting her pilot at a pub. Well, there was none of that at all. There was *before* and there was *after*, but not whilst the battle was on, there wasn't. There was no relief whatsoever. Oh, we were moved as a squadron up north for a week, but that was only in order to refurbish and get some new pilots in and give them a quick bit of training, and then go back again [to Hornchurch]. We were on 'readiness' or we were so bloody tired we were just dead. There was no glamour about it, really. That seems trite, but there wasn't any at the time. We didn't feel much glamour, I can tell you."

In 1948, Warner Brothers returned to the fray with *Fighter Squadron*, directed by Raoul Walsh and starring Robert Stack and Edmund O'Brien. With a script that had "orders from above" prohibiting the USAAF P-47 pilots jettisoning their long-range drop tanks in combat, credibility took a beating from the word go. Colonel Lee Gover was assigned to the *Fighter Squadron* project and he recalled the

I can only say that as a fighter pilot myself, living in mess on fighter stations from mid-1940 continuously to almost the end of the war in Europe, I found my contemporaries to be perfectly normal young men of their time. Of course they were high spirited, but they were of normal intelligence. We had affairs with young women and enjoyed a party. That is surely what one would expect of young men who were volunteers, who met exacting medical standards, who withstood for long periods the hazards both of flying and of war, of which they were quite frequently reminded by the loss of their friends in accidents or in battle.
—Air Vice-Marshal Edward Crew, former night fighter pilot

After each war there is a little less democracy to save.
—Brooks Atkinson

drop tank matter: "They asked us [during the war] to bring the belly tanks home if we could because they were scarce at first. But when we got into a dogfight we didn't give a damn who said don't drop 'em! We dropped them."

Actor Jack Larson played the part of Shorty, the youngest pilot in the squadron. Of the director Larson recalled: "Raoul Walsh was a very imposing personality, tough with that tough voice of his. He wore boots and riding pants and had that eye patch [he had lost an eye filming an early western]. He never really rehearsed you. He was interested in timing and dialogue and didn't deal with the actors much. He never gave you any direction except to say, 'Pick it up kid, the scene's on its ass', or 'I could drive a truck through that pause.'"

James Farmer wrote of *Fighter Squadron*: "Leaving Hollywood for the last time in July, Gover, who appears as an extra in the film's pub sequences, returned home with mixed emotions. Although satisfied with the flying scenes that he led in the air, Gover remained dissatisfied with much of the script. The sense of frustration would grow as veteran pilots, friends who had flown for the film and knew and felt what it had really been like in the war, were killed. For many of these men, it was their last chance to see the story told before giving their lives during the Korean conflict. Commenting on the film Gover admitted: 'I knew the movie wasn't very good, just too much Hollywood nonsense in the damn thing. I told them at the time, but no one would listen.'"

"Certainly there were some 'mad' fighter pilots, also tank men, submariners and others. I believe that you had to have a good deal of 'derring-do' even to undertake training as a fighter pilot, knowing what you were expected to do at the end of your training. A good number of fighter pilots 'didn't give a damn' for anybody or anything. Certainly I never knew or met a fighter pilot who didn't like women. I feel the 'non-intellectual' idea came from

'brains' or people who thought they were clever, who could not visualize themselves doing what fighter pilots did. So they said, 'They must be really dumb.' Of course, hard-drinking, go for the girls, who cares about tomorrow attitude... makes for good copy for stories and papers. I think journalists may have over-reacted."
—Flight-Lieutenant Douglas "Duke" Warren, RCAF (Ret), formerly with No. 66 and No. 165 Squadrons, RAF

Colonel John Cunnick, USAF (Ret), flew Mustangs with the 55th Fighter Group at Wormingford in World War II: "A fighter pilot is all balls and no forehead. If he thinks at all, he thinks that he is immortal; God's gift to women and his airplane. On a mission, he is too damned busy to be frightened because he is alone and has to do it all... at all times he has to know where he is on the chart, set his armament switch for the occasion, scan his instruments and the entire sky constantly, cover his leader's six o'clock, fly his aircraft, and at some crucial time try to relieve himself. Finding your pecker when it is minus 60 degrees is all but impossible. Then, of course, he must shoot down the enemy, strafe the airfield, train or any other targets of opportunity, etc. When the fighter pilot returns to base, that's when the bullshit starts. Yes, they were cavalier because a fighter pilot who thought about dying usually did die."

"All the fighter pilots I ever knew were sober, God-fearing men who were kind to little old ladies crossing the road and would much prefer to retire to bed early with a cup of cocoa and their aircraft manual than go on a run ashore and get stoned."
—Captain Alan J. Leahy, RN (Ret), formerly with No. 810 Squadron

"Young men away from home for the first time are a product of their upbringing. A few go off the deep end unless their peers intercede. As a rule,

Left and above: Living conditions for USAF pilots in the Gulf War varied considerably.

I think most of the good fighter pilots I have known were pretty much "devil-may-care" types...especially during wartime. I'm sure it was partially to avoid becoming too obsessed with the inherent dangers of being a pilot in combat. Although they were not very intellectual, they were extremely intelligent and, in most cases, team players. Of course, the successful ones were exceptionally competent aviators and knew their aircraft's capabilities as well as it's limitations. They all really enjoyed flying and particularly aerobatics.
—Lieutenant Commander H.B. Moranville, USN (Ret)

March 15, 1944
Dear Folks & Bro. John,
I have just arrived at a new station and I'll scribble you a few lines tonight so you'll get my new address soon. I have written you a V-Mail also which you may get before this.

I consider myself a very lucky guy to land in this Squadron. It's the oldest American fighter unit in England. It was the famed "Eagle Sqd." I don't think I need to say more. These boys really know their business and they are a swell bunch. This squadron just started using the plane I fly so I have a lot more time in the plane than the older boys but there is a he__ of a lot I can learn from them on other things. By the way, I do hope you have the radio working or have a newspaper cause we are making history over here and if you can hear reports on what "my plane" is doing you will get a picture of my activities.

This station is known as the best in England as far as personal comforts go. We live in regular hotels with steam heat, bathrooms, etc. Our mess hall has the air of a banquet hall—white linen tablecloths and more *continued*

Right: Pilot-Officer Albert G. "Day" Lewis of Nos. 85 and 249 Squadrons, RAF during the Battle of Britain. Lewis appeared in a *Life* magazine article on RAF fighter pilots early in World War II.

however, most young men, fighter pilots, like to drink and chase girls. I found that those I knew did not drink to excess except on a rare occasion. When in combat I flew ten days of combat and was given three days off. I made it my practice not to drink the night before a combat mission for obvious reasons. A good many of the young men never drank before entering the service and their drinking in the service was limited. However, the older group did their share of drinking. The younger group of fighter pilots were nineteen to twenty-five years of age. The older group were five years older. Fighter pilots by nature are cocky, aggressive and self-assured. How else would one go into war all by himself in a fighting machine?"
—Lieutenant-Colonel Robert M. Littlefield, USAF (Ret), formerly with the 55th Fighter Group, 8 USAAF

"Naturally, when you put together a bunch of young men (most were between twenty and twenty-five years old) who were brought up in different countries and cultures, you are going to get a mixed bag. Most of the pilots were single, and I think those who weren't sometimes wished they were. Spitfire pilots flew in the daytime, so nights were used to let off steam and enjoy themselves. You must recognize that there was a different mindset during the war years, not just among servicemen and women, but also the civilian population. The pubs in England were great places for socializing, and each squadron seemed to have its own favourite pub and the local girls knew this also. It wasn't the Hollywood-style 'eat, drink and be merry for tomorrow we die', but it was close to it. There was definitely a carefree attitude among the populace in those years.

Of course, there were also the quiet types who preferred to stay back at the RAF base and write letters home. I wasn't one of them and I think, in retrospect, that they were in the minority. I think

the average fighter pilot was a bit of a hell-raiser."
—Flight-Lieutenant Charles M. "Ack" Lawson, RAF (Ret), formerly with No. 165 Squadron

"When a fighter pilot walked into a pub or a hotel bar, he let those inside know who he was by having the top button of his tunic unbuttoned. That was his trademark; it signified that he was an aerial warrior and that he flew fighters. He was, of course, immediately spotted by the opposite sex, young and old, and was instantly admired."
—Colonel Steve Pisanos, USAF (Ret), formerly with the 4th Fighter Group, 8 USAAF

"I have a habit when I am frightened of talking to myself silently—but the words are so plain in my head that it's almost as if they were echoing there with real sound. 'Now, boy,' I'd say to myself, or call myself 'Squirt' or 'Son', and tell myself to just take it easy and I'd be all right. But whatever I told myself that day I kept thinking, 'Oh Mama!'

"We went along fast in a good, tight formation, like a bunch of killers going to town, I guess, but I kept sitting up there in the middle of the posse looking like one of the boys, no doubt, but thinking what a kid I was. I was twenty-one years old then, and what was I doing here, I asked

myself, when where I wanted to be was at home in my mother's lap."
—Major Don S. Gentile, formerly with the 4th Fighter Group, 8 USAAF

"Derring-do was the fiction of aged fighters, often writing years afterwards—trying to depict themselves as above it all. Nonsense! We were kids, trying to get through it! We were scared to death on every mission—particularly when going in to bomb a strongpoint such as a marshalling yard. We were almost as scared of real women as we were of flak!"
—Flying-Officer E.A.W. Smith, formerly with No. 127 Squadron, RAF

"We... all contribute to the squadron newspaper fund. Every morning, a pristine copy of the *Telegraph* appears in the crew room, along with an assortment of 'comics'—the *Sun*, the *Mirror* and a couple of other tabloids. When the papers are thrown away the next morning, the *Telegraph* remains... pristine. The only time it is opened is to photocopy the crossword. Meanwhile fights break out over the comics, with everyone desperate to immerse themselves in sex, scandal and soap opera. Such is the intellectual might of the men of 31!"
—from *Tornado Team* by RAF Flight-Lieutenants John Peters and John Nichol

"I think *Top Gun* came out before I actually joined the Air Force. It was out when I was applying to join the University Air Squadron, and I think it was the big, glamourous 'look what I can do, this is great, and we're all wonderful heroes' and everything is happening at twice the speed. I wouldn't say the job is mundane... it's not at all, but it [the movie] is exaggerated. Some of the flying sequences are great to watch, but they're not realistic as far as what happens day to day on the squadron. The actual stuff that goes with it... all the big talk and everything, I don't know. The Americans themselves might find some of it a little

more akin to what they do. But as far as the RAF... we operate on a completely different level to what *Top Gun* is showing you. It's something that people watch and they know all the lines to, and it's good fun to throw 'em around every now and again. It's good fun to watch. I don't think there's anybody [on the squadron] who hasn't seen it, or anybody who would object and say, 'Oh, I'm not watching it. It's rubbish.' It's more of a laugh. Pilots like watching aeroplanes flying on screen and it always looks brilliant when you see it with the cameras, but I don't think the way they interact with each other is anything quite like what goes on on the squadron."
—Flight-Lieutenant Helen Gardiner, No. 43 Squadron, RAF

"Looking back now from my vantage point after some hundreds of scraps with the Germans—of bouncing them and of being bounced and of the bangs and prangs and clobberings and of being clobbered—I would say now that in those ancient days of 1942 and 1943 the confidence I had in my ability to kill the Nazis and to keep them from killing our men was misplaced.

"I know now how much remained for me to learn before I could handle myself in the rough, fast, big-time company they have operating over Europe. But in those days I didn't even know how little I knew.

"After I had a few fights under my belt and made a few scores I became again what I had been before the war—a kid full of beans, who, when he sits in an airplane, feels there is nothing in the world that can master him. Fortunately for me, our side of the war was up against a situation in those years that prevented me from acting on my belief in myself. Otherwise, I probably would have had my beans cooked in some gasoline fire long before I learned how much there is to know besides flying about this business of fighting."
—Major Don S. Gentile, formerly with the 4th Fighter Group, 8 USAAF

silverware than I quite know how to use. We also have pretty civilian girl waitresses which adds spice to things (Ha).

I'll write again very soon and give you more detail. Right now that big soft bed in my room looks very inviting. We rode all day on the train. I had the misfortune of being placed in charge of the group and it was my duty to see that we caught the right trains, etc. We only changed trains nine times so you can see the job I had. The English do things backwards and their method of train travel is no exception. No, I'm tired!

Bye for now,
Love to all,
Don

The real issue today is between the frenzy of a herded, whipped-up crowd-begotten cause, and the single man's belief in liberty of mind and spirit, and his willingness to sacrifice his comforts and his earnings for its sake.
—Archibald MacLeish on World War II

IN THE LATE 1930s, the British Air Ministry believed that with the Vickers-Supermarine Spitfire and the Hawker Hurricane, both Rolls-Royce Merlin-powered fighters, they could meet RAF Fighter Command's requirement for the defence of Great Britain. They had no particular interest in any other fighter types and certainly none in anything being produced in the United States. There was simply no match for the speed, manoeuvrability and fire power of the Spitfire at that time. However, the Spit was rather short on range, and as the European war entered its fifth month it became clear to some in the British defence establishment that the RAF needed a fighter of greater range to meet the Italians' very real threat to Egypt and that of the Japanese to Singapore. The Air Ministry decided that it required 1000 fighters for delivery in 1941, and placed an order with Brewster in the United States for the Buffalo. Brewster could supply no more than 170 Buffalos during 1941, and the Air Ministry had to look elsewhere.

By the end of 1939, France too needed new fighters and agreed with the Curtiss Company of New York to purchase 420 Hawk H75A and 259 H81A fighters, an export version of the US Army Air Corps P-40. The French were hoping that by 1941 the US Army would let them buy P-38s and P-39s.

A joint Anglo-French Purchasing Commission (AFPC) was formed. After many complex and frustrating twists and turns featuring such players as Bell Aircraft, Lockheed and Republic, in addition to Curtiss, the Commission finally decided to order 667 export models of the Lockheed Model 322, a P-38 variant. However, it could not be delivered in quantity until late 1941.

In June 1940, after France had fallen to the Germans, the RAF inherited the Curtiss aircraft ordered by the French, and came to regret the AFPC's commitment to the Lockheed 322. Furthermore, in late May Curtiss had changed its

production plans, and was now offering the P-40D. Both the Army Air Corps and the RAF believed that this was a better plane than anything else available, and, what is more, it had an earlier delivery date. The RAF bought 471 of one version and 560 of a second, naming them the Tomahawk and the Kittyhawk.

However, the British still had a fighter requirement. The RAF needed more fighters than Curtiss alone could build and, even before the Curtiss Kittyhawk production programme had begun, went shopping for another source of P-40 production. On 25th February 1940, they approached North American Aviation in Los Angeles, whose Harvard I trainer had served them impressively since 1938, and asked the company's president, J.H. "Dutch" Kindelberger, to consider building P-40s for them.

Kindelberger's chief designer, a forty-year-old German engineer named Edgar Schmued, who had emigrated first to Brazil and then to the United States in 1930, had worked for North American since February 1936. His fellow designers regard him as quiet, friendly and methodical—and as a man with a burning ambition to design and build the best fighter plane in the world. He had been working on design ideas for several months, using a German engineering handbook called *Huette*, together with his own small notebook of technical formulae. Rumours that the British wanted North American to build P-40s for them had been circulating in the Los Angeles (Inglewood) factory and Schmued was well prepared when Dutch Kindelberger dropped by his office one afternoon in early March. He asked the designer: "Ed, do we want to build P-40s here?" Schmued responded: "Well, Dutch, don't let us build an obsolete airplane. Let's build a new one. We can design and build a better one." Kindelberger replied: "Ed, I'm going to England in about two weeks and I need an inboard profile, three-view drawing, performance estimate, weight estimate, specifications and some detail drawings on the gun installations to take along.

THE HORSES

My saucepans have all been surrendered, / The teapot is gone from the hob, The colander's leaving the cabbage / For a very much different job. / So now, when I hear on the wireless Of Hurricanes showing their mettle, / I see, in a vision before me, A Dornier chased by my kettle.
—*Salvage Song (or: The Housewife's Dream)*
by Elsie Cawser

Left: The cockpit panel of a Curtiss P-40 Warhawk in 1991. Below: The grave near Eastleigh, Hampshire of Spitfire-designer R.J. Mitchell.

Then I would like to sell that new model airplane that you develop." Kindelberger told the designer to make it the fastest plane he could, and to "build it around a man that is 5 feet 10 inches tall and weighs 140 pounds". He said that it should have two 20mm cannons in each wing and should meet all design requirements of the US Army Air Corps. With that, North American Specification NAA SC-1050 was issued, and work on the new fighter began on 15th March 1940. Armed with the papers he had requested, Kindelberger left for Britain later that month, and Ed Schmued and his design team started to build a paper and plaster of Paris mock-up of the new plane. On Thursday, 11th April, Sir Henry Self, director of the AFPC, signed a letter of intent to purchase 400 Model NA-50B, NAA Spec 1592 fighters. The greatest fighter of the war had been launched.

Lend-Lease had not yet started, and Britain wanted to keep its costs down on the new plane, which was to be powered by an Allison engine. The agreed unit price of $40,000 was not to be exceeded by the manufacturer, who also undertook to deliver 320 aircraft between January and the end of September 1941, and fifty per month thereafter. It was estimated that the actual cost to Britain would be $37,590 per plane.

By merging his earlier fighter design concepts and a new laminar flow airfoil, Schmued shaped the model NA-73. The RAF contracted with North American for 320 of the new model in late May 1940, although final official British approval was not given until 20th July, after the fall of France and the start of the Battle of Britain.

The design assignment was apportioned to several specialized groups under Schmued's supervision. He estimated that a hundred days would be needed to build the first experimental airplane. The British required North American to have the airplane flight-tested, debugged and in production within one year. Within the company there were many concerns about the new wing and

how it might perform. Exhaustive testing proved its viability, and brilliant scheduling and co-ordination resulted in that first airplane being completed by both engineering and the shop in 102 days, almost exactly as promised. In 1984 Schmued reflected: "We could never build another plane today in a hundred days as we did then. Today they just don't have what it takes. There are too many levels of authority within the building companies. They have a president, a vice-president, another vice-president and many other levels. We had formed an exceptional group of engineers. There was an enthusiasm in this group that was unequalled anywhere. We worked every day until midnight. On Sundays we quit at 6 p.m., so we knew we had a 'weekend'. "

Unfortunately, the Allison people at their plant in Indianapolis failed to deliver the engine for the new fighter test airplane, and it was a further eighteen days before it arrived for installation in the airframe. The Flight Test Division of North American then prepared the necessary instrumentation and on 11th October 1940 the aircraft, NA-73X, was given initial engine run-up tests.

Initial flight testing began on Saturday, 26th October, and continued until 20th November. On that day the test pilot neglected to put the fuel valve on "reserve", and ran out of fuel after fifteen minutes of flight. He was forced to put the precious prototype down on a freshly ploughed field. As he landed, the wheels dug into the soft ground, causing the airplane to flip on to its back. The pilot was uninjured, but NA-73X was badly damaged and required a time-consuming rebuild. Schmued's team decided to have the second airplane on the shop line, which was actually scheduled to be the first production airplane, prepared for flight test, so as not to delay the gathering of the critical test data needed immediately if the new plane was to be produced on time.

Before NA-73X was flown for the first time, the

Far left: James H. "Dutch" Kindelberger headed North American Aviation through the lengthy development and production phases of the Mustang. Left: The North American Dallas, Texas P-51 assembly line in 1944. Bottom left: A P-51D Mustang of the Indiana Air National Guard. Below: Edgar Schmued, designer of the Mustang, as a student in Landsberg, Germany.

Right: A Packard Rolls-Royce Merlin engine manufacturer's identity plate from a Mustang. Below: The North American AT-6 trainer, this example at Duxford Airfield near Cambridge, England in 1998. The AT-6 Texan is considered to be the greatest trainer in history. It was the most widely used, safest single-engine trainer of World War II. Most US and British Commonwealth fighter pilots received their advanced phase training in it, or its Harvard variant.

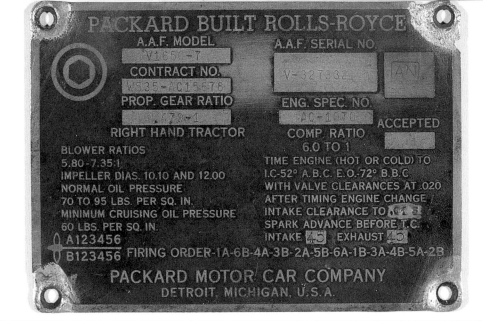

British ordered an additional 300 planes, making a new total buy of 620. A letter from the British purchasing authority to North American on 9th December 1940 referred to the fighter as Mustang, its new official name. In August 1941, the first Mustang I, AG346, to be accepted for delivery to the British was crated and shipped via the Panama Canal from Long Beach, California, to England, where it was assembled and test flown on 11th November. During August and September, the US Army had also accepted several of the new planes, the first being designated XP-51. It was flown to Wright Field in Ohio for additional testing and evaluation, while at the same time the North American Flight Test Division continued to test two examples at the California facility.

All 620 aircraft of the British order were completed and delivered by July 1942, and Mustang Is were in service with fifteen RAF Army Co-operation squadrons by December 1942. They were used primarily for reconnaissance on low-level cross-Channel dashes in which they shot up German trains, barges and troop concentrations, and did valuable photo reconnaissance work. The RAF pilots flying these Mustang Is liked the airplanes and thought them easily "the best American fighters to have reached Britain". Compared with the Spitfire Vb, the Mustang was faster up to 25,000 feet and had twice its range. However, the Spit Vb, could go much higher, had a better rate of climb and turn rate, and owed its high-altitude superiority to its Rolls-Royce Merlin engine. When Rolls-Royce test pilot Ronald Harker was invited by the RAF to Duxford airfield near Cambridge on 30th April 1942 to fly the Mustang I, he was impressed by the American fighter's handling qualities, fuel capacity (three times that of the Spitfire V) and by the positioning of the guns in the wing, which he felt gave greater accuracy. His report to the RAF Air Fighting Development Unit on the Mustang's general performance was very positive. It was in this report that Harker

suggested that a really special fighter might result if this exceptional airframe were to be combined with the proven and fuel-efficient Rolls-Royce Merlin engine. But the report and his subsequent lobbying of officials in his company and in the Air Ministry met with little initial enthusiasm. Few of them wanted anything to do with an American-built aircraft. Nonetheless, Harker was ultimately able to convince senior people at Rolls-Royce that his idea of mating the Merlin to the Mustang was not only likely to result in a wonderful new weapon against the Nazis, but would also produce a great deal of new engine business for Rolls. Influential executives at the engine maker then persuaded the RAF to provide three Mustangs for Merlin installation at the Rolls-Royce Hucknall factory.

Next came a series of modifications, conversions and redesigns of the cowling and the cooling system, along with other detail changes which, in the end, produced a Merlin 65-powered Mustang designated Mk X, a highly successful realisation of Ronald Harker's inspiration.

Rolls-Royce sent its performance and factory installation data on the Mk X to North American's design staff, who began preliminary adaptive designs to incorporate the marvellous Merlin into production-line Mustangs. Agreements were reached with the Packard Motor Car Company and Continental Motors for the mass production in the United States of the V-12 Merlin engine under licence from Rolls-Royce, to supplement the British production of the power plant. Among the many changes required by the Merlin-Mustang installation was the move to an enormous, four-bladed 11 foot 2 inch Hamilton Standard Hydromatic propeller.

By November 1942, General 'Hap' Arnold had been convinced of the promise of the rapidly developing Mustang and ordered more than 2200 of the new fighters for the US Army Air Corps. By this time, North American was inundated with orders for its B-25 Mitchell bomber and AT-6 Texan

...the Bf 109 was simply a well-conceived, soundly-designed fighter that maintained during maturity the success that attended its infancy; its fundamental concept facilitated the introduction of progressively more powerful armament and engines which enabled it to stay in the forefront of fighters for three-quarters of a decade. The Bf 109 always brought to my mind the adjective 'sinister'. It has been suggested that it evinced characteristics associated with the nation that conceived it, and to me it looked lethal from any angle, on the ground or in the air; once I had climbed into its claustrophobic cockpit it *felt* lethal! The cockpit was small and narrow, and was enclosed by a cumbersome hood that was difficult to open from the inside and incorporated rather primitive sliding side panels. The windscreen supports were slender and did not produce serious blind spots, but space was so confined that movement of the head was difficult for even a pilot of my limited stature. The armourglass of the windscreen gave the impression of being slightly smoked and was obviously of much poorer quality than that of earlier Bf 109s that we had tested, this sign of deterioration in quality indicating the 1944 production vintage of the particular aircraft. The *continued* engine starting system was of the inertia type whereby a flywheel was wound up by one of the groundcrew turning a handle until sufficient revs were obtained to engage the starter clutch control by the pilot pulling out a handle positioned beside his left knee. The Daimler-Benz DB 605A engine emitted a pleasantly powerful throaty roar as it warmed up at 1,900 rpm while the magneto, fuel pumps and pressures, and temperatures were checked. Its response to throttle movement was particularly good. The forward view for taxying was terrible but at least the aircraft was easily steerable owing to its positive toe pedal-operated wheel brakes, and using 15 deg of flap and 1.3 ata boost the take-off was commendably short and certainly superior to that of the Spitfire IX in distance of run. The strong swing to port could easily be held on rudder, but it was advisable to raise the tail as quickly as possible owing to the poor forward view. This could be done fairly coarsely without fear of the airscrew hitting the ground as the high thrust line of the inverted-vee engine gave ample clearance. The Gustav had *continued*

Right: The cockpit of a Focke-Wulf Fw 190, the finest German piston-engined fighter of World War II.

trainer, as well as for the Mustang now designated P-51B. It began to construct expanded manufacturing facilities at Inglewood, a new plant for Mustang production in Dallas (the plane built there was designated P-51C but was identical to the Inglewood product), and yet another new plant at Tulsa, Oklahoma.

Mustang production at the North American plants proceeded smoothly after initial delivery delays of Merlin engines from Packard had been overcome. Performance testing of the early Merlin production airplanes proved the brilliance of Ronald Harker's idea. The new plane had a top speed of 441 mph, more than 50 mph faster than the Allison-powered Mustang. It showed greatly improved performance in virtually all other categories as well.

The first American fighter group in the European Theatre of Operations to get the P-51B was the 354th FG, based in England at Greenham Common, Berkshire. Their initial Mustangs arrived on 11th November. Thereafter, the new fighters underwent field modification to ready them for combat operations. These included the addition of external additional fuel capacity in the form of droppable aluminium and compressed paper tanks. Some Mustangs also received an 85 US gallon fuel tank in the fuselage right behind the pilot, as a field modification, a change that became a production standard with the last 550 P-51Bs.

The Mustang encountered teething problems as it took on its primary long-range escort role. Prolonged high-altitude operation soon resulted in the freezing of certain oils and greases, oxygen starvation, ice build-up on windscreens, coolant loss and the resultant engine overheating condition, and fouled plugs and jammed ammunition belts during high-G manoeuvres. All these were ultimately fixed, most of them in the field, by crew chiefs. North American field representatives passed information about the

various problems and the fixes employed in the field back to the company and modifications were soon incorporated into the production-line planes.

With the arrival of General James Doolittle as the new commander of the Eighth Air Force in early January 1944, some of the escort fighters were released from their full-time commitment to the bombers they were shepherding, and for the first time were given the freedom to attack and destroy German fighters both before and after the Germans attacked American bombers. Now the Mustang began to show what it had. More American fighter groups were equipped with the slender, agile aircraft, and by 3rd March 1944, when Mustangs escorted bombers of the Eighth all the way to Berlin, a trip of more than 1000 miles, the Americans knew that they finally had the long-range fighter they needed to defeat the German Air Force.

In an on-going effort to improve this already splendid air weapon, North American modified a P-51B from its Inglewood line to carry a bubble or 'teardrop' canopy for greatly enhanced visibility. The canopy became the most notable feature of the next Mustang version, the P-51D, which also featured a strengthened airframe, a standard 85 US gallon fuselage fuel tank, slightly modified cowling, a landing gear modification, wing armament standardized to six .50 caliber Browning machine guns, and a V-1650-7 Merlin engine of 1695 hp (war emergency rating). These D models quickly began to arrive at the American squadrons in England and other war theaters.

The widespread availability of this newest and most highly evolved Mustang to date gave the Mustang groups a new target priority. If German aircraft could be successfully attacked and destroyed while still parked on their airfields, if their hangars, runways and other airfield facilities could be rendered unserviceable, the Allied cause in the air war would be considerably advanced.

Jimmy Doolittle was quick to support this new priority by releasing some P-51 squadrons to hit the enemy airfields and other surface targets. The Mustangs proved extremely effective in this added role, but at a stiff price. For the remainder of the war in Europe, significantly more P-51s were lost to German ground fire than to aerial combat. The German Air Force was efficient in the defence of their airfields, which were heavily ringed with anti-aircraft weapons. The Mustangs were particularly vulnerable to hits in the cooling system, and many were shot to pieces or brought down by shrapnel hits to the radiator or cooling tubes while attacking the German aerodromes. In spite of the increased losses from ground fire, the Mustang was considered quite effective in the ground-attack role, if somewhat less so than the heavier, radial-engined P-47 Thunderbolt.

As dominant as the P-51 had quickly become in the skies over German-occupied Europe, its pilots were soon facing fearsome new technological weaponry from the other side. Jet and rocket-propelled fighters in the form of the Me 262 and Me 163 respectively were appearing with increasing frequency in the defence of the Reich, and their performance, though limited and erratic, was startling and devastating. They went through the American bomber formations like a hot knife through butter, often destroying two or more heavy bombers in a single pass. But while the speed and performance of the Me 262, for example, was considerably superior to that of the Mustang, they were never available to the German Air Force in great enough numbers to overcome the powerful presence of the P-51s.

In the Pacific theater, the new Boeing B-29 Superfortress long-range bombers, with their massive incendiary loads, were starting to bring the terror and fury of the man-made firestorm to the Japanese home islands, which were fiercely defended by their fighter force. This was the

to be flown off as any attempt to pull it off the ground early resulted in aileron snatching as the wing slats opened unevenly. The Bf 109G-6 climbed well and at a steep angle. A shortcoming was the lack of any rudder trimming device. This meant that it was necessary to apply moderate right rudder during the climb and considerable left rudder during a dive. Thus, although the Bf 109G pilots tended to use a bunt into a steep dive as an escape manoeuvre in dogfights, they had some very heavy rudder and elevator control forces to contend with as speed built up and pull-outs at low altitude had to be made with considerable circumspection. This manoeuvre was employed against early marks of Spitfire and Hurricane which could not follow without the Merlin engine cutting in the bunt, but with the availability of the negative-g carburettor, some RAF fighting pilots, finding a Messerschmitt on their tails, took to deliberately diving to ground level in an attempt to lure their antagonist to disaster. At its rather disappointing low-level cruising speed of 240 mph (386 km/h) the *Gustav* was certainly delightful to fly, but the situation changed as speed increased; in a dive at 400 mph (644 km/h) the *continued*

supreme test for the P-51D. It was required to operate in the vital escort role, flying with the B-29s over thousands of miles of lonely and cruel sea. An oft-quoted remark about the early Superfortresses was "three turning, one burning", a reference to their inclination to develop engine problems. The Mustangs frequently had to escort B-29s crippled by mechanical failure while simultaneously fending off the attacks of Japanese fighters looking for easy pickings among the big bombers. Still, the B-29s efficiently practised the fire-bombing technique on more than sixty key Japanese target cities, all but burning them to a fine ash by the end of the War. They were accompanied to and from their objectives by P-51s operating mainly from a precious little SeaBee-built airfield on the hard-won island of Iwo Jima. It was from Iwo that the Mustangs took final control of the airspace over Japan, which they maintained until the atomic-bombing of Hiroshima and Nagasaki ended the Pacific war in August 1945.

The Mustang continued to be developed through a succession of variants until the end of World War II and was, without question, among the most successful and highly-regarded fighters in the entire history of aviation. By the end of the War, Mustangs of the USAAF, the RAF and the other Allied air forces had destroyed nearly 5000 enemy aircraft in the European theater alone. The combat life of the plane was extended in the Korean War in 1950, in Arab-Israeli wars, and in other conflicts in many different air forces.

More than 200 Mustangs are still flown today worldwide—the careful, loving restorations of proud enthusiasts who continue to appreciate the charms and performance of an airplane that many believe contributed more to the winning of World War II than any other.
  Eighty-five-year-old Ed Schmued, the kind, quiet, modest, brilliant designer of the Mustang, died of

heart failure on Saturday, 1st June 1985. His body was cremated and on 15th June, at the request of his wife, Christel, his ashes were flown from Los Angeles International Airport out to sea where they were released. Ed's last flight took place in a Mustang, the airplane that he created and loved to the end.

At seventeen, Cecil Lewis earned the wings on his Royal Flying Corps tunic and, with a total of thirteen flying hours to his credit, left for France to join No. 56 Squadron in February 1916. He quickly learned about air fighting and about the fighter planes of the day: "At Martlesham, I realized a long-cherished ambition—to fly scouts. My attempt with the Bristol Bullet at St Omer in the spring of the previous year had been disastrous. Since then no opportunity had come along; but one day the Sopwith Triplane arrived at Martlesham for tests.
  "Of all the machines, the Triplane remains in my memory as the best—for the actual pleasure of flying—that I ever took up. It was so beautifully balanced, so well-mannered, so feather-light on the stick, and so comfortable and warm. It had what was then a novel feature, an adjustable tail plane to trim the machine fore and aft. Set correctly, with the throttle about three-quarters open, the Tripe would loop, hands off, indefinitely. Not for this, but for its docility, the lack of all effort needed to fly it, and yet its instantaneous response to the lightest touch, it remains my favourite. Other machines were faster, stronger, had better climb or vision; but none was so friendly as the Tripe. After it I never wanted to fly anything but a scout again, and on active service I never did."

Like most radical new designs, the Vought F4U Corsair was born with a lot of inherent problems. More than a hundred separate modifications were required just to correct problems with lateral stability and aileron control. But the United States

Below: A variant of the World War I Sopwith Pup. The Pup was underpowered and underarmed, but in spite of engine problems and gun-jamming, it was one of the few British scout planes able to deal effectively with the German Albatros types.

Navy knew it had something very special when in 1940 the XF4U-1 prototype achieved more than 400 mph in level test flight, the first American combat aircraft to do so. That early test airplane had just been rebuilt after suffering a devastating crash landing during a previous test flight.

When Vought were developing the Corsair, they chose to employ the new and highly promising Pratt & Whitney R-2800 engine to power their new bird. It was a brilliant match, even though both engine and prototype aircraft were plagued by teething troubles that took up a lot of development time. In the process, General Hap Arnold, who had been watching the progress of the new P & W power plant, was so impressed that he told the engine maker to drop its work developing a liquid-cooled engine for the US Army and concentrate entirely on the R-2800 and other radial aircraft engines.

The Corsair featured a unique new inverted 'bent' gull wing design made necessary by a very large 13 foot 4 inch propeller that transferred the power of the big R-2800 engine. Such a large propeller mounted on an airplane with a conventional wing would have resulted in an unacceptably high angle of attack in landing and take-off. The bent wing brought other advantages to the new fighter. Vision from the cockpit was improved, and the folding point of the wing meant that the plane took up less room on board a carrier, where aircraft storage space was limited. The inverted gull wing also offered a reduced drag factor, further adding to the Corsair's fine performance.

The combat record of the Corsair is legendary. It destroyed 2140 enemy aircraft during World War II against a loss of 935 Corsairs (190 in aerial combat, 350 from anti-aircraft fire, 230 from other causes and 165 in crash landings). A further 692 were lost on non-operational missions. The Corsair was built by Chance Vought (7829), Brewster (735) and Goodyear (4017). The US employed the majority of the Corsairs, while Great Britain operated 2020 and

Left: The Vickers Castle Bromwich Spitfire assembly plant at Birmingham, England in World War II.

controls felt as though they had seized! The highest speed that I dived to below 10,000 feet (3,048 m) was 440 mph (708 km/h) and the solidity of control was such that this was the limit in my book. However, things were very different at high altitude, and providing the *Gustav* was kept where it was meant to be (i.e. above 25,000 feet/ 7620 m) it performed efficiently both in dogfighting and as an attacker of bomber formations. A number of dummy attacks on a co-operative Lancaster and a friendly skirmish with a Mustang flown by one of the RAE pilots revealed the fact that the slipstream of these aircraft caused the intermittent operation of the Bf 109G's slats so that accurate sighting became an impossibility.

The Mustang III possessed a clear speed advantage at all altitudes. The Gustav offered a marginally better climb rate up to 20,000 feet but between this altitude and 25,000 ft the Mustang had a very slight advantage. When dived and then pulled up into a climb there was little to choose between US and German fighter, but the Mustang could steadily outdive the Bf 109G-6 and had no *continued*

difficulty in out-turning the Messerschmitt. One of my rashest ventures was to fly the Bf 109G-12 tandem two-seater from the rear cockpit. I was interested to ascertain what sort of view the instructor had for landing. The answer was none! I had to make three very frightening attempts before regaining *terra firma*. The periscopic sight in the rear cockpit was of no use whatsoever in the vital final stage of flare, touch-down and landing run. One can only assume that Luftwaffe instructors finding themselves in a Bf 109G-12 acquired a fatalistic acceptance of an inevitable reliance on their pupils for the finale of each training flight. I would certainly not recommend the ultimate solution that I adopted of a split-S turning dive at the runway and then a burst of power to avoid cratering the tarmac, and making tail-up contact on the mainwheels. After the tail dropped it was anybody's guess as to the direction in which the aircraft was heading. I certainly had not the vaguest idea.
—from *Wings of the Luftwaffe* by Captain Eric Brown

New Zealand 430.

According to Captain Alan J. Leahy, RN (Ret), his favourite aircraft was the one he happened to be flying at the time: "What you had to do was identify the aircraft's good points [and] then build your tactics round them.

"The Corsair was rough and tough, but in no way could you think of entering a one-on-one dog fight with a Zero. Get in quick and get out quick was the preferred method of attack.

"The Sea Fury [was] the second fastest propeller-driven aircraft in the world. Highly manoeuvrable, it was a delight to fly and fight. It would outmanoeuvre any jet and the MiGs in Korea soon learned not to try to mix it, and used the fast-in-fast-out philosophy.

"The Sea Hornet was the fastest propeller-driven aircraft. It had a high rate of climb and could accelerate and dive at high speed, but it could not outrun the Sea Fury. The Sea Hornet could mix it with jets, but that was never put to the test in war. Ideal as a fleet fighter, it had long range and endurance, and with the cockpit right up front between the two engines it was perfect for deck landings, giving the pilot an excellent view of any impending accident."

No combat plane is perfect in all respects. Knowing an aircraft's limitations is as fundamental to combat survivability as knowing its capabilities. The most serious limitation of the P-47 Thunderbolt was its comparatively slow rate of climb. It was, however, a remarkably rugged airplane, armed with a wing-mounted battery of eight .50 caliber Browning machine guns. Underwing rockets and bombs could add to its firepower for the ground-attack role. It was the biggest single-seat, single-engined Allied fighter of World War II, and its shape soon earned it the nickname Jug: with its bulbous front and tapering fuselage it certainly resembled a milk jug.

If the Thunderbolt did not climb very well, it could surely dive. Its pilots attributed this characteristic to what they called the milk-bottle effect. Gravity and the massive Pratt & Whitney Wasp R-2800 engine driving a huge four-blade propeller made its dive impressive by any standard. The P-47's great size, though, made the first impression on pilots new to it: "Gee," said one Spitfire veteran as he looked into a Thunderbolt cockpit for the first time, "you could walk around in there!"

The Thunderbolt was more than just big, it was an ace-maker. In it, many Eighth and Ninth Air Force pilots achieved that status. It was the airplane with which the high-achieving 4th and 56th Fighter Groups first became famous. Once the early engine and radio problems common to the aircraft had been overcome, the Thunderbolt became an outstanding fighter—appreciated by its pilots and respected by the German Air Force.

In the 1990s, a magnificently restored P-47 is still flown regularly by Stephen Grey of The Fighter Collection, at Duxford, Cambridgeshire, England:

"Settle into the cockpit and space plus comfort prevail. Start the 2800 engine and it begins to feel like a 'class act'. Taxi to the hold and it feels like a beautifully damped Mack truck. At run-up it purrs rather than barks.

"Put the hammer down for take-off and there is no kick in the back or dart for the weeds. It runs straight and true—if sedately.

"Put the wheels in the wings and it turns into a crisp-handling fighter, with beautiful ailerons, outstanding controls, great visibility and a sensation of pedigree.

"True, it does not climb with the best of them, but stuff the nose toward the greenery and the air-speed indicator will wind to the stop and stay there faster than other prop fighters that I have flown. Circuit work, landing and ground handling are docile and beautifully mannered.

Left: The Republic P-47D Thunderbolt, a fine airworthy example from The Fighter Collection at Duxford Airfield, England. When the 56th and 78th Fighter Group pilots learned her little ways in 1943, they began to score heavily against their German Air Force opponents. The last Thunderbolt variant was the P-47N which was used effectively in escorting B-29s to Japan. Below: A new P-38 on the Lockheed ramp at Burbank, California during World War II.

Right: Captain Stanley "Swede" Vejtasa flew a Wildcat (far right) with VF-10 from the USS *Enterprise* in World War II, downing seven enemy aircraft in a single sortie in October 1942. Below: Hawker Hurricanes of an RAF Eagle Squadron at their Kirton-in-Lindsay airfield in Lincolnshire, England during World War II.

"Fortunately, or regrettably, I have not had to fight in the Jug. However, from a little 'arm wrestling' with others behind the hangar I know that the Jug could fight incredibly well, if differently. If I were able to transpose myself back to the 1940s and had a choice, I feel my survival instincts would tell me to choose the Jug but my competitive instincts would tell me only to fight on my terms with a lot of airspace underneath me.

"The sheer rugged, technical quality of the airplane is its charm, the handling a joy. When I climb out and walk away, I always find myself looking back at the P-47 with affection—what a character."

"My personal favourite fighter is the F-16. I flew it for fourteen years. It is small, agile and powerful. It is also very easy to fly, wonderful for low-level aerobatics and a fine weapons platform, with perfect visibility."
—Gidi Livni, formerly a Colonel in the Israeli Air Force

Pilot-Officer Nick Berryman of No. 276 Squadron, RAF, was a "Hurricane man". Although he never flew one operationally, he remembers the airplane vividly: "Friday, 16th October 1942. Flew Master for twenty minutes, then pushed off in a Hurri. Very careful indeed. Twenty minutes for cockpit check which I carried out about five times. Eventually ready to go. Got off OK, but unable to find undercart lever. Terrible moments expecting to spin in any minute. Aircraft bucking about all over the place. Climbed to 1000 feet, then selecting 'wheels down' found myself at 1700 feet. Forgot radio procedure completely and unable to remember call sign. Suddenly, a crosswind coming in to land. All became calm and she came in as gentle as a bird. Now, at long last, a Hurricane has flown me.

"Not exactly a macho way of describing one's first flight in a fighter aircraft, but that is exactly how it was. Over a beer in the bar that night I probably said, 'Hurricanes? A piece of cake.' "

Like so many Hurricane pilots, Berryman learned to love and respect the airplane: "Give it half a chance and it would do its best to safeguard the pilot. There was little or no swing on take-off and in flight it was comfortable. Apart from the undercarriage, all the tits and knobs were in the right places. It was delightfully steady in all attitudes and steep turns were a joy. So, too, were aerobatics, which I could carry out more accurately on Hurricanes than Spits, which I tended to over-aileron. I'm told that 15 degrees of flap milked down in a dogfight situation would leave your tail-chasing adversary wondering why he could not stay with you. Landing was no problem. One bounce it would absorb without a murmur. Two bounces it would remind you to be careful and I never saw anyone bounce three times. If you did that, it would take over and drop in fairly straight on its wide legs. Without doubt, the Hurricane helped me to a state of proficiency I would never have achieved on any other fighter. It was a winner all the way. And yes, the airplane was probably more capable than many of the pilots who flew it."

Wing-Commander Geoffrey Page, formerly of No. 56 Squadron, RAF, shares Berryman's opinion of the Hurricane. Page flew it in combat: "In the Hurricane we knew that the Me 109 could out-dive us, but not out-turn us. With that knowledge one obviously used the turning manoeuvre rather than trying to beat the man at the game in which he was clearly superior. With a 109 sitting behind you, you'd stay in a really tight turn and after a few turns the position would be reversed and you'd be on his tail. In short, I'd say that the Hurricane was a magnificent airplane to go to war in."

The Fw 190A-8 was the favourite mount of Oscar Boesch, German Air Force (Ret), a former Feldwebel of *Sturm Staffel* I, IV/JG3 "Udet". In his career as a fighter pilot, Boesch was credited with

There is no doubt in my mind that no aircraft in the world was better suited for its job than the F6F Hellcat. The Hellcat was an extremely stable gun platform with few if any bad flight characteristics. It was an easy aircraft to fly and had no hidden quirks like stalling in slow speed turns like the early F4U Corsair. It had one of the most reliable and easily maintained radial engines, the R2800, which was exceptionally rugged and could withstand a great deal of damage and continue to operate, many times getting a pilot home safely when other fighters would have fallen out of the air. The aircraft itself was also tough and able to sustain massive damage from enemy fire and continue to fly. Although several WWII fighters were slightly faster than the Hellcat, the difference was not enough to make for an appreciable advantage. In air combat the F6F would out-maneuver almost any Allied fighter except the Spitfire. Although most Japanese fighters could out-maneuver the Grumman, here again the difference in maneuverability did not overcome other Hellcat advantages.
—Lieutenant-Commander H.B. Moranville, USN (Ret)

The sound of these old aircraft is music; the smell of them is perfume; flying them is pure pleasure.

For most who flew R.J. Mitchell's wonderful Spitfire, it is their first flight in the type that remains their most enduring memory.

John Nesbitt-Dufort: "I strongly suspect that most pilots experienced the same slight feeling of awe as I did when gazing out for the first time over the apparent yards of engine that separated me from the propeller. Brakes on, petrol on, rad shutters open, fine pitch, switches off. I gave her three full dopes on the priming pump, nodded to the airman on the trolley ack and he held his thumb up. 'All Clear!' Opening the throttle a shade I threw the booster-coil switch and then ignition, and pressed the starter button. After about two revolutions there was a puff of black smoke as she caught with a roar. I immediately throttled back and switched off the booster coil. The trolley ack was disconnected and after a brief warming-up I ran up, checked mags and pitch and then waved away both chocks and the windswept character who had draped himself over the tail.
I saved time by carrying out my preflight checks as I taxied, weaving wildly, to *continued*

Right: CF-18 Hornets of the Royal Canadian Air Force. The Hornet is the American state-of-the-art strike fighter of the 1990s.

destroying six B-17s, two B-24s, one P-51, one Spitfire and eight Russian aircraft. He experienced four bail-outs, four crash-landings, two mid-air collisions, and for three days was a prisoner of the Russians until he managed to escape: "We considered the Fw 190 superior to the Mustang and Thunderbolt. The Fw 190's robust construction and its flight characteristics made it an excellent fighter. It had excellent handling qualities and manoeuvred superbly. It had two fuselage-mounted 13mm machine guns and a 20mm cannon in each wing root. In addition, there was a 30mm Mk 108 cannon in each wing.

"I never had a problem dogfighting with any opponent. The only fighter that might have had an edge on manoeuvrability was the Spitfire, with the Mustang a close second. The big air-cooled BMW 801D engine provided the power, and in some variants we even had extra horsepower provided by a booster. The large, robust radial engine also provided much protection for the pilot and could take severe punishment before it seized from being shot up.

"Our tactic against the bombers was to attack from behind regardless of the deadly defensive fire. If we couldn't down the bomber with a firing pass, then we were to ram. All *Sturm Staffel* pilots signed a declaration to do our duty to the utmost of our ability. About the ramming tactic... this was always considered a last and final option for downing the enemy. The decision to ram was left up to the individual. It was a last-ditch method to stem the bomber tide, but at the same time we knew we were of greater value to our country alive than dead. The Fw 190 was known throughout the Luftwaffe as the *Würger*, which means Butcherbird. In *Sturm Staffel* I, we called it the *Sturmbock*, which equates to Ram. We thought this an appropriate name for the aircraft."

Captain Eric Brown, RN (Ret), served as a Fleet Air Arm fighter pilot in the World War II and in January

84

1944 became the Royal Navy's Chief Test Pilot at the Royal Aircraft Establishment, Farnborough. There he flew many captured German aircraft and, at war's end, his position and his command of the German language led to his interrogating some of Germany's most successful aircraft designers, including Messerschmitt, Heinkel and Tank. He was designated Officer in Charge of German Aircraft Reception at Farnborough, and in his time there he flew some fifty-five different types of German World War II aircraft: "If asked to nominate the most formidable combat aircraft to evolve in World War II, I would unhesitatingly propose Messerschmitt's Me 262. I say 'unhesitatingly' advisedly, despite having flown the Spitfire in virtually all of its variants, the Mosquito, the Lancaster, the Mustang and even Mitsubishi's Zero-Sen—all warplanes that might be considered as contenders for this accolade.

"It [the Me 262] was a fantastic aeroplane from several aspects, and its eleventh hour debut in the *Götterdämmerung* of Germany's Third Reich provided as dramatic a movement as any the great Wagner himself could have composed. In this case, however, the 'composer' was one Professor Willy Messerschmitt, whose Bf 109 fighter, after blooding over Spain, had provided most of the vertebrae of the German Air Force's spinal column throughout the entire war. The same fertile brain had given birth to the Bf 110 and the Me 410, both very useful twin-engined combat aircraft, but its *pièce de résistance* was unquestionably the Me 262, which was both turbo-jet-driven and swept-winged—a truly startling combination in 1944.

"I was immediately struck by its beautiful yet sinister lines, which reminded me of those of a shark. I was very keen to get airborne in this aircraft, but interrogation of some of the German Air Force pilots led our team to proceed with some caution.

"My first cursory glance around the cockpit of the Me 262 had revealed what was, by 1945 standards,

a complex but neat layout. The dashboard carried the flight instruments on the left and the engine gauges on the right. The left console carried the throttles, fuel cocks, trimmers, ancillary controls and their emergencies, while the right had the electronics, starters and radio equipment. All this compared pretty closely with British practice.

"Once the rigamarole of starting had been completed, and assuming that both engines *were* functioning, the process of taxiing could begin.

"The view from the cockpit was excellent, and every upper part of the aircraft was within the pilot's field of vision. The mainwheel brakes were operated, as on all German aircraft, by toe action, and the Me 262 embodied the somewhat odd feature of a hand-operated nosewheel brake, which, I assume, was needed when the aircraft was fully loaded, German brakes never seeming too positive in their action.

"The take-off preparations were simple enough. At full power fumes or smoke invariably penetrated the cockpit, and, as the canopy had to be closed for take-off, the sensation was, to say the least, disturbing. The nosewheel was raised at 100 mph, and the aircraft pulled gently off at 124 mph.

"The take-off run was long, and the aircraft gave one the feeling that it was underpowered, as indeed was the contemporary Meteor I.

"Our interest in the Me 262 at RAE Farnborough was threefold. First, we were intrigued to discover if the performance really did match the capabilities claimed by the Germans; second, we were anxious to discover the behaviour of the swept-wing configuration at high Mach numbers; and, third, we wanted to know if this aircraft provided a good gun platform. We soon ascertained that the German performance figures were by no means extravagant, but the high Mach performance must, of course, be related to the contemporary state of the art, to use an Americanism.

"The normal range of flight characteristics from aerobatic manoeuvres to the stall revealed the Me

Left: *Floogie*, a Mustang of the 357th Fighter Group based at Leiston, Suffolk, England in World War II.

the downwind side of the airfield. Coarse weaving was an absolute necessity as the Spit was completely blind dead ahead with the tail down. Stopping the regulation forty-five degrees out of wind I had a final check around the cockpit. Taking a deep breath I gently pushed the handled throttle fully open. There was an immediate and pronounced tendency to swing to the left but this was easily checked by coarse use of opposite rudder, and with a centralized control column the tail appeared to come up on its own.

"Now for the ticklish part: Changing hands I selected 'up' and with my now free hand I pumped up the undercarriage avoiding, I hoped successfully, the novice's tendency to pump the control column at the same time. After closing the canopy I adjusted boost and revs climbing at 160 mph. This was the fastest airplane that I had ever flown and I was duly impressed; throttling back to cruising boost and revs I felt all the controls in turn, elevators very light, ailerons and rudder not quite so light but all sensitive and very positive. All the controls stiffened up appreciably, but in no way unpleasantly, as *continued*

Below: From the World War II flying log book of US Navy Lieutentant Tom Harris, an F6F-5 Hellcat pilot who flew with VF-17 from the carrier *Hornet* (CV-12). Below right: Bits of metal fly off as a US Navy Corsair crash-lands on the deck of carrier during the Korean War.

262 as a very responsive and docile aeroplane, leaving one with a confident impression of a first-class combat aircraft for both fighter and ground attack roles.

"The Me 262's landing run was long and was always accompanied by that unpleasant suspicion of fading brakes that one had with all German aircraft of the period.

"The Me 262 [was] variously known as the *Schwalbe* and the *Sturmvogel*, but whatever the appelation it was in my view unquestionably the foremost warplane of its day; a hard hitter which outperformed anything that we had immediately available but which, fortunately for the Allies, was not available to the German Air Force in sufficient numbers to affect drastically the course of events in the air over Europe. It was a pilot's aeroplane which had to be *flown* and not just heaved into the air. Basically underpowered and fitted with engines sufficiently lacking in reliability to keep the adrenalin flowing, it was thoroughly exciting

to fly, and particularly so in view of its lack of an ejector seat. I was reminded vividly of this aircraft when I first flew the F-4 Phantom some twenty years later. This later-generation US aircraft offered its pilot that same feeling of sheer exhilaration, but the Phantom possessed the added attractions of safety and reliability which perhaps kept the pulse at a somewhat lower tempo than it attained when flying the Me 262 in those now-distant days of 1945."

Neither the Royal Navy nor the US Navy had the front-line fighter they needed in the early part of World War II. The Corsair was on order and promised the qualities both naval air arms required, but they did not know if the new Chance-Vought plane would perform up to its specifications, and so the Americans decided to buy some insurance. The Navy purchasing people asked Grumman to build an improved and updated version of the Wildcat, and in the effort something entirely new and much

March 45 — CV-12

Date	Type of Machine	Number of Machine	Duration of Flight	Character of Flight	Pilot	PASSENGERS		REMARKS
1	F6F-5	72981	3.5	STRIKE	Self. Iwo	85	CL	OKINAWA
3	"	71510	2.3	N	"	86	CL	(REPLACEMENT PLANE) IE SNIMA
14	"	70546	3.3	K	..	87	CL	DROP NAPOLM
8	..	71742	3.5	STRIKE	Konoya–Kyushu	KYUSHU 88	CL	✳ ZEKE ✳ ZEK..
18	"	72832	3.5	STRIKE	Kanoya	KYUSHU 89	CL	OVER CHIRAN AND TAKE YAMA AIRFIELDS
19	..	71071	2.7	SWEEP	Kure	Kure Naval Base-Honshu	CL	✳ TONY ✳ ZEKE
21	..	72822	4.3	CAP	..	91	CL	SCRAMBLE TURKEY SHOOT FOR JIM PEARCE.
23	..	71538	3.8	SWEEP	Okinawa	92	CL	OKINAW..
23	..	70338	3.3	STRIKE	Okinawa	93	CL	ON 18th MAR. A total of 35
24	..	70082	2.3	STRIKE	Okinawa	94	CL	Jap planes were shot down
25	..	72274	3.3	CAP	..	95	CL	on 19th March, 25 Jap planes
25	..	72822	3.3	CAP	..	96	CL	were shot down. Also
27	..	70582	3.8	CAP	-	97	CL	"SKIP". Chuck Weiss, Edmund, SCRAMBLE
27	..	71582	3.0	CAP	..	98	CL	Hannah, and Pappy Matthe.. were shot down.
28	-	70113	3.1	CAP	..	NITE 0.3 99	CL	" In 1945 heard that

better resulted—the XF6F-1, later called the Hellcat. Designed by Leroy Grumman and William Schwendler, the prototype airplane was first flown in June 1942 at Grumman's Bethpage facility on Long Island, New York. That first airplane left a lot to be desired. It was underpowered by 25 per cent. The first engine was replaced with a Pratt & Whitney R-2800, which fixed the speed and rate-of-climb problems. But the plane had a tendency to flutter in high-speed dives and it required too much trim adjustment between flaps up and flaps down. These and other early problems were corrected, and Grumman moved rapidly to set up a new production line for the Hellcat. Production of the new fighter actually progressed faster than completion of the factory housing the assembly line. The new production version, the F6F-3, was given an R-2800-10 engine rated at 2000 hp at 2700 rpm.

The Hellcat was sturdy and built to take the shock of carrier landing and the punishment of enemy fire. With six .50 caliber Colt-Browning machine guns,

and 400 rounds for each gun, it could dish it out as well. Hellcats were delivered to US Navy fighter squadrons and to the Royal Navy in quantity during 1943, and they immediately showed their worth in action. The F6F was the first naval fighter of the war to meet the Japanese Zero on equal terms. Excepting tight turns, the Hellcat gave at least as well as it got. Its toughness made it popular with Allied naval aviators, if not with the opposition who now had something substantial to worry about. The Cat was also popular with mechanics and repair personnel. Her engine and systems were easily accessible. Maintenance and repairs were normally done quickly and with little fuss or strain.

As early as August 1940, General Clare Chennault was warning the US military about the startlingly superior performance of the Japanese Zero. He was talking about the model 11 Zero. By 1942, the best aircraft of US Navy fighter squadrons were still being shot to pieces by the Zero, now the model

the speed built up. Medium and steep turns in either direction and then daringly a roll—she went round as though she had been on rails! The little airplane handled beautifully, her flying characteristics what one might expect from such delightful lines.

"Time to come in again. I located myself quite a distance from the airfield and closed the throttle to test for a stall with the gear and flaps up. Even with the nose held fairly high the speed took a long time to fall off. Then after a definite shudder the nose dropped smartly but cleanly at just under 84 mph. Ye Gods! I thought, that's a bit quick. For some silly unknown reason I didn't test for stall with gear and flaps down, which would have reassured me, but instead headed to join in the circuit with about twenty pupils in Oxfords and Harvards and after snapping down the flaps came whistling in at 100 mph over the hedge. Far too fast! I floated, pump-handling furiously across two-thirds of the field to eventually sit down firmly at just over 72 mph to finish my run only 20 yards from the boundary. I was sweating profusely and more than somewhat ashamed of my performance; still, with not a little pride I made the first entry of the magic words 'Spitfire Mk I No. N3174' in my log book."

New Zealander Al Deere flew many Spitfire marks into combat through the entire course of the war. He had no doubt about its superiority over the Messerschmitt Me 109.

"The Spitfire was a better aircraft than the 109. Not in all respects, but overall a better aircraft. Anything the 109 could do we could do better...except a dive. They could run away from us then but in a turn or sustained climb we could match them. Top speed or cruise was much the same, but the Spitfire just had the edge."

21. In the Zero, the Japanese had a battle-tested, proven fighter of impressive performance and capability. In it they were confident and ready to go to war.

As early as November 1937, the Imperial Japanese Navy knew what it needed in a future first-line fighter, and it gave its requirements to the Mitsubishi and Nakajima aircraft companies. The Navy wanted a plane with a top speed of at least 310 mph, outstanding manoeuvrability, the ability to climb to 10,000 feet in 3.5 minutes and a better range than that of any existing fighter. The armament had to be two cannon and two machine guns, a requirement that both manufacturers felt was unrealistic, and Nakajima pulled out of the competition to build the new plane. The contract went to Mitsubishi, who agreed to try to solve the gun problem. However, it turned out that Nakajima had been right, and in the end the armament requirement was modified.

An intially underpowered prototype Zero was completed in a little more than a year using a tough new lightweight alloy called Extra-Super Duralumin (ESD).

Testing in the spring of 1939 identified some relatively minor problems which were soon resolved, and on 14th September 1939 the Zero was accepted by the Imperial Navy as the A6M1 carrier fighter. The armament now consisted of two 20mm cannon in the wings and two 7.7mm machine guns set in the upper cowling and firing through the propeller. She was good—but she was going to be better.

Mitsubishi designers were waiting for a new engine, the 925 hp Nakajima NK1C Sakae 12, to pass its naval acceptance so they could install it in what was now the A6M2 Zero. The new engine gave the already impressive plane a significantly improved performance, and the new weapon presented the Allies with a staggering challenge until well into 1943 when the Hellcat and the Corsair arrived.

Right: A twin-engined Dornier Do 335 at Neubiburg, Germany in the summer of 1945. It was transferred to the RAF in September and, early in 1946, an in-flight rear-engine fire caused it to crash, killing the pilot, Group-Captain Alan Hards. The Do 335 was a twin-engined (tandem) fighter capable of *continued*

I was standing near a display in the World War II wing of the Smithsonian's National Air and Space Museum in Washington DC some years ago. Next to me were three men in the uniform of the German Air Force. Two of them were in their early twenties, and the third was a very senior officer of many years' service. We began a conversation about the aircraft we were all admiring, an Me 109G, and I asked the elderly officer if he had flown the Messerschmitt. He told me that he had flown it in the War, and I asked his opinion of the plane. He thought it an excellent fighter, every bit as good as most marks of the Spitfire, and better than many of its other opponents. Then he was silent for a moment and admitted that he had lost a great many friends, fellow Me 109 pilots whose aircraft had been shot up in aerial combat: "In most cases," he said, "they died because they were unable to get out of the tiny cockpit of the Messerschmitt in the few seconds left to them before it was too late—they had been trapped."

The Me 109, known officially in German plans and technical documents as the Bf 109, began life in 1934 when the German Air Ministry let contracts for prototypes of a new single-seat monoplane fighter to four aircraft manufacturers: Arado, Heinkel A.G., Focke-Wulf Flugzeugwerke, and Bayerische Flugzeugwerke (Bf). The latter's Bf 109 prevailed in the competition, which was influenced by German military intelligence reports from Britain. The new fighter offered advanced controls, an enclosed cockpit, automatic leading edge slats to provide extra lift on take-off, and slotted flaps and ailerons. Bf's chief designer, Professor Willy Messerschmitt, had produced a very advanced aircraft, but it was a long way from achieving wide acceptance. It was something less than a hit with the experimental test pilots who experienced a variety of failures with all ten of the initial aircraft ordered for trials at the Rechlin Experimental Establishment.

By July 1937, most of the bugs had been worked out of the 109. At this point, Dr Josef Göbbels and Hermann Göring decided that the time was right for a practical demonstration of what Göbbels had called "the wonder plane", and the German Air Force re-equipped two *Staffeln* with 24 new Bf 109Bs and sent them off to Spain to fight in the Spanish Civil War as the Condor Legion. In full production now, the 109 attracted a lot of attention from the international press covering the war in Spain, and much of what they wrote and photographed was extremely bad press for the plane, the plane maker and for Germany. More than 1500 109s had been lost before the Spanish war in take-off and landing accidents owing to excessive torque, and historical records show that many more were lost during the Civil War itself. Subsequent C and D versions of the 109 were essentially exercises in additional problem-solving. By the time of the Battle of Britain the E model was out in strength and proved itself to be one of the finest fighter aircraft of World War II.

The Bf or Me 109E had an 1100 hp Daimler-Benz 601A engine with direct fuel injection, an enormous advantage over its Spitfire and Hurricane opponents, whose Rolls-Royce Merlin engines tended to cut out when flying inverted. Where the odds changed in favour of the RAF was in the matter of the limited flying time of the 109 from its bases in western Europe. It had a maximum of one and a half hours in the air when escorting bombers to attack targets in England, with only about ten minutes of fighting time over the target area. The fighters of the RAF were defending and fighting over their own land, and could easily land, refuel, rearm, and be back in the air to fight again as many as five or six times in a day. Many German fighter pilots found themselves running on empty on their return trips, and getting their feet wet in the English Channel.

Between 1936 and the end of the war in Europe, Messerschmitt produced more than 33,000 Bf 109s through many different marks and changes in

477 mph, it was powered by two 1900-hp Daimler-Benz DB 603G 12-cylinder liquid-cooled engines. It first flew in autumn 1943. It was armed with a 30mm cannon and two machine guns and had under-wing racks for light stores. 90 aircraft were built.

power, armament and performance. The plane operated in various campaigns including western Europe, Britain, Africa and Russia.

For much of the war, Generalleutnant a.D. Günther Rall flew 109s in Russia: "The war had been raging in Russia for two years. It was a different one than in the west—ideologically motivated, brutal and destructive—in a battle where no quarter was given. After my crash following an aerial fight on 28th November 1941, I was seriously injured with three broken vertebrae in the spine, paralysis and head injuries. German tank drivers had pulled me from the wreckage of my downed Me 109 at a freezing temperature of minus 40 degrees Centigrade (about minus 24 degrees Farenheit). Following nine months of rehabilitation in military hospitals in Bucharest and Vienna, I was declared fit and ready for action. Back with my squadron, VIII/JG52, I was just in time for the push to the Caucasus mountains, the retreat and new action in Stalingrad at Christmas 1942. Then more retreats. Action on the Crimea and Kuban bridgehead. I then received additional treatment for my paralysis in a Vienna field hospital. There a telegram reached me calling me back to the front as the new group commander of III/JG52. Then to action at Bjulgorod over the Pocket of Kursk. I reached my fighter group shortly before the attack started—the biggest tank battle of all time. It was summer 1943 and we were flying as many as five missions a day.

"One day in the late afternoon I was flying with my adjutant as wingman in pursuit over the Pocket. I was looking from west to east and spotted two aircraft silhouettes flashing against huge cumulus clouds lit up by the late afternoon sun. With full throttle I closed behind the two radial-engined fighters and fixed the left one in my sight. He did not see me. I could have shot, but I was in doubt. A few days earlier a Fw 190 group was moved to that part of the front. I had never seen an Fw 190 in the air. Were the two in front of me Fw 190s? With

additional speed I pulled up to the left and looked down. I could see the red star and the dark green colour—Russians!

"A Lagg 5. Too late to pass him... then I would be the hunted. So, I closed and attacked from above at a short distance and shot. After a short burst of fire I pulled out of a dive and my Me 109 stalled. After a hit and a bang—which I will never forget as long as I live—the right wing of the Lagg flew by. She was spinning out of control below. My engine was vibrating as if it was breaking up. I tried to find the best rpm to reduce the tremendous engine vibration after this midair collision, to avoid the danger of the airplane breaking up. At an altitude of 4000 metres, I was more or less heading towards the German lines. I found a meadow and, in a gentle turn, came to a landing with the gear down. After landing, a mechanic showed me a 1 metre cut on the underside of the Me 109. I had been lucky to survive."

Pilot Officer Leo Nomis, formerly with No. 71 (Eagle) Squadron, RAF, in World War II, flew the Me 109 for the Israelis in 1948–49: "It was all they could get at the time. Got them from the Czechs. Nobody else would sell the Israelis anything. Had to smuggle them in. They modified the 109Gs and they were real tricky to fly, with a lot more accidents. Didn't lose any in air-to-air. Lost about five to ground fire. The problem was, you had to go to Czechoslovakia to check out on them because you couldn't just check out on 'em like you would a regular fighter. They had a helluva lot of real dangerous habits. They had changed the centre of gravity on it. They changed the engine and the whole airframe. Then they put a 211 Jumo engine in it, which was a Ju 88 engine. They had to change it from one side to the other and the prop went the other way and it had a helluva torque on it. You'd be takin' off into the tents and the jeeps. And then, when it landed, it had a helluva swing on it if you didn't catch it right away. It would groundloop on

Left: The cockpit of a German Air Force F-4F Phantom of 71 "Richthofen" Fighter Wing based at Wittmund, Germany. Now in its fourth decade of service, the big, twin-engined jet has been operated by Air Force and Naval squadrons in a variety of roles. It is still being flown by the Air Forces of Greece, Turkey, Israel (as the F4-2000) and Germany. It is expected to be operational well into the next century.

Bob Hope once called the F-4 Phantom "the largest distributor of MiG parts in the western world."

Comparing the F3 Tornado and the F-4 Phantom...the F3 has a big cockpit; there seems to be a lot of glass there; it's very quiet, and ergonomically, it's very nicely set out. With the F-4, we are looking back at the 1950s. It's hot, it's sweaty, it's not particularly well layed-out, it's not very user-friendly...but it's a damned sight more fun. I joined the Air Force to fly Phantoms. There's just something about the aircraft. OK, it's getting old. It's a museum piece, but it's still great fun. When you walk up to the Phantom, you look at it and it says, 'Don't mess with me,' whereas the F3...and I hate to say this... seems more effeminate really, and that's being polite.
—Flight-Lieutenant Gary Dunlop, 712 "Richthofen" Geschwader, German Air Force, on exchange from the Royal Air Force

you. In Israel we used to call it 'the battle of the Messerschmitts'. "

"In my opinion, without question, the best fighter of the war was the Merlin-engined Mustang. It had the range, high cruising speed, good vision, powerful armament. The Germans I talked to said the same thing."
—Flight-Lieutenant Douglas "Duke" Warren, RCAF (Ret), formerly with No. 66 and No. 165 Squadrons, RAF

RAF pilot Tony Mead flew the F-86 in the post-war years at Wildenwrath, Germany, where the 2nd Tactical Air Force had established a small conversion unit to which RAF pilots went for their first experience on the Sabre: "When we arrived in early 1954, there were some dog-eared copies of the Pilots' Notes, several laid-back Flight-Lieutenant instructors who went through the notes in an appropriately relaxed manner, took us to the aircraft, helped us to strap in, and leaning into the cockpit actually started the GE J47 engine for us 'because otherwise you'll just burn the back off the bloody thing'. Jet engines of the time had very simple fuel systems and start-up was very much a manual affair, fiddling with the throttle at minimum to try and achieve a fuel flow compatible with a cool light up, which was not easy. Once achieved, however, and with the engine stabilised at an appropriate level, the instructor would say simply 'see you when you get back'. There were, of course, no F-86 two-seaters in the RAF fleet.

"The cultural change to this completely American swept-wing transonic fighter from the British Meteors and Vampires that we had flown up to then was daunting. First, used as we were to sitting in our Vampires with our bottoms practically scraping on the runway, we now found ourselves sitting high in the air looking out at first floor level. Gone too was our nice tidy standardized RAF instrument flying panel and in its place a bunch of

Left: Chopped, stacked and ready for scrapping, P-40s await their fate shortly after the end of World War II. Overleaf: The cockpit of a MiG 15 fighter of The Old Flying Machine Company at Duxford, England. When flown by a capable pilot, the MiG 15 proved a formidable airplane. But to the F-86 Sabre pilots of the US Air Force who faced the bulk of these Russian jets, many appeared to be operated by pilots with little experience. This impression was supported by the high kill ratio of the Sabre over the MiG in the Korean War.

I have been flying the F-4 Phantom for ten years. The particularly interesting thing about flying the F-4 is that there is no computer limiting you, like in most of the modern jets where the computer says 'OK, no maneuvering beyond this point!' That is the biggest advantage of the F-4. Even though more modern avionics would help in stabilising the aircraft, we can outmaneuver somebody by going into extreme flight parameters where others can't go because their computers say No. Also, it has very forgiving engines. I mean, a German Tornado... if it sucks up something, that's it. It has been proven that the F-4 can take in two Canadian geese and still fly along.
—Hauptmann Mike Herrling, 712 "Richthofen" Geschwader, German Air Force

I really enjoyed flying the F-86 above all others. It was a great aircraft for its time, and is still among the best ever built. It had plenty of fire power, excellent range and it was a first line fighter. It was certainly comfortable for the pilot. Although I didn't last too long during the Korean War, that air war was more enjoyable than anything I have ever done before or after. We hear many stories comparing the F-86 and the MiG 15, and lots of pilots have the view that the MiG was better. Not so. Chuck Yeager did performance evaluations on a MiG 15 [that] a North Korean pilot brought to the South during the war. Anyone reading the results of his evaluation will have a true picture of the two aircraft. I became engaged in dog fights several times with MiGs and in every case I was confident that I could outperform and outfight the enemy. It had nothing to do with pilot ability, it was the aircraft that did it. Best of all, the pilot was comfortable in the F-86. I believe [that] the combat average between the F-86 and the MiG proved conclusively which aircraft was better, even though it also had a lot to do with the training our pilots received.
—Colonel Walker M. Mahurin, USAF (Ret), formerly with the 56th Fighter Group and the 4th Fighter-Interceptor Group

Above: Colonel Walker M. Mahurin and his F-86 Sabre at Suwon Air Base during the Korean War.

dissimilar instruments arranged around the cockpit in apparent confusion—at least to *our* trained eye. The control column had so many knobs, nipples, buttons and switches that, although an ergonomic marvel, it was grasped with some trepidation. Cleared by the tower, we taxied out of our dispersal using nose-wheel steering for the first time in our lives, and it was pure delight. The marvellous steerability on the deck gave immediate confidence. With the Sabre now lined up on the runway and unable to find any further excuse for delay there was nothing for it but to open the throttle to maximum power and release the brakes. There followed a seemingly wild acceleration and before realizing it we were airborne, wings wagging furiously due to an aileron sensitivity never before experienced, and climbing away at a frightening rate. Almost at once and whilst cleaning-up, the cockpit began filling rapidly with white smoke! Calling an immediate re-entry for 'HEAVY SMOKE IN COCKPIT!' provoked a prompt if laconic 'adjust conditioning control, port console, to warm', which once found and done, thank God, rapidly dispersed the cloud. It is strange how water vapour can smell so decidedly of burning.

"Most of us honestly admitted that for the first flight or so in the Sabre we were not really fully in control but, surprisingly, practically the entire RAF conversion programme of all the 2nd TAF pilots to the F-86 was achieved without incident.

"Notwithstanding its complexities, this graceful and manoeuvrable aircraft rapidly became a much loved and respected mount with a reliability highly appreciated by the 'chaps'. It had its idiosyncrasies of course, a propensity for engine over-temperaturing on start-up and a tendency to surge during anything but a most gentle throttle opening. It was, in fact, common practice on take-off to open the throttle fast, which frequently caused an engine surge. By easing off a bit and opening wide again, chasing the rumble up the quadrant, a clean 100 per cent was then achieved. This enabled you to catch up with your leader who never really gave you sufficient time to tuck in properly for a formation take-off. The ground-attack role was helped by the innovative wing slots. Unfortunately, they didn't help its performance as an interceptor day fighter at high altitude and so 'hard edges' were fitted. These, in turn, required a great deal more airspeed in the circuit and on finals which, sadly, led to one or two incidents.

"Firing the six Browning machine guns in unison made a tremendous noise, smell and vibration, and the radar gun-sight ranging ring leapt about furiously. Counting coloured bullet holes in the 'rag' [target sleeve] later was, however, a great satisfaction. If there weren't any, the Squadron

It was an anathema to some pilots and sheer ambrosia to others. There were those pilots that acclaimed it as the best single-seat fighter of any nation to emerge from WW II; there were pilots that pronounced it a vicious killer equally dispassionate towards killing its pilot as his opponent. Indeed, few fighters were capable of arousing within those that flew them such extremes of passion as was the Corsair. Oddly enough, the Royal Navy was not quite so fastidious as the US Navy regarding deck landing characteristics and cleared the Corsair for shipboard operation some nine months before its American counterpart. The obstacles to the Corsair's shipboard use were admittedly not insurmountable, but I can only surmise that the apparently ready acceptance by their Lordships of the Admiralty of the Chance Vought fighter for carrier operation *continued*

Commander was inclined to comment that 'a fighter pilot that can't shoot is a contradiction in terms'.

"The Sabre was a fine aircraft and platform, and allowed its pilot considerable latitude. Flying it gave us the right to a special illuminated address and a lapel pin, certifying us to be 'A member in good standing of the Mach Buster's Club', having exceeded the speed of sound in an F-86 Sabre Jet. However, this was achieved only by removing the wing tanks, climbing to 40,000 feet, rolling upside down, and pulling through to the vertical with the engine at full power. Diving vertically the airspeed built rapidly and following some buffet at Mach .96–7, and a tendency to roll to port, easily corrected by gentle aileron, one slid through to Mach 1.03–4, at which point it was time to throttle back and start the pull-out. This transonic capability was more of a curiosity than operationally useful, but all of us stood just a wee bit taller after doing it for the first time."

Former USAF pilot John Lamb has more than 1500 hours flying different versions of the F-4 Phantom: "The first thing that struck me about the F-4 was the size. I had been flying the A-37 for four years including 400 combat missions in South-east Asia. The A-37 had great power/throttle response and turning capability, so the transition to the Phantom was initially just a matter of getting used to the new cockpit. I'll never forget the first time... taxiing on to the runway beside another F-4 for my first formation take-off. What a big, powerful machine!

"Over my career, I was fortunate to fly every model of the F-4 that the USAF operated. Originally, I flew the RF-4C with the Alabama Air National Guard in Birmingham. For a while we had an F4-C on loan at Birmingham, so I picked up a few hours in it. The 'recce' [reconnaissance] mission was a lot of fun if you like flying close to the dirt with your hair on fire. The greatest assets of

must have been solely due to the exigencies of the times, for the landing behaviour of the Corsair really was bad, a fact to which I was able to attest after the briefest acquaintance with the aircraft. A curved approach was very necessary if the pilot was to have any chance of seeing the carrier, let alone the batsman! When the throttle was cut, the nose dropped so that the aircraft bounced on its main wheels, and once the tail-wheel made contact, the aircraft proved very unstable directionally, despite the tail-wheel lock, swinging either to port or starboard, and this swing had to be checked immediately with the brakes. On one approach, I tried a baulked landing and discovered that the sudden opening of the throttle at 80 knots (148 km/h) produced a torque stall. I needed no more convincing of the wisdom of the US Navy in withholding the Corsair from shipboard operation! Oh yes, the Corsair could be landed on a deck without undue difficulty by an experienced pilot in ideal conditions, but with pilots of average capability, really pitching decks and marginal weather conditions, attrition simply had to be of serious proportions. There can be no doubt that the Corsair was one of the fastest naval aircraft of WW II and few of *continued*

Left: The US F-15 Eagle was designed from the outset to be the finest air superiority fighter in the world. Two 24,000 lb thrust Pratt & Whitney turbofan engines give it an incredible power-to-weight ratio. Pilots love the visibility it affords and the ease of flying, as well as the avionics and weapons control systems, and the integral Vulcan cannon. On 7th August 1990, the 1st Tactical Fighter Wing, USAF, began deploying forty-eight F-15C Eagles from their Langley, Virginia base to Saudi Arabia for Gulf War service. The grueling trip took fourteen hours with nine aerial refuellings.

Below: US Navy F-14 Tomcats worked as air-superiority fighters in the Gulf War. Right: Hawker Hurricane in three-view.

its pilots criticised it from the performance standpoint. It had good range, adequate firepower, an extremely reliable engine and it could absorb a lot of punishment. However, in my view it left much to be desired as a fighter from the viewpoint of manoeuvrability and this same shortcoming was apparent in the dive-bombing role in which it saw widespread use. Finally, it had a very dreary track record as a deck-

the RF-4 were clean aerodynamic lines and power... she was a very fast machine.

"In 1988, I was assigned to Spangdahlem AFB, Germany. As a reward for finding a highly sensitive and classified ALQ 131 jamming pod which had fallen off one of our aircraft, I was given a chance to fly the F-4G 'Wild Weasel'. The Weasel mission is the most demanding thing I have ever attempted. It required air-to-air skills as well as conventional air-to-ground weapons delivery, in addition to the primary role of SAM [surface-to-air missile] killer. The co-ordination and trust required between the pilot and the electronic warfare officer (EWO) was of the highest order. The Weasel EWOs, and some of the backseaters I flew with in the Guard who had been former Navy/Marine RIOs [radar intercept officers],

were some of the best and most respected aviators I have ever known."

US Air Force Major Jonathan Holdaway has flown the F-15 Eagle for seven years and now in 1998 he is nearing the end of a three-and-a-half-year exchange tour with the RAF, where he is flying the F3 Tornado with No. 43 Squadron at Leuchars: "I love the F-15. That's my first love. Flying the Tornado with the Brits has been fun but deep in my heart I'll always be an Eagle driver. It's a great airplane to fly. It's optimized for one mission—to kill other airplanes. It's the greatest air-to-air fighter in history and, until the F-22 comes out and proves itself, the F-15 will be the king of the skies. Talk to any country that flies them, particularly the Israelis. They have done some very, very good work in some of their conflicts with the F-15. Combining our kills in

Desert Storm with the kills the Israelis have had in their conflicts, its kill ratio is well over 100 to nothing, which no other airplane in the world can even come close to matching. I love it. It's an airplane designed by fighter pilots for fighter pilots and I just can't say enough good things about it.

"One of the big things I had to get used to in coming to this exchange (with the RAF) was the difference between the F-15 and the F3. We do the same mission—shoot down and kill other airplanes. The Eagle is much easier to fly than the T-38, which is the airplane that we fly in training. The basic skills of taking off, flying from point A to point B, and landing in an F-15 are very simple. The airplane is very responsive to the pilot controls, with big, powerful engines out the back, and she'll do basically whatever you ask of her. The F-15 doesn't have all the fancy fly-by-wire systems and computers controlling the flight controls like some of the new airplanes. It's an airplane that was bridging the gap between the old-style fighters like the F-4 Phantom of Vietnam days and the new fighters with fly-by-wire computer-driven software systems. Flying the F-15 is very easy but, because it was designed for single-seat operation, the guy flying it and operating it has a relatively high workload. He has to work the weapons system and fly the airplane at the same time—a very different concept from what I do now with the Tornado.
I have a guy in the back seat, a navigator, who controls the radar. He searches the sky, he finds us targets and then tells me where they are; he locks down to them with the radar and tells me when they are in range to shoot. He's also responsible for the navigation. To be quite honest, the cockpit of the F3 Tornado is much less pilot-friendly than that of the F-15. The F3 is much harder to fly. Just getting the airplane airborne, from A to B, and landing it is much more difficult than with an F-15. As I'm flying the

Tornado, I have to be devoting part of my concentration to keeping the thing airborne and flying where I want it to fly. The F-15 almost flies itself and I can concentrate more of my energy and attention on doing my mission—finding and destroying other airplanes.

"There is a fundamental shift in design philosophy that McDonnell-Douglas took from the Panavia consortium which designed and built the Tornado. The F-15 was designed to fly high and relatively fast, to have very good turn performance and a very high thrust-to-weight ratio, and to operate at medium to high altitudes. The F3 Tornado was designed as a follow-on to the GR1, which was designed as a low-altitude striker to penetrate the Warsaw Pact defences back in the Cold War; to take out enemy airfields, strategic targets, that sort of thing. The F3, as a derivative of that design, shares a lot of that heritage. It has very high wing-loading with a very small wing. As a result, it doesn't turn very well. It bleeds energy quite quickly when you start manoeuvring it hard. It doesn't have the same G capability that the F-15 has. It doesn't like medium-to high-altitude flight because it was designed to fly down low. If, for instance, we are training against F-15s, F-16s or F-18s, if we can drag them down into the low altitude arena, we can eliminate or reduce some of their advantages because that is where the F3 was designed to operate... low altitude, within 1000 feet of the ground. The F-15s and F-16s don't like to get down there with us because it eliminates some of their advantages, so they try to keep the fight up high and let their missiles— the AMRAAM, AIM 7, and AIM 9—come down and take us out at low altitude. But, if we can defeat those long-range shots and get them to come down with us, then it's a little bit of a different fight. The bottom line, though, is that if an F3 is flown to its maximum performance and an F-15 is flown to its maximum performance—well, you know who is going to win that one... the F-15."

landing aircraft; many were the pilots that lauded its high-speed performance but decried its lack of affinity with a carrier deck.
—from *Wings of the Navy* by Captain Eric Brown, RN (Ret)

The Air Force began phasing out the "Wild Weasel" Phantoms in the early 1990s and I delivered aircraft 69-250 to the AMARC "boneyard" in Tucson, Arizona in December 1991. "250" had the most SAM missile kills during the Gulf War. The only thing wrong with the aircraft when we signed it over was that the autopilot would not hold altitude. It was a tremendously emotional experience to see such a wonderful airplane retired.
—John Lamb, USAF F-4

LIFE ON LEISTON

Below: Believed to be Sergeants R. Ollerton and J. Kuykendall, 363rd Fighter Squadron maintenance inspectors. Ground crewmen got little recognition in World War II for their invaluable contribution to the performance and safety of the aircraft they maintained. Right: This 357th Fighter Group P-51D was flown by Lieutenant William Gruber.

MASTER SERGEANT Merle Olmsted, USAF (Ret), was a crew chief at Leiston, only 80 miles across the North Sea from the German-occupied Netherlands. He remembers the daily grind on his fighter station: "Dawn has not yet broken through the cold and swirling mist at Leiston airfield in the county of Suffolk, on the coast of England's East Anglia bulge. It is January 1945, and many of the 1500 men of the fighter group and its supporting units are still secure in their cots. Many others, however, have been awake all night as numerous shops and offices at Leiston require twenty-four-hour manning.

"Among those awake, and hopefully alert, are the CQs, which means 'Charge of Quarters', an old Army term for the non-commissioned officers who man every unit's Orderly Room during off-duty hours. It is a job that rotates among all the unit's NCOs. With the coming of daylight the three squadron CQs go forth from the Orderly Room to rouse the pilots and ground crews. They had been jarred from late-night lethargy by the telephone call from Group Operations which at some time during the night had received, by teletype machine, the Field Order for the coming mission from 66th Fighter Wing.

"The Field Order (FO) originating from Eighth Air Force Headquarters spells out the mission objectives, units involved, bomber routes to the target, fighter rendezvous times and locations, radio codes and all other information needed for the unit to play its part in the continuing air assault on Germany.

"As the CQ goes from hut to hut the routine is the same. He steps through the blackout door, flips on the light switch and says in a loud voice: 'Briefing 0700, maximum range, maximum effort'. Normally, only the wake-up time varies depending on the pilots' briefing time. In the case of the pilots' barracks, he wakes only those scheduled to fly today.

"The first item on the agenda is breakfast at the big consolidated mess hall or the officers' mess.

From there it is off to the flight line via GI truck, bicycle, or on foot, a distance of about 1 mile. With the crews on their way to the Mustangs huddled under their covers, and the pilots drifting into Group Briefing, the day's activities begin to accelerate.

"For centuries large military bases have tended to be self-contained cities. Leiston airfield, USAAF Station F-373, like dozens of other Eighth Air Force installations which sprawl across East Anglia, is no exception.

"The 1500 men (and half a dozen women who run the Red Cross Club) provide all of the usual town services and a few others of a more warlike nature. The mission of these 1500 men is to place a few to as many as sixty-five P-51 Mustang fighter planes and their pilots over Europe every day if ordered to do so, to enable them to take on the German military and win World War II. Everything on the station revolves around some ninety Mustang fighters and their pilots.

"These few pilots, and some 900 others, are all members of the USAAF's 357th Fighter Group—

The Yoxford Boys, who have been in residence for about one year. The point of this piece is to tell something about the daily routine on an American fighter base in World War II England, from the perspective of the ground crews. Air operations are not really what we are talking about here. It is, however, worth noting that the 357th, our host today, is among the three highest-scoring fighter groups in the Eighth Air Force.

"January 1945 is proving to be the coldest, and one of the most difficult, months for flying weather the group has so far experienced. For eighteen days of the month, the ground and runways have either been frozen or covered with snow and ice.

"On the 14th of this month, a date which has since become known as 'the big day', the 357th became engaged in a great air battle in the Berlin area and was credited with fifty-five and a half enemy fighters shot down, the highest one-day score ever among US fighter groups.

"Today we have left the ground crews on their way to their individual aircraft. It is not always obvious to those outside aviation (or to some in it)

Left: Briefing room of the 357th Fighter Group. The map shows the flight route to Berlin on 14th January 1945. Below: Lieutenant Ed Hyman who flew a P-51 Mustang called *Rolla U* with the 362nd Fighter Squadron at Leiston.

Centre: Captain William O'Brien flew three hundred combat hours in seventy-seven missions including escort, fighter sweeps and ground strafing with the 357th Fighter Group in the European Theater of Operations in World War II.

how critically important quality maintenance is in the operation of airplanes. In military operations it can mean the difference between success and failure of the mission, and the spectre of aircraft and crew loss due to mechanical failure is always uppermost in the minds of the ground crews. Across the North Sea from Leiston, German Air Force commander Reichsmarshall Hermann Göring said of his ground crews: 'Without their service, nothing can be achieved. I must say that their endurance, their skill, their patience, although different, is in every way the equal of that of the aircrews.' Certainly, that praise applies equally to the ground crews of all the air forces in the War.

"In the 357th, there are two levels of maintenance, the flight line crews assigned to individual aircraft, and the hangar crews which handle heavy maintenance such as engine changes. A third, higher level, on the Leiston base, the 469th Service Squadron, does the more complicated jobs that the squadrons are not equipped to do.

"When ground crews are mentioned, which is seldom, the reference is usually to the crew chiefs. Most Eighth Air Force fighter units assign three men to each airplane. Besides the crew chief (usually a staff sergeant), there is an assistant crew chief (a sergeant or 'buck sergeant') and an armament man (a corporal or sergeant). Those selected as crew chiefs are usually in their twenties, or the very elderly—in their thirties. Unless one is on 'other duty', both the crew chief and assistant arrive at their aircraft at the same time.

"Their first duty is to remove the cockpit and wing covers and the pitot tube cover. Then the propeller is pulled through its arc a few times and the pre-flight inspection is started. The P-51 is remarkably simple. Nevertheless, the pre-flight, as laid out in the manual, is quite lengthy. Most of it consists of visual inspections, many of which have been completed during the post-flight inspection the day before. All reservoirs are checked for fluid level, coolant, hydraulics, battery, engine oil and fuel. An inspection is always made under the aircraft for coolant leaks, which frequently occur due to temperature changes. It is often difficult to tell coolant from water, but touching a bit of the fluid with the tongue will reveal the difference, as coolant has a bitter taste (and is poisonous if consumed in quantity).

"If all visual and servicing checks are satisfactory, the engine run is done, using the battery cart to save the airplane's internal battery. Because the seat is rather deep (to accommodate the pilot's dinghy pack), a cushion in the seat helps one to reach the brakes and to see out from the cockpit. Now the brakes are set and the seatbelt fastened around the control stick to provide 'up elevators' during the power check. The flaps are left down, the fuel selector is set to either main tank, the throttle cracked open, and the mixture control set to the idle cut-off position. After yelling 'clear' to be sure no one is near the nose of the plane, the starter switch is engaged (the P-51 has a direct-

Right: On 11th April 1944 Lieutenant Mark Stapleton and the pilots of the 364th Fighter Squadron, 357th Fighter Group, were engaged in a fierce dogfight over the city of Leipzig, Germany: "My guns jammed after each short burst but thanks to an experimental hydralic gun charger that had been installed in my plane, I was able to clear the jam and fire again. My guns jammed and were cleared at least seven times. I overran the enemy aircraft at which time Lieutenant Sumner closed and observed hits on the enemy aircraft which crashed and exploded."

Stretched out in the shade on the grass, / Talking with others who'd gathered around, Crew chiefs were waiting for time to pass Until their planes were back on the ground.

All night long some of them had worked, / Making their birds ready to go; / They knew o'er enemy skies what lurked... / And so the tension began to grow.

Five hours now and nary a sign / Of their fighters in friendly skies; Each was dying to shout: "There's mine!" / There were only
continued

drive starter), along with engine prime. As soon as the cylinders begin to fire, the mixture control is moved to 'run'. The propeller is already in full increase rpm for the warm-up. Various additional checks are now carried out, including checking that the engine oil and coolant temperature instruments are registering 'in the green'. The engine is run up to 2300 rpm and the magnetos are checked. With each mag off, the maximum allowable rpm drop is 100. The propeller governor is also checked at this rpm. The maximum rpm is 3000, but this is for take-off and is not used on the ground run.

"After the engine is shut down and everything has checked out OK, it is mostly a matter of waiting. The fuel and oil trucks cruise the taxiway and all tanks are topped off after the run. Now the windshield, canopy and rear view mirror are all polished—for the tenth time today. The armament man has long since arrived and charged his guns, so all aircraft on the field have 'hot' guns long before take-off. The gun switches in the cockpit are off, of course, but occasionally one has been left on and the pilot gripping the stick could fire a burst, terrifying everyone within range, including himself.

"The pilots usually arrive fifteen to twenty minutes before engine start time, via an overloaded jeep or weapons carrier. After the pilot is strapped in with the help of the ground crew, his goggles and windshield are given a final swipe. Engine start time comes and sixty Merlins cough into life around the airfield hardstands. Then the wheel chocks are pulled and, with a wave of his hand to the ground crew, each pilot guides his fighter out to the proper place on the taxi strip in a snake-like procession toward the active runway.

"The ground crews, and everyone else in the airfield area, seek a vantage point to watch the take-off—always an exciting event. The sight and sound of sixty or more overloaded Mustangs getting airborne is impressive.

Below: Major Leonard "Kit" Carson signals pairs of P-51s at the take-off end of the active Leiston runway at the start of the 357th's final combat mission of World War II, 25th April 1945. Right: A 362nd Squadron beer party in their hangar.

nervous glances and sighs.
Then a speck was spotted
far off, / Joined by others as
they streaked down; / They
swooped low and an engine
did cough... / That crew
chief wore a worried frown.

A six-hour mission, they
peeled up to land / And all
came back except for one
lad; His mechanic friend
tried to understand...
Slowly he walked away,
tearful and sad.
—One Is Missing
by Bert McDowell, Junior

"Much of the weight the planes are carrying today is represented by two long-range fuel drop tanks, so vital to the success of the US fighters in Europe. Most of these tanks are made of paper composition units (though some are metal), each holding 108 US gallons and built in huge quantities by British companies. They are installed on the wing racks for the next day's mission the night before and are filled at that time. During operation they are pressurized to ensure positive feeding at altitude, by the exhaust side of the engine vacuum pump. The piping for this and the fuel flow is rubber tubes with glass elbows which will break away cleanly when the tanks are dropped. Even though the drop tanks are pressurized, it is necessary to coax fuel into the system during the pre-flight. After switching to the drop tank position, the engine will often die, and the selector switch must quickly be put back to 'main' and then to 'drop tanks' until they feed properly. On the mission they are always dropped when empty, or earlier if combat demands it. With all fifteen fighter groups operating, Eighth Air Force

fighters can require 1800 drop tanks per day.

"At mid-day, while the mission aircraft are out, the line crews are in a state of suspended animation. It is mostly free time, time to attend to laundry, read the squadron bulletin board to see when mail call was, and to see if your name has appeared on any unwanted, but unavoidable extra duty rosters. There is also time to drop into the Post Exchange for a candy bar, and to take in noon chow at the big consolidated mess hall.

"Regardless of what they have been doing while the mission was out, the aircraft ground crew always 'sweat out' the return of their particular airplane and pilot, and when both return safely it is a great relief.

"Whether a crew has a close relationship with their pilot depends on several factors—how long they have been together, the pilot's general attitude towards enlisted men, and if he is an outgoing individual.

"Although the word 'hero' probably never occurs to the ground crews, they are well aware that it is their pilot who is doing the fighting, and

sometimes the dying. In most cases, there is considerable affection for their pilot and they are proud of his achievements. There is always a period of depression when an aircraft and pilot fail to return from a mission, and often the cause doesn't filter down to the ground crew. In a day or two, a new P-51 arrives, and a new pilot, and the war goes on.

"An average mission of the 357th Fighter Group lasts about four to five hours and by the ETR [estimated time of return] everyone is back on the hardstands. If the group comes into sight in proper formation and to the rising snarl of many Merlins, it is probable that there has been no

combat. If they straggle back in small groups, or individually, it is certain that there has been some kind of action. Missing red tape around the gun muzzles is a final confirmation.

"As each P-51 turns into its parking place, the pilot blasts the tail around and shuts down the engine, the wheels are chocked and the mission is over—one more toward completion of his tour.

"Now he brings any aircraft malfunctions to the attention of the crew, and departs for debriefing. For the ground crews there is considerable work ahead to complete the post-flight inspection and repair the aircraft. If luck is with them, their airplane can be 'put to bed' in time for evening chow, and the work day will have come to an end. Often, though, it does not work out that way, and their jobs continue into the night."

"Our narrative has started before dawn on a dreary January day. On another day this month, the 16th, two days after the group's astounding success over Berlin, Major Guernsey Carlisle leads fifty-four Mustangs on a heavy bomber escort mission. He reports: 'Takeoff 0924, down approx 1600 at various bases on continent. Group rendezvoused with bombers at 1100 Zwolle at 24,000. Left bombers at 1400 at Strasbourg. Weather bad. 10/10 cloud over target. Group instructed to land on continent, returned to UK on 19th January. Lieutenant William Thompson, 363rd, killed in crash near Framlingham.'

"Thompson is a victim of the bad weather, only a few miles from home base. He is one of seven who die during January. One of these is Staff Sergeant Melvin Schuneman, a crew chief and the only 357th ground crew man to die in an aircraft accident. He is killed on the 27th in another weather-related crash, along with pilot Lieutenant Walter Corby, in the group's AT-6.

"Leiston airfield was within a few miles of the North Sea coast, and was often the first airfield seen by American and British pilots of battle-damaged aircraft. Many such cripples landed there with varying degrees of success. One of these incidents ended in a fiery spectacle in late May 1944 and is described here by Captain William 'Obee' O'Brien, USAF (Ret): 'After a mission flown in the early afternoon, I was in the cockpit of my plane, and my crew chief, Jim Loter, was standing on the wing. We saw a P-47 taxiing from south to north on the perimeter track on the 363rd squadron side of the field. The Jug was

moving fairly slowly, and he then pulled into an empty hardstand just across from where I was parked. As he turned, I could see white smoke starting to come from the lower fuselage, well back from the engine, about where the turbo supercharger exit was located. I told Jim to try and get to the Jug with our fire extinguisher as the pilot shut down the engine. The smoking aircraft was facing to the west, and about this time its guns started to fire and the pilot was out of the plane and standing on the hardstand. It is well

Below: Ground crewmen of the 99th Fighter Squadron, 332nd FG, await the return of their Mustangs, the Red Tail Angels, a black fighter unit of the 15 USAAF in World War II. The photo is by Vogue fashion photographer Toni Frissell, while she was on a wartime assignment in Italy with the US Army Air Force.

Right: P-51 Mustangs in the 1997 Flying Legends airshow at Duxford, England. The Mustang was the primary front-line fighter of the 357th FG at Leiston in World War II.

GOD BLESS AMERICA

—o—

REPEAT OFTEN, DAILY, SINCERELY.

LET'S GO! U.S.A. KEEP 'EM FLYING!

UNCLE SAM NEEDS PILOTS
BE A U. S. ARMY
FLYING CADET

Strike 'em Dead

REMEMBER PEARL HARBOR

CLOSE COVER BEFORE STRIKING

known that the Jug had eight .50 machine guns. All eight were firing and believe me, that was the first and only time I'd ever heard that much firepower released. Needless to say, neither Loter or I could get to the Jug, which proceeded to burn and fire its guns. I imagine everyone within 4 miles wondered what the hell had happened. The story I got was, the Jug pilot was short on fuel—to the extent that he might not make it, and landed at the first base he saw, planning to refuel and then proceed to home base. He got refuelled all right and was taxiing to take off when he heard a loud bang, so he pulled into the nearest hardstand. He had been doing some strafing on the way home from his mission. The 'loud bang' was probably a 20mm or larger shell that had been lodged in the fuselage and finally exploded, possibly caused by taxiing across a rough spot, which was enough to activate the fuse. This Jug pilot was one lucky man!'

"Gunfire of a more serious nature hit Leiston airfield two weeks later. Compared with the experience of the RAF during the Battle of Britain, and the German ground crews in 1944–45, life on an Eighth Air Force airfield was a relatively safe existence. Our pilots, the only ones on station doing the fighting, faced death or capture every day, but only once in the fourteen months of wartime service did Leiston airfield encounter hostile gunfire.

"On the night of D-Day (6th–7th June), the Luftwaffe struck back at the Allies in retaliation for the invasion. According to RAF records, several bombs fell on Tuddenham, and five bombs were dropped in the vicinity of Parham and Framlingham (both only a few miles from Leiston). Three night-flying B-24s were attacked and one was shot down just after midnight. An RAF 25 Squadron Mosquito encountered and shot down an Me 410 40 miles east of Southwold.

"Shortly after midnight a German intruder struck at Leiston airfield. The field, like all of England

114

then, was blacked out, but apparently the door to the mess hall, then serving midnight chow, had been left open. Attracted by this light the intruder fired a burst of cannon fire into the building, doing little damage other than making a few holes.

"Among those present there has always been much confusion and disagreement about the details of the event. The type of German aircraft has never been authenticated. Group records indicate it was probably an Me 410, but two men who were outside and got a close look at it say that it was a single-engine type, an Me 109 or Fw 190. Since neither of these types was really suitable for night raids on England, it was probably an Me 410, possibly the same one shot down by the 25 Squadron Mosquito.

"Sergeant James Frary made a detailed entry about the incident in his diary: 'I was standing outside the Orderly Room (I was CQ that night) and there was a red alert on at the time. I heard the plane coming in low from the south. I didn't think about it being German until he reached the edge of the field and I could see him silhouetted against the sky. Just as a precaution I crouched down in front of the door. About then our AA guns started to fire. Pink tracers were going all around the enemy ship. Just as he got almost out of my range of vision he banked around to the east and cut across the communal site. It was then that he cut loose with his guns, putting three holes in the mess hall and ploughing up the baseball field with his 20mm guns. The AA fired about 300 rounds of caliber .50 and 8 rounds of 40mm at him as he crossed the field. They apparently hit him as a gas cap and some scraps of metal were found later.'

"Sergeant Emery Gaal, who had been working in the 364th Squadron area, recalls his view that night from the mess hall: 'Around midnight I was sitting in the mess hall with Karnicke, having a snack. We heard the plane coming and then a big boom like cannon fire. It blew a big hole just

below the roof. As all of us hit the deck the benches and tables flew all over and we were hollering at the cooks to shut off the lights, which they did. After the lights went on, I found a cut on my leg from a heavy table which had fallen on me.'

"Out on the flight line, Claude Allen of the 363rd Squadron remembers: 'It was about midnight and I had just been to the mess hall, and then to our squadron area to pick up the mail and some blankets as several of us from 'A' flight usually slept out on the line near the ships. I was driving the bomb service truck and a Sergeant Van Tyne was riding with me. While returning to the flight line we stopped at the radio shack just off the perimeter track and were informed that an alert had been in affect, but as all seemed clear, I pulled back on the perimeter track toward 'A' flight area. Suddenly we heard this loud drone overhead which sounded like an aircraft making a sharp turn, coming in from the direction of Leiston, and we could see the flash from the aircraft's guns. This is when I went out of the left side of the truck, my partner out the right side. About the time we were flat on the ground, the ack-ack opened up. When it was over we found the truck which had gone only a short distance before stopping, but did not see any damage to it.' "

"The fourteen months on Eighth Fighter Command's Leiston airfield was a unique experience for the ground crews, and probably the high point of life for many. Most of us, however, did not appreciate this at the time, and wanted only to get it over with and go home. Only in later years did some realize what a fascinating time it had been, and many of us have returned several times to the now tranquil land that once housed a fighter group at war."

I am grateful to my friend Merle Olmsted for generously sharing his memories of life on Leiston airfield in World War II. PK

I think that these moments just before the clash are the most gloriously exciting moments of life. You sit there behind a great engine that seems as vibrant and alive as you are yourself, your thumb waits expectantly on the trigger, and your eyes watch the gun sights through which in a few seconds an enemy will be flying in a veritable hail of fire. And all round you, in front and behind, there are your friends too, all eager and excited, all thundering down together into the attack! The memory of such moments is burnt into my mind for ever.
—Flight-Lieutenant D.M. Crook of No. 609 Squadron, RAF

Left: The top shooters of the 357th Fighter Group, left to right: Richard A. Peterson, Leonard K. Carson, John B. England and Clarence E. Anderson. "Two months after the Normandy landings", states Carson in his book *Pursue and Destroy*, "German fighter units in France had ceased to exist, period. Shot up on the ground, knocked out of the air, grounded for lack of fuel, because trucks could not move on the roads, they simply disappeared. Just as their land forces were retreating, so was Germany's defensive fighter arm pulled back to the borders of the Fatherland itself."

HAWKEYE

GOOD EYESIGHT was vital to the achievement and survival of the successful fighter pilot. In World War II a fighter pilot who could focus on the speck of an enemy aircraft several miles away had the advantage. He had time to position himself in such a way as to make his adversary take the defensive. If his marksmanship was fairly good, this superior position frequently led to a kill.

Erich Hartmann was the highest-scoring fighter pilot in history, and all 352 of his kills during World War II were verified either on film or by other pilots who witnessed them. While it is true that the majority of the opponents he faced were relatively inexperienced Russian pilots, others were highly trained airmen. Another factor in Hartmann's extraordinary score was the Luftwaffe's policy requiring nearly all its fighter pilots to serve continuously in action for the duration of the War, or until killed or incapacitated. As a result, the skill and achievement of those who managed to stay in the fight grew dramatically. Many years after the War Hartmann recalled: "Today I am sure that 80 per cent of my kills never knew I was there before I opened fire. My dogfights were fast and simple on that account. But one factor always worked for me more than any other. I found I could spot enemy planes long before my comrades—sometimes minutes before them. This was not experience and skill, but an advantage with which I was born. My rule for air fighting is this: *the pilot who sees the other first already has half the victory.*"

Feldwebel Oscar Boesch, German Air Force (Ret), formerly of IV/JG3 "Udet": "Eyesight was most important for life or death. Many lost out by being approached in the blind area."

Colonel John W. Cunnick, USAF (Ret), formerly with the 55th Fighter Group, 8 USAAF: "The successful fighter pilot had to be at the right place

Below: On 27th December 1944 Feldwebel Oscar Boesch and his fellow IV JG 3 "Udet" pilots were attacked by more than fifty USAAF Mustangs over the Ardennes. Many of the Fw 190s were shot down. The event is portrayed in the painting *War Wolf* (right) by Canadian artist Robert Bailey.

at the right time. Exceptional eyesight was a great help. It seems that several of our squadron always called in bogies before the others saw them."

"Much of what has been written about fighter pilots is pure malarkey! As in any other profession, their traits run the gamut from calm, cool and collected to plain stupid. It certainly helped to have 'radar eyes', but normal eyesight with an aggressive nature was more important."
—Colonel Dewey F. Durnford, Junior, USMC (Ret), formerly with VMF-323 and on exchange with the 4th Fighter Group, USAF, Korea

Between the start of World War II and the end of 1941—including the British retreat from Dunkirk, the Battle of Britain and the initial German attack on Russia—General Adolf Galland scored more than seventy kills. He was appointed General of the Fighter Arm of the German Air Force in the summer of 1941, at the age of twenty-nine. From his comments to me, and his book *The First and The Last*, come his view of the air war in the west in the summer of 1940: "In the opening encounters [of the Battle of Britain] the English were at a considerable disadvantage because of their close formation. Since the Spanish Civil War we had introduced a wide-open combat formation in which great intervals were kept between the smaller single formations and the groups, each of which flew at a different altitude. This gave us a number of important advantages: greater air coverage; relief for the individual pilot who could now concentrate more on the enemy than on keeping formation; freedom of initiative right down to the smallest unit without loss of collective strength; reduced vulnerability, as compared to close formation; and, most important of all, better vision. The first rule of all air combat is to see the opponent first. Like the hunter who stalks his prey and manoeuvres himself into the most favorable position for the kill, the fighter in the opening of a

121

Left: Sergeant George Unwin (third from left) and pilots of No. 19 Squadron, RAF at Fowlmere, Cambridgeshire, England in 1940, Below: The Vickers-Supermarine Spitfire in identification three-view.

A very large German Shepherd named Flash was the mascot of No. 19 Squadron at Fowlmere in 1940. Flash belonged to Flight Sergeant George Unwin, DFM and Bar. Flash lived with the pilots of A Flight in a Nissen hut at Fowlmere Farm and seemed to believe that he was supposed to run with them to their Spitfires whenever they were ordered to scramble. As the Spits took off, Flash would run across the field with them and watch them until they disappeared from view. When the fighters returned to land, he would meet each plane until he found the one with George Unwin in the cockpit, and would leap onto the wing to welcome him back.

Right: USAF fighter pilots being briefed for a Gulf War mission in 1991, Below: A USAF F-16 Fighting Falcon about to launch on a strike during Operation Desert Storm from a Royal Saudi Air Force base in 1991. F-16s from Air National Guard units in New York and South Carolina were among the first of nearly 200 US Falcons in action at the start of the Desert Storm battle. They were extremely effective tactical strike fighters.

dogfight must detect the opponent as early as possible in order to attain a superior position for the attack.

"The British quickly realized the superiority of our combat formation and readjusted their own. At first they introduced the so-called 'Charlies': two flanking planes following in the rear of the main formation, flying slightly higher and further out, on a weaving course. Finally, they adopted our combat formation entirely. Since then, without any fundamental changes, it has been accepted throughout the world. Werner Mölders was greatly responsible for these developments.

"From the very beginning the English had an extraordinary advantage which we never overcame throughout the war: radar and fighter control. For us and for our Command this was a surprise and a very bitter one. The English possessed a closely knit radar network conforming to the highest technical standards of the day, which provided Fighter Command with the most detailed data imaginable. Thus the British fighter was guided all the way from take-off to his correct position for attack on the German formations. We had nothing of the kind. In the application of radio-location technique the enemy was far in advance of us. Under the serious threat for England arising from the German victory in France—no one described it more forcefully than Churchill in his memoirs—the British Command concentrated desperately on the development and perfection of radar. The success was outstanding. Our planes were already detected over the Pas de Calais while they were still assembling, and were never allowed to escape the radar eye. Each of our movements was projected almost faultlessly on the screens in the British fighter control centres, and as a result Fighter Command was able to direct their forces to the most favourable position at the most propitious time. Of further outstanding advantage to the English was the

fact that our attacks, especially those of the bombers, were, from sheer necessity, directed against the central concentration of the British defence. We were not in a position to seek out soft spots in the defence or to change our approaches and to attack now from this direction, now from that, as the Allies did later in their air offensive against the Reich.

"For us there was only a frontal attack against the superbly organized defence of the British Isles, conducted with great determination. Added to this, the RAF was fighting over its own country. Pilots who had bailed out could go into action again almost immediately, whereas ours were taken prisoner. Damaged English planes could sometimes still reach their base or make an emergency landing, while for us engine trouble or fuel shortage could mean the end.

"Morale too and the emotions played a great part. The desperate seriousness of the situation apparently aroused all the energies of this hardy and historically conscious people, whose arms in consequence were directed toward one goal: to repulse the German invaders at any price!"

"I was returning from a mission one winter day, all by myself. I had gone back to strafe a German locomotive and lost the rest of the squadron.

"The weather was very hazy... you could see the ground by looking straight down, but not at an angle straight ahead. I found my base, Wormingford airfield, and saw that there was a constant stream of green flares being shot up at the end of the runway.

"I buzzed low over these flares and peeled up into a landing pattern, keeping the flares in sight at all times. I landed with no difficulty and reported to Squadron Operations for de-briefing.

"I was asked, 'Didn't you see that other plane?'

"Aghast, I answered, 'What other plane?'

"Then I was informed that another plane came in to land at the same time as I did, only he was using

Excellent sight was needed, and normal medical examination ensured that we all had it. As night fighter pilots we were also tested for night vision, starting about 1941. Excellent vision was and is certainly a *sine qua non*, but only one of several important requirements. Fighter pilots were not selected by attempting to compare the visual acuity of one man with that of another.
—AVM Edward Crew, former night fighter pilot

Above: The Irvin flying jacket of Group-Captain Peter Townsend of Nos. 43 and 85 Squadrons, now on display at the Tangmere Military Aviation Museum in Sussex, England.

the other runway.

"I was told that when we both zoomed up in the pattern, there was not enough clearance between the two planes to see daylight between them.

"I nearly fainted. I guess it was just not my time to go."
—Colonel Bert McDowell, Junior, USAF (Ret), formerly with the 55th Fighter Group, 8 USAAF

Spiros 'Steve' Pisanos spoke no English when he arrived in Baltimore on a Greek merchant ship from Athens in April 1938. Working in bakeries and restaurants in New York, he earned enough to pay for flying lessons, gained a pilot's licence, and was Johnny-on-the-spot when the Clayton Knight Committee sponsored his entry into the RAF after flight training in California. (At the behest of RCAF Vice Marshal Billy Bishop, Knight, a widely respected American pilot who had flown with the Royal Flying Corps in World War I, established a committee to screen and evaluate pilots—at first clandestinely and then openly—for possible service with the RAF and RCAF prior to America's entry into World War II.)

A member of No. 71 (Eagle) Squadron, RAF, Steve Pisanos later transferred to the 4th Fighter Group, where he accounted for ten enemy aircraft before his Mustang experienced engine failure and crash-landed south of Le Havre near the French coast. For six months he evaded capture by the Germans, and was aided by sixteen French families. After the war, Major Pisanos served as a test pilot in the P-80 jet programme. Later, he served with the US Air Force in Viet Nam, retiring with the rank of Colonel in 1973: "The successful fighter pilot of World War II had not only exceptional eyesight; he had guts and great determination. He was clever and he knew by heart the rules and tactics of air fighting. He knew the capabilities and limitations of his aircraft and of the aircraft the enemy flew. He flew his fighter with the feeling that the machine was part of him and he of it. The successful fighter

pilot was daring, yet cautious and observant, and had a brilliant and aggressive mind that he used [to good effect] in an engagement with an opponent. He was not the reckless type because a careless fighter pilot didn't live. The successful fighter pilot who attacked a superior force and got away, unscratched, with a kill, was an outstanding tactician and a good shooter whose mind and eyes worked like lightning. He had to be daring and aggressive in an attack on a foe. He was smooth, precise, calm and steady, and he didn't start firing until he was close to his target."

In the late morning of 19th June 1944, US Navy Ensign Daniel Rehm, Junior, flying in a four-plane Combat Air Patrol from VF-50 of the light carrier *Bataan*, was vectored to intercept a very large force of Japanese aircraft approaching from the west. The famous Marianas Turkey Shoot of the First Battle of the Philippine Sea was about to begin. In the course of that first encounter, Ensign Rehm destroyed three Zero fighters and the pilots of VF-50 that day achieved ten aerial victories: "There seemed to be burning aircraft all over the sky, falling down to the sea. I observed several enemy parachutes deployed. The whole area looked like a large Christmas tree with its lights turned on."

"I started the battle by picking the best man I could get to fly on my wing—Johnny Godfrey, of Woonsocket, RI, who doesn't like Germans. They killed his brother, Reggie, at sea, and the name Johnny has painted on his plane is *Reggie's Reply*. He means it, too. The point about him is that he not only is a fierce, brave boy, but he knows his business as well.

"To show how a team works even when a big brawl has boiled the team down to two men flying wing on each other, Johnny and I spent twenty minutes over Berlin on 8th March and came out of there with six planes destroyed to our credit. I got

Left: Mark Hanna of The Old Flying Machine Company at Duxford in Cambridgeshire, England, flying a Mk IX Spitfire in 1989. Below: Commander Edward G. Wendorf, US Navy, flew with VF-16 from the carrier USS *Lexington* in World War II, participating in the Marianas "Turkey Shoot." On his first day of combat, and after his aircraft had been hit by a 3-inch shell which disabled his radio and compass, he shot down a Japanese Betty bomber and two Zeros before being wounded by another Zero. Bleeding badly from head and back wounds, Wendorf managed to elude his pursuers and return to his carrier where he landed into a barrier without the aid of flaps, brakes or tail hook. That night a Japanese aerial torpedo damaged the sick bay where he was confined and he was saved by one of his shipmates as that compartment was flooded.

Exceptional eyesight was important, but a killer spirit was more important.
—Lieutenant-Colonel John F. Bolt, USMC (Ret)

a straggler, and Johnny got one, and then I got another one fast. A Hun tried to out-turn me, and this was a mistake on his part. Not only can a Messerschmitt 109 not out-turn a Mustang in the upstairs air, but even if he had succeeded, there was Johnny back from his kill and sitting on my tail waiting to shoot him down. He was waiting, too, to knock down anybody who tried to bounce me off my kill.

"There were Huns all around. Berlin's air was cloudy with them. The gyrations this dying Hun was making forced me to violent action, but Johnny rode right along like a blocking back who could run with the best. After two Huns had blown up and another had bailed out, Johnny and I formed up tight and went against a team of two Messerschmitts. 'I'll take the port one and you take the starboard one,' I told Johnny, and we came in line abreast and in a two-second burst finished off both of them. They were dead before they knew we were there.

"Then a Messerschmitt bounced Johnny. Johnny turned into him and I swung around to run interference for him. The Hun made a tight swing to get on Johnny's tail, saw me and rolled right under me before I could get a shot in. I rolled with him and fastened to his tail, but by that time we were very close to flak coming up from the city. The Hun wasn't so worried about the flak. I was his immediate and more desperate woe, but flak wasn't my idea of a cake to eat, and I didn't dare go slow in it, but the Hun took a chance and put his flaps down to slow to a crawl.

"Then I got strikes on him. Glycol started coming out of him, and I had to pass him. But Johnny had fallen into formation right on my wing and he took up the shooting where I had left off. He put more bullets into the Hun while I was swinging up and around to run interference for him. Then he said his ammunition had run out and I said, 'Okay, I'll finish him,' and I followed the Nazi down into the streets clobbering him until he pulled up and

bailed out.

"Teamwork is the answer to any man's score, but in the meantime there was plenty of competition within the team. Once a battle started there were a great many of the boys who saw in it what I saw—the chance to make a record that would come in handy later in life."
—Major Don S. Gentile, formerly with the 4th Fighter Group, 8 USAAF

"Seeing the enemy first, or at least in time to take correct tactical manoeuvres, was very important. Most important, however, is the 'guts' to plough through an enemy or enemies and fight it out. There are no foxholes to hide in... there is no surrendering. I know of no Navy fighter pilot in the war who turned tail and ran."
—Commander Richard H. May, USNR (Ret), formerly with VF-32

"Excellent eyesight was necessary in the past to achieve a first kill, but an outstanding fighter pilot is measured by his ability to achieve a second and third kill. The better pilots achieved three or even four kills in a single aerial combat, and I'm talking about in the jet age!

"Often, after scoring the first kill, all the tension which has built up before the combat breaks down. The ability to skip, and refocus on a new target depends on the motivation and aggressiveness of the fighter pilot. A real shooter must have an aggressive character and will seek a fight in any circumstances.

"Now, perfect eyesight has lost some of its crucial importance. Modern fighters are equipped with high-quality radar systems that target long-range missiles at the enemy far beyond visual range. Nevertheless, good vision is still essential when a dogfight gets closer, and eye contact is a primary factor in the kill and survival."
—Gidi Livni, formerly an F-16 pilot and Colonel in the Israeli Air Force

43(F) SQN

JONATHAN HOLDAWAY

Left: An RAF Sergeant pilot in the cockpit of a Spitfire during the Battle of Britain. Above: US Air Force Major Jonathan Holdaway, who is currently (1998) on exchange with No. 43 Squadron, RAF, at Leuchars, Scotland. Major Holdaway: "Flying the Tornado with the Brits has been fun but deep in my heart I'll always be an Eagle driver. It is optimized for one mission—to kill other airplanes. It's the greatest air-to-air fighter in history." The pilots of F-15s and other front-line fighters meet in competition at annual exercises in Nevada called Red Flag where today's fighter tactics are mastered. As one Red Flag pilot put it: "In our business second best is dead last."

NIGHTFIGHTER

As I walked out that sultry night, / I heard the stroke of One. / The moon, attained to her full height, Stood beaming like the sun: / She exorcized the ghostly wheat / To mute assent in love's defeat, Whose tryst had now begun.
—from *Full Moon*
by Robert Graves

"He died who loved to live," they'll say, / "Unselfishly so we might have today." / Like Hell! He fought because he had to fight; / He died that's all. It was his unlucky night.
—by Wing-Commander Dennis McHarrie, RAF

Right: Members of RAF Bomber Command's Nightfighter escort group in World War II. The Mosquito crews are discussing their upcoming intruder patrol over Germany.

MOST FIGHTER PILOTS of World War II did not enjoy night flying. They were not comfortable doing it and felt awkward up there in the darkness. Night flying was a thing to be avoided if at all possible. Perhaps because pre-war air force pilots did not do very much night flying, airfield lighting was not well developed, and night navigation aids, other than brightly lit cities, were non-existent. In addition, the blackout restrictions imposed after the start of the war made night flying all the more difficult. Clearly, new and effective techniques had to be developed in a hurry.

General Bill Vincent, RCAF (Ret), flew Mosquito and Beaufighter aircraft as a Sergeant pilot on No. 409 (RCAF) Nightfighter Squadron in the European theatre of World War II: "Prior to receiving my Wings in Canada, my Pilot course was extended one month [in order] to add to our instrument and night flying time before we left for overseas duty. My night flying in the UK began in earnest when I arrived at the OTU [Operational Training Unit]. I soon learned that you had to know your aircraft cockpit extremely well in order to feel comfortable about night flying. And one needed to night fly frequently to retain that comfortable feeling.

"I experienced one of those moments of stark terror while night flying in a Blenheim Mk IV at the OTU. After a spell of night cloud flying at 17,000 feet I broke into the clear. On my return to base while descending to a lower altitude, the Blenheim rattled and shook as though I was being fired upon. My mouth became very dry and visions of enemy aircraft shooting down sprog pilots at training schools were central to my thoughts. My mouth remained dry until I figured out that my propellers had been iced up and the lower altitudes and warmer temperatures were allowing the props to throw off the ice, which was hitting the extended nose of the Mk IV Blenheim. Scary stuff for an inexperienced pilot, at night, flying an

When you're frozen blue like your Spitfire / And you're scared a Mosquito pink, / When you're hundreds of miles from nowhere / And there's nothing below you but drink.

It's then that you'll see the Gremlins, / Green and Gamboge and Gold, / Male and Female and Neuter, Gremlins both young and old.

It's no use trying to dodge 'em: / The lessons you learned in the Link / Won't help you evade a Gremlin, Though you boost and you dive and you jink.
—from *The Gremlins*, anonymous

Right: Nightfall at a former World War II fighter station in East Anglia.

unfamiliar aircraft.

"More serious was a mid-air collision [I had] with another Beaufighter while in training at the OTU. This one almost finished me off. Night fighter tactics were such that the (GCI) controller would create a curve of pursuit attack, bringing the fighter into the rear of the target, slightly below on the same heading at 4 miles' range (maximum range for the early airborne radar). The fighter crew took over the intercept, the navigator working the radar and giving directions to the pilot as to range, target position by clock reference and overtake speed. When at minimum radar range (about 300 yards), and with speeds synchronized, the pilot would, or should, be able to see a target as a black blob, and then visually identify it as 'friend or foe' *before* opening fire. Initially, we practised this approach tactic in daytime to gain experience in the procedure, in pilot aircraft handling and in navigator radar techniques. For training purposes we would be paired with another aircraft and crew, and we alternated being fighter and target. This was referred to as 'banging heads'.

"It was while we were acting as target that the other crew in the fighter role closed in to our stern, and my navigator informed me of the fighter's whereabouts. My navigator's demeanour suddenly changed as he shouted that the fighter was 'bloody close' and directly beneath us. Then all hell broke loose as the fighter pulled up in front of our aircraft in a slight left turn, and slightly to the right of our nose. A normal break-off on completion of an intercept consisted of a peel-off left or right, not coming in fast underneath and pulling up in front, thus throwing the target into violent slipstream, the situation in which we found ourselves.

"My right prop chopped off his left tail plane, with wood flying everywhere (the Beaufighter II had a three-blade, wooden, variable pitch prop). The violent slipstream flipped my aircraft on its

130

back and, by the time I regained full control, we had dropped from 10,000 feet to 4000. The engine mounts had been damaged in the collision and my right engine was skewed on the wing, with the three blades of the prop now splintered stubs.

"At the time of impact all I could see was this enormous Beaufighter in my windscreen, and the alarmed face and eyes of the navigator staring back at me from his fuselage-bubble canopy. Then my aircraft began its gyrations brought on by the slipstream. When I informed Ground Control of the accident, I was sent to Winfield, the OTU satellite airfield from which the final OTU Beaufighter phase conducted operations. When handed over from GCI control to the tower, I informed them that I was on one engine, and why. Due to a breakdown in ground communications between the GCI and my airfield, of which I was not aware, I did not know that the airfield had not been apprised of the accident. However, the fire trucks, Station Commanding Officer and the Chief Flying Instructor were all there to meet me on landing. It took some time to unravel the specifics of the accident because of the communications problem, but, once it was all cleared up, I was without blame. Unfortunately, the pilot and navigator [of the other aircraft] did not bail out in time for their parachutes to deploy and were killed. I expect that they had a hair-raising ride down without full elevator control, if they had any at all. I learned later that this pilot had pulled the same trick on others during training missions. After that experience, it took me awhile to become comfortable being 'target' during intercept practice.

"In 1943, the squadron was moved to Acklington, 13 Group, in the Newcastle area, exchanging airfields with No. 410 (RCAF) Night Fighter Squadron. They had been re-equipped with Mosquito night fighters, which were said to be a better aircraft for night fighting. They had the same radar equipment as the Beaufighter, but the Mosquito had less firepower.

"Our CO managed to wangle a limited number of special duties operations to keep us active. These were known as 'Ranger' operations and were conducted during the full-moon period each month (about five nights). The radar had to be removed from the aircraft as it carried a secret classification. These were straight navigation trips with railroads, road traffic and enemy HQs as targets of opportunity. A limited number of crews would be selected, usually three, and they deployed to forward bases to carry out intruder-type sorties over the Continent. Routes and take-off times were assigned to the crews. This was certainly more exciting than carrying out standing night fighter patrols in north-east England, where enemy activity was but sporadic. They were especially exciting as there was minimal training organized to prepare us for this type of work. As a result, we lost a few crews during February, March and April 1943. It was then decided to remove the squadron from this type of activity, to concentrate on night fighting, and await our turn to convert to the Mosquito.

"Serete was another option. This utilized Mosquito aircraft (with the radar removed) equipped with electronic devices that could 'home' on enemy electronic transmissions. The aircraft would go out with our bombers and attempt to intercept enemy night fighters that were attacking the bombers. This met with limited success and we suffered a considerable loss rate. Many crews volunteered for this duty but few were selected.

"The decision not to allow the night fighters airborne-type radars over enemy territory was probably correct considering the speed with which the 'boffins' on both sides could figure out what made various [enemy] devices work. 'Our' radar in enemy aircraft would probably have been even more devastating to our night bomber missions. However, greater use, without radar, of our Beaufighter and Mosquito night fighters could

Flight-Lieutenant John Cunningham of No. 604 Squadron was flying the fighter version of the twin-engine Blenheim from Middle Wallop during the Battle of Britain. It was then that he acquired the nickname "Cat's Eyes". As word of his nightfighter successes spread, the rumour quickly followed that his achievements were due to his heavy consumption of carrots, the vitamins from which had sharpened his night vision. The Air Ministry would say only that he had "exceptional night vision." The carrot rumour followed. It proved to be of interesting propaganda value against the Germans and helped in Lord Woolton's (the Minister of Food) campaign to make the case for vegetables in the rationed wartime British diet.

Left: Women at work on the "Wooden Wonder", the DeHavilland Mosquito which contributed so much to the effort of the RAF in the vital nightfighter role during World War II. Before that War, women had almost no experience working in large manufacturing plants. With the outbreak of war they came into the factories with an enthusiasm and sense of purpose that led to great productivity, especially in the aircraft industry. They proved superior to men in the finer aspects of aircraft construction and their efficiency was higher than that of the male workers.

Below: The plotting table in the meticulously restored operations room of No. 11 Group, RAF Fighter Command, at Uxbridge, Middlesex, England.

have disrupted operations around the enemy's night fighter airfields. It would have made their departures and arrivals more hazardous.

"In early 1944, we were assigned to the 2nd Tactical Air Force and we converted to Mosquito aircraft with the latest in radar equipment. We went under canvas and practised mobility exercises in preparation for D-Day.

"In the Mosquito, the pilot and navigator sat side by side. This was different from the Beaufighter, where each air crewman had an area that he could call his own, with the pilot in the front and the

navigator in a rear area of the fuselage with a bubble canopy for his observation. In the Mosquito, I was able to teach my navigator the rudiments of flying in order to improve our scramble time. There were times when a crew was scheduled a take-off time to proceed to a patrol area. If some activity occurred earlier on the GCI radar, this crew would be scrambled from standby. I then proceeded with all haste to our aircraft and took off as quickly as possible, not bothering to fasten my parachute or safety harness. While I was busy starting engines and taxiing, my navigator warmed up the radar and fastened himself in. After becoming airborne and establishing radio contact with the control agency, my navigator would reach across and fly the aircraft, freeing me to fasten my parachute and safety harness. This speeded up scrambles considerably. The safety aspect was an accepted risk, but, as you knew your own aircraft, and had completed a thorough walk-around inspection and had flown the aircraft earlier on a night flying test, the safety risk was minimal.

"Being assigned to the 2nd Tactical Air Force meant living and operating under canvas. The squadron was moved to West Malling, south-east of London, about a month before D-Day. No. 409 was designated to be the first night fighter squadron to deploy to the Continent after D-Day. At this time we were one of five crews who had been on the squadron for twenty months or more, and we knew that it would be touch-and-go whether we would be declared 'tour-expired' before D-Day. Our luck held and we participated on D-Day and for about a month afterwards.

"The V-I buzz bombs began arriving on 13th June 1944, and their route was directly over West Malling to London. This posed a problem for the squadron and the airfield. We had to maintain a very narrow corridor from West Malling to and from Beachy Head on England's south coast while proceding at night to and from the Normandy

beachhead. To stray from this route meant we might be shot at by the flak guns that had been positioned in that part of England to combat the buzz bombs. There were also barrage balloons located south-east of London to help defend against the buzz bombs at night and in bad weather. It became prudent for our squadron to be moved out of 'buzz bomb alley' and we were re-deployed to Hunsdon, north-east of London.

"While conducting operations over and around the beachhead during June 1944, our squadron shot down a number of German aircraft at night that were bombing the beachhead or laying mines in the adjacent waters. Our manned GCI units were [on] floating barges, towed into position on D-Day, one of them located off Fécamp on the eastern end of the beachhead, and another off Cherbourg on the western end. This was rather frightening duty for the controllers as they were sitting ducks for German bombers and fighters. You could detect their concern in the tenseness of their radio transmissions.

"Night fighter squadrons assigned to the beachhead maintained fighter patrols under GCI control, behind and in front of the beachhead, from dusk to dawn and during inclement weather. Enemy activity was not as intense as expected, but I was able to engage a Ju-188 on its way either to bomb the beachhead or lay mines in the nearby waters. I identified the enemy plane and shot it down using deflection as it turned in towards the beachhead. This was not a normal night fighter attack pattern, but I was able to use deflection because the 'target' was silhouetted against the light sky to the north as it turned south towards the beachhead. If I had hesitated, it would have been me silhouetted against the sky. We got him before he unloaded his bombs or mines, and the kill was confirmed by the GCI that was controlling us at the time."

"Here, in my opinion, are the main points about night fighter operations in World War II.

Top: Oberstleutnant Hans Joachim-Jabs flew an Me 110 "Destroyer" nightfighter, scoring forty-seven victories during World War II. In March 1944 he became *Kommodore* of NJG 1, his nightfighter unit. He flew a total of 510 day and night sorties in his combat career.

"1. Night fighter crews during World War II were the first to use airborne radar as a means of detecting aircraft at night and during bad weather (cloud conditions).

"2. When the Beaufighter arrived on the squadrons, it was designed especially for night fighting and was equipped with the new airborne radar. It was heavily armed with four 20mm cannon and six machine guns.

"3. Unfortunately, airborne radar for night fighting purposes was not in use until after the Battle of Britain, during which it could have been a great deterrent to the German night bombing attacks on London. It was, however, very effective against German intruder operations in the south and east of England, which were conducted on a sporadic basis throughout the war, and against some of the more intense German raids on Britain's cathedral towns during 1942.

"4. German airborne radar was not as advanced as the British version and, so as to maintain this advantage, our night fighters were not permitted to fly over enemy territory with the radar on board. This ban was maintained until D-Day. Without this restriction, our night fighter tactics would have been developed to support the night bombing missions both as an integral part of the bomber stream and in harassing the German night fighter bases while the night bomber force was on its way to and returning from its targets. If we had been permitted to use our night fighters in this manner, I am sure that Bomber Command would not have suffered such terrible losses due to German night fighters.

"5. After the war, radar development for a variety of military uses made great advances, and the result is today's sophisticated fire control systems which equip our all-weather fighter aircraft, providing pick-up ranges of over 20 miles and the capability to fire the armament from any angle of attack, from ground level to in excess of 55,000 feet, climbing or diving, through 360 degrees. It has created a capability for conducting intercepts on up to six targets at once with the computerized fire control system calculating the intercepts and automatically firing the ordnance best suited for the type of attack and the target type. In addition, the modern radar cockpit scope presentation can be tied into the aircraft's auto pilot so that all the pilot has to do is throw on the 'lock-on' switch, connecting the fire control system with the auto pilot, and hold the trigger in the 'fire' position. Everything else is automatic. I speak from experience when I say that the fire control system and the aircraft's auto pilot flies the intercept better than the pilot can manually.

"6. The British revealed their secrets of airborne radar in [or about] 1942 to the Americans, and the American technicians then improved on the British invention, producing airborne radars with ranges of more than ten miles and attack capabilities other than stern attacks. It was excellent radar, and was in service by 1944 in British and American night fighters.

"7. The most hazardous part of night fighter tactics was in the final stage of the interception, when, with your speed synchronized with that of your target, the range usually at 300 yards or less, in the black of night, you had to recognize and identify the black blob of the target as an enemy aircraft before opening fire. Making this identification on a black night was not easy, and the night fighter was often a sitting duck for the enemy rear gunner. Records show that many 'unknown' type aircraft were claimed as destroyed, probably destroyed or damaged, especially in the early part of the war when certain German and British aircraft were easily mistaken for one another. An identification device known as IFF [Identification Friend or Foe] was later installed in our bombers and the electronic transmission from this device could be received and identified on our night fighter radar. This procedure had to be carried out to confirm the identity of an enemy aircraft."

I am the enemy you killed, my friend. / I knew you in this dark; for so you frowned yesterday through me as you jabbed and killed. / I parried; but my hands were loath and cold. Let us sleep now...'
—from *Strange Meeting* by Wilfred Owen

Ah, love, let us be true / To one another! for the world, which seems / To lie before us like a land of dreams, So various, so beautiful, so new, / Hath really neither joy, nor love, nor light, Nor certitude, nor peace, nor help for pain; / And we are here as on a darkling plain / Swept with confused alarms of struggle and flight, / Where ignorant armies clash by night.
—from *Dover Beach* by Matthew Arnold

Left: A P-61 Black Widow nightfighter believed to have been a 9 USAAF aircraft during World War II, after a landing accident. Arriving in the combat theaters in 1944, the Black Widow was the first aircraft designed expressly as a nightfighter. It was armed with four 20mm cannon and four machine guns. It could achieve 366 mph at 20,000 feet and had a combat radius of 1000 miles. With a combat weight of 28,000 pounds, it was the heaviest fighter of the War.

SHOOTER

"IT ISN'T ALWAYS BEING FAST or accurate that counts, it's being willing. I found out early that most men, regardless of cause or need, aren't willing. They blink an eye or draw a breath before they pull a trigger. I won't."
—John Bernard Books, title character in the film *The Shootist*

"When you've got a good hold on the enemy's tail and are clobbering him well, it seems then he never will die. Each part of a second then doesn't feel like time at all, but is slow, so very slow and so endless. Armour-piercing incendiaries hit him all over. They cloud him up all over and go all over him like snake tongues. That's what they look like—little red snake tongues, hundreds of them, flicking him poisonously all over. That goes on and on, each little flick quick as a twist, but the whole thing so slow, so endless.

"Then black smoke starts out of him and goes slowly and endlessly out of him. At first it comes as if you've squeezed it out of him and then a cloud of it appears. Glycol is the fluid that keeps the motor from overheating. You can't fly more than a minute or so without it. It comes out into the air looking white, and when you see it coming out well, in a pour, then that's the end.

"The wind of death blowing up to storm proportions in him. It's a small pour at first, usually thin, like a frosty breath; then bigger, bigger, bigger and always slow and endless and stuck into your eyes and stopped there like a movie held still.

"And after that, sometimes when you're really clobbering him and are really all over him, hammering his guts out, pieces start coming off him. It's nuts-and-bolts stuff at first, then bigger things, big, ripped-off-looking things as if you're tearing arms and legs off him and arms and legs and the head of him are going slowly, endlessly

I know that I shall meet my fate / Somewhere among the clouds above; / Those that I fight I do not hate, / Those that I guard I do not love; / My country is Kiltartan Cross, My countrymen Kiltartan's poor, / No likely end could bring them loss / Or leave them happier than before. Nor law, nor duty bade me fight, / Nor public men, nor cheering crowds, / A lonely impulse of delight / Drove to this tumult in the clouds; I balanced all, brought all to mind, / The years to come seemed waste of breath, / A waste of breath the years behind / In balance with this life, this death.
—*An Irish Airman foresees his Death*
by William Butler Yeats

Preceding page: An F/A-18 being guided into a dispersal point. US Navy Hornets operated from the aircraft carriers *Midway*, *Saratoga*, *America*, *Dwight D. Eisenhower*, *Theodore Roosevelt* and *Independence* during the Gulf War. "Hornets, bandits on your nose, 15 miles!" was the call from an E-2 Hawkeye airborne monitoring aircraft heard by Lieutenant-Commander Mark Fox and Lieutenant Nick Mongillo on their mission of 17 January 1991. They approached the MiG-21s at Mach 1.2 and Fox fired a Sidewinder missile which took out the first MiG. Mongillo shot a Sparrow missile downing a second Iraqi MiG. Left: A US Navy F-4 Phantom is prepared for launch from the carrier USS *Kittyhawk* in the Viet Nam War.

141

over your shoulder."
—Major Don S. Gentile, formerly with the 4th Fighter Group, Eighth USAAF

Thomas J. Moore flew Mustangs with the 361st Fighter Group, which was based at Bottisham, Cambridgeshire, and Little Walden, Essex in England: "I do not think [being a 'shooter'] is the fighter pilot's most important asset. I think the more important aspect would be the ability to get into position to fire at the enemy. If a pilot was able to get into position behind the enemy or even [for] a deflection shot, this would enhance a chance for victory. A pilot might miss on a deflection shot but still might be able to get behind the enemy or [get] a more accurate small angle shot."

"I started flying the American Curtiss P-36 with 1/5 Groupe de Chasse of the French Air Force. The P-36 handled very well and was well armed and better than any of the French aircraft of that time.

  On 12th May 1940 over the town of Sedan, I saw that a bunch of Ju 87s [Stukas] were dive-bombing the town. I didn't even notice that they were protected by some Me 109s as I positioned myself behind one of the Stukas. He went down from only two short bursts of my gun. In four minutes I brought down four Ju 87s using less than 250 shells altogether. I did not open fire until I was less than 100 yards behind the German planes. One Me 109 fired at my plane, but it didn't seem to be badly damaged and I flew back to our airfield. On landing, a German bullet was found that had passed through my fuselage and stopped in the protective steel plate by where my neck had been. Only then did I realize how close I was to my death, and my knees turned to jelly."
—Generalmajor Frantisek Perina formerly of No. 312 (Czech) Squadron, RAF

Group-Captain Al Deere, formerly with No. 54 Squadron, RAF: "Personally, I was never a good shot. I know from my work with a shotgun. I was an average shot, whereas Colin Gray, my fellow New Zealander in No. 54 Squadron, was above average, so it was easier for him than me. Each chap worked out his own tactics. I soon worked it out, but I had to get bloody close, otherwise I wouldn't have got the guy down. The range was supposed to be at 400 yards, which was ridiculous. You had to be able to shoot, but you didn't have to be an exceptional shot. It's no good shooting well if you can't fly the aircraft well. So, if you could fly the aircraft well you could, to a degree, overcome your lack of ability in natural shooting. The best shots in the [Royal] Air Force were chaps who could shoot birds on the wing with a shotgun. I could, but not to their extent. The best shot in the Air Force, I think, was 'Sailor' Malan. He was a contemporary of mine at Hornchurch."

Colonel John W. Cunnick, USAF (Ret), formerly with the 55th Fighter Group, Eighth USAAF: "In our day, fighter pilots spent many hours shooting skeet and trap to learn about leading and lagging our targets. However, after reviewing hundreds of kills on gun camera film, I believe that more than 90 per cent of them were made from dead astern. Every fifth round in our ammo belts was an incendiary tracer. Their primary use was to ignite fires; the secondary use was to give us a look at where our ammo was going. In fact, the incendiary trajectory wasn't the same as our standard rounds."

Feldwebel Oscar Boesch, formerly with *Sturm Staffel* I, IV/JG3 "Udet": "To be a good shot was essential. Every dogfight is a duel, and deadly."

The pilot of a Spitfire recently attacked and shot down an Me 109. On returning to his aerodrome he began a victory roll, got into a spin and failed to

Far left above: Frantisek Perina, who flew with the Czech Air Force and the RAF in World War II. Far left below: Generalmajor Perina in 1998. Left: A "blood chit" as carried or worn by most members of the American Volunteer Group in Burma and China, the Flying Tigers, during World War II. The chit informed Chinese civilians of the American identity of the downed pilot enlisting their help for him, requesting that he be protected from the Japanese and pledging a reward for his assistance. This example bears the signatures of several former pilots of the American Volunteer Group.

We were not, thank God, involved in the intimate, personal killing of men which is the lot of the infantry—though we fired with the same bloody end in view. The men inside the aircraft must be killed or maimed or taken prisoner, otherwise they would return to battle. Very few of us thought of it that way, and this gave to our battle in the air the character of a terribly dangerous sport and not of a dismal, sordid slaughter.
—Group-Captain Peter Townsend, No. 85 Squadron RAF

Right: Lieutenant Walter J. Konantz of the 55th Fighter Group based at Wormingord, Essex, England, is credited with being the first American pilot to shoot down an Me 262 jet fighter, on 13th January 1945 over the Geibelstadt airfield in central Germany. Far right: One of the most unusual photos to come out of World War II. Below: A gun-camera sequence showing the downing of an Me 262 jet by a 55th Fighter Group pilot near the end of the War.

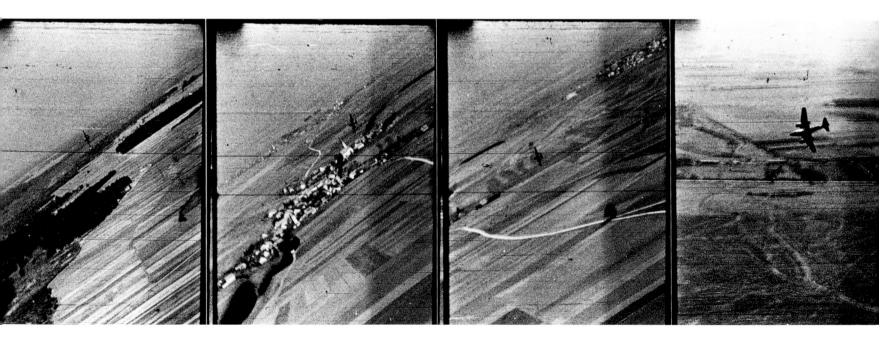

recover. Net result: all square—instead of one Jerry down. A perfect example of what Major "Mick" Mannock, V.C., called "bad arithmetic".
—from *Tee Emm*, June 1942

Captain Harvey Mace, USAF (Ret), formerly with the 357th Fighter Group, 8 USAAF: "It [marksmanship] was important, but most kills were made by virtually poking the gun barrels up their butts."

Colonel Walker M. "Bud" Mahurin, USAF (Ret), came from Fort Wayne, Indiana. One of his mathematics teachers once wrote to him: "I never was impressed with your ability to solve algebra or geometry problems. The fact is, I didn't think you'd ever amount to a damn."

In World War II, Mahurin spent most of his combat career with the 56th Fighter Group, "Zemke's Wolf Pack". It is probably fair to say that Hub Zemke and Bud Mahurin were something less than close friends. Mahurin found himself in trouble with his commanding officer on a number of occasions. Bud was naturally aggressive and was never shy about showing initiative in the Group.

While he was flying missions from Halesworth in his P-47 Thunderbolt, it was VIII Fighter Command policy that its fighters, when assigned to escort the B-17s and B-24s of Eighth Bomber Command, were to stay with the bombers... period. On several missions, however, Mahurin decided that if he saw a German fighter, he was going to go get it: "The first two that I got were some distance from us, queuing up to go into the bomber stream. Later, Hub was going to court-martial me for leaving the bomber stream. When he went down to see General Kepner about charging me, the General said: 'Well, you go ahead if you feel you want to, but in the meantime I'm gonna give him a Silver Star.'

"The excitement and the thrill associated with shooting down an enemy airplane is indescribable. I always liken it to a big-game hunt, only here the quarry has the same advantage as you. Boy, it's touch and go, but Jesus, is it thrilling! I think the most fun and the most excitement I *ever* had was flying an F-86 in Korea against the Russians. That was just sheer delight and pleasure.

"In Europe though, we were bore-sighted for 300

Kazimierz Budzik, flew Spitfires with No. 308 (Polish) Squadron RAF. His combat record includes two operational tours and a score of kills and probables. But he dismisses any suggestion of heroism. "Heroes? I don't know what they are. There were many brave deeds done, of course. Mostly, though, heroes were born out of spur-of-the-moment actions. Most of the time, like everyone else, I was just concerned with self-preservation."

What counts is not necessarily the size of the dog in the fight—it's the size of the fight in the dog.
—Dwight D. Eisenhower, 1958

yards, and at that range the pattern would be a square of about 12 feet. The natural tendency was to fire way out of range. With the first two airplanes I got, I came home with German oil on my airplane and on the windshield. But lots of times I fired out of range. Lots of times I took 'snap shots' and didn't have the presence of mind to slow down and take things easy and really get things lined up. But the more experienced one became, the closer one got to the enemy airplane, and as more inexperienced German pilots were encountered, the easier it was.

"But the perspective—we just didn't have training aids that were good enough to simulate ranges as the range would look in the gunsight... to show, for example, what a 109 would look like out there at 600 yards, so you could get a perspective. In theory, we were supposed to be able to control the circle so you could set it for the wingspan of, say, a Focke-Wulf Fw 190, and if the airplane filled the circle, you were within range... except, how the hell are you gonna do that when it went this way and that way and up and down and sideways? You just couldn't do it.

"I was in several dogfights. With the Me 110s, most of my kills were rear-quartering stern shots; most were real stern chases where they were wide open, and they knew we were behind them and we were closing very slowly. If you couldn't get into that kind of position, your chances of hitting the guy would be a question of how good you were at aerial combat, and most of us weren't that good.

"I've been on any number of missions where there was fighting going on all over the sky and I couldn't find out where the hell they were. Bob Johnson, or Gabreski... I'd hear those guys shooting, but it was happening in a different part of the sky, and by the time I got over there, there wasn't any more fight because it had happened so fast. You had to be in the right place at the right time. One of the advantages that Hub Zemke and the 56th Fighter Group had was that we were one

of the three senior groups in England and we got the P-47s first and had had them in the United States beforehand. We were allowed to escort the lead box of the bombers so we were up in front, and since we were in front, and the Germans were gonna attack the lead box, we had more exposure than the other wings did, and that was very, very important, as far as victories went."

"Being able to shoot accurately was, of course, important but I would not say it was the one most important asset [of a successful fighter pilot]. The P-38 [which I flew] was probably one of the most stable platforms of the various American fighters, and its cone of fire was such that it was quite forgiving of slight miscalculations in range since the streams of fire from the five guns went straight ahead and were not dispersed, as was the case with wing-mounted guns."
—2nd Lieutenant Robert N. Jensen, USAF (Ret), formerly with the 55th Fighter Group, 8 USAAF

"Fighter pilots have to be good shooters, by born ability or by increasing experience. But certainly we couldn't select pilots according to those qualities as we were short on fighter pilots."
—Generalleutnant a. D. Günther Rall, German Air Force (Ret)

"Being a great shooter... important, yes! Most important, no. Give a poor marksman a good shot and he will get you."
—Captain William O'Brien, USAF (Ret), formerly with the 357th Fighter Group, 8 USAAF

"With the exception of [Albert] Ball, most crack fighters did not get their Huns in dogfights. They preferred safer means. They would spend hours synchronizing their guns and telescopic sights so that they could do accurate shooting at, say, 200 or 300 yards. They would then set out on patrol, alone, spot their quarry (in such cases usually a

Above: Loading .50 caliber machine gun rounds into the wing of a P-51B Mustang of the 4th Fighter Group at Debden, Essex, England during World War II. Right: Linked ammunition belts are carefully laid into the wing channels of the 56th Fighter Group P-47 Thunderbolt of Lieutenant-Colonel Francis Gabreski.

Single combat, a duel with another machine, was, performance apart, a question of good flying. Two machines so engaged would circle, each trying to turn inside the other and so bring his guns into play. Ability to sustain such tight vertical turns is the crucial test of a fighting pilot. Once the balance of the controls is lost, the machine will slip, lose height, and the enemy will rush in. Then, by all the rules of the game, you are a dead man.

But when a number of machines had closed and were engaged in a "dog-fight", it was more a question of catch as catch can. A pilot would go down on the tail of a Hun, hoping to get him in the first burst; but he would not be wise to stay there, for another Hun would almost certainly be on *his* tail hoping to get him in the same way. Such fights were really a series of rushes, with momentary pauses to select the next opportunity— to catch the enemy at a disadvantage, or separated from his friends.

But, apart from fighting, when twenty or thirty scouts were engaged, there was always a grave risk of collision. Machines would hurtle by, intent on their private battles, missing each other by feet. So such fighting demanded iron nerves, lightning reactions, snap decisions, a cool head, and eyes like a bluebottle, *continued* for it all took place at high speed and was three dimensional.

At this sort of sharpshooting some pilots excelled others; but in all air fighting (and indeed in every branch of aerial warfare) there is an essential in which it differs from the war on the ground: its absolute coldbloodedness. You cannot lose your temper with an aeroplane. You cannot "see red," as a man in a bayonet fight. You certainly cannot resort to "Dutch" courage. Any of these may fog your judgement—and that spells death.

Often at high altitudes we flew in air well below freezing point. Then the need to clear a jam or change a drum meant putting an arm out into an icy 100 m.p.h. wind. If you happened to have bad circulation (as I had), it left the hand numb, and since you could not stamp your feet, swing your arms, or indeed move at all, the numbness would spread to the other hand and sometimes to the feet as well. In this condition we often went into a scrap with the odds against us— they usually were against us, for it was our job to be "offensive" and go over into enemy country looking for trouble— coldbloodedly in the literal sense; but none the less we had to summon every faculty of judgement and skill to down our man, or, *continued*

two-seater doing reconnaissance or photography), and carefully manoeuvre for position, taking great pains to remain where they could not be seen, i.e. below and behind the tail of the enemy. From here, even if the Hun observer did spot them, he could not bring his gun to bear without the risk of shooting away his own tail plane or rudder. The stalker would not hurry after his quarry, but keep a wary eye to see he was not about to be attacked himself. He would gradually draw nearer, always in the blind spot, sight his guns very carefully, and then one long deadly burst would do the trick.

"Such tactics as those were employed by Captain McCudden, VC, DSO, and also by Guynemeyer, the French ace. Both of them, of course, were superb if they got into a dogfight; but it was in such fighting that they were both ultimately killed." —from *Sagittarius Rising* by Cecil Lewis, No. 56 Squadron, RFC

US Marine Corps pilot John F. Bolt was a member of Marine VMF-214, Gregory 'Pappy' Boyington's *Black Sheep* squadron from June 1943. Jack Bolt flew the F4U Corsair with 214. In the Korean War he flew F9F-4 Panthers and F-86 Sabres on an exchange tour with the US Air Force. He remains the only jet ace in Marine Corps aviation history and the only man in US Navy aviation history to become an ace in two wars: "It takes a while to develop real expertise in a combat situation. You're not very effective on your first few contacts with the enemy. I estimate that I have been in fifty firing contacts with enemy fighters—with either me shooting at them or them shooting at us—in World War II and the Korean War. After you've been in ten to fifteen contacts, you're a different person. The ones who are most frightened are the ones most at risk. I was certainly a slow learner.

"Most kills were made by sneaking up on a guy. He would be preoccupied with what was going on all around him, and he would not be watching the very narrow cone through his tail from which he

was most vulnerable. If we had a good speed advantage, we would try to get down low as we came in behind him because he could not see there. It was more difficult [for him to see us] than when we were higher up. If we got within firing range, we closed in to tail him until we were ready to fire, and being 50 or 100 feet below him put us in his blind area. If he knew we were coming, he was really hard to kill. There was just that narrow little shooting position, in behind him, from which he was going to get killed."

For the last two weeks of February 1944, Flight-Lieutenant Douglas "Duke" Warren, temporarily posted to No. 58 OTU at Grangemouth in Scotland, was assigned to attend a skeet shooting course in Bournemouth, Dorset: "The idea was that I would become the skeet shooting instructor. It was thought that if pilots learned the basics about leading a moving target they could apply this in air-to-air combat. So to Bournemouth I went. There were about six or seven on the course, and the instructor had been the skeet-shooting champion of England for several years. We fired hundreds of rounds, and because I was not holding the shotgun correctly my shoulder got very sore. However, in a short time I could see where my shot was going, and make corrections. The pellets looked like a small 'see-through' shadow in flight. Later on I found that 20mm cannon fire gave one the same impression. My assessment from the course basically said I was not a very good shot, but was a good instructor."

Never forget in air fighting, / Close range and accurate sighting. / Range judging done on Spitters Makes a Heinkel give you jitters. / Four hundred yards looks right / Because the span half fills the sight. / But this Hun is so much bigger / That you must not press the trigger / Till you seem too ruddy close / Then let go—he's had his dose! / Never forget in air fighting / Close range and accurate

at the worst, to come out of it alive ourselves. So, like duelling, air fighting required a set steely courage, draining of all emotion, fined down to a tense and deadly effort of will. The Angel of Death is less callous, aloof, and implacable than a fighting pilot when he dives. —from *Sagittarius Rising* by Cecil Lewis

Left: Colonel Walker M. Mahurin, a twenty-two-victory ace in World War II. After seventeen months in combat, Mahurin was shot down and evaded capture with the help of the French underground. In the Korean War he was credited with 3 1/2 MiG 15s, was shot down and spent sixteen months as a prisoner of the North Koreans. Above: Colonel Steve Pisanos, 4th Fighter Group ace in World War II, finished with ten kills.

Below: The cockpit of a Mk IX Spitfire. Right: *Battle Over Malta, 1942* by Denis Burnham. Far right above: The armoury section at the former Goxhill, Lincolnshire fighter station in England. Far right below: The gun button and spade grip of a Hawker Hurricane in the Fighter Collection at Duxford airfield, Cambridgeshire, England.

sighting. / The Hun is protected behind / Why—
(That thought is most unkind) / Still you've got to
shoot from the side / And you may think you're
taught to aim wide. / But the bullet moves slower
than light / And if you're shooting is right / You
shoot where the Hun *will* be / That is, just prior to
hitting the sea. / Never forget in air fighting / Close
range and accurate sighting. Good shooting!
—from *Tee Emm*, October 1941

"Whatever may have been previously written, it is
fact that fighter pilots never found deflection
shooting easy for a variety of reasons. Some of the
'aces' were better at it than the majority, but in the
main, the enemy were shot down by attacking
fighters 300 yards astern and a three second burst
of machine gun fire 'right up the arse'."
—Pilot-Officer Nick Berryman, RAF (Ret), formerly
with No. 276 Squadron

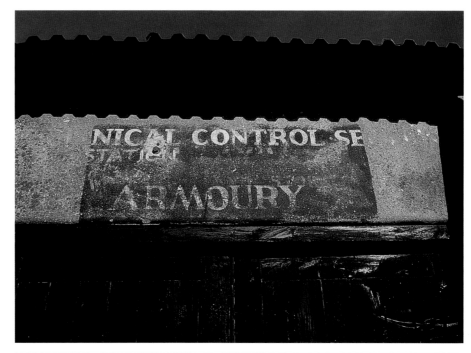

19th July 1940 was a scorcher across England. As
the day wore to a close the Hurricanes of A Flight,
No. 43 Squadron, RAF, rose from the Tangmere
runway, buffeted by blasts of hot and turbulent air,
climbing eastward to 10,000 feet. There John
Simpson spotted a dozen Me 109s just above his
Flight and heading in the opposite direction
through a thin, wispy cloud layer. The six A Flight
Hurricanes continued their climb into the sun, and
then they turned and dived on the Germans. Six
against twelve: "Well, there were six Hurricanes
actually daring to attack twelve Me 109s. The truth
was, we knew we were better than the Me 109s if
they would stay and 'mix it'. We could turn faster.
The 109s could beat us in the dive and in the
climb, and they were nearly always above us. That
is where the danger lay."

  All eighteen fighters chased one another in and
out of cloud, and at one point a 109 presented
Simpson with an irresistible target. "He seemed to
be dreaming... I gave him a short burst which
damaged him... I flew in closer for a second dose...

151

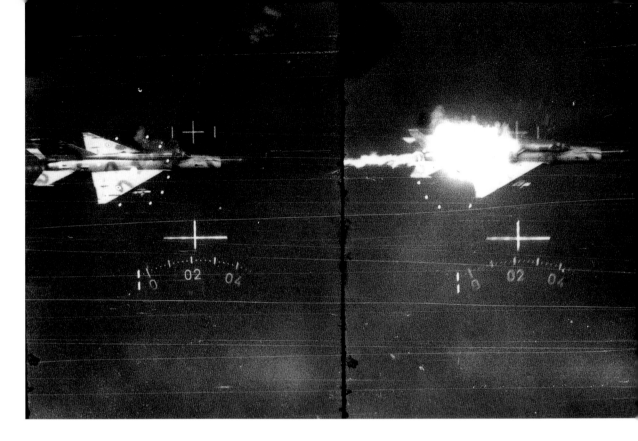

Right: During the Yom Kippur War Israeli Air Force Colonel Gidi Livni, flying a Mirage, destroyed this Egyptian MiG 21MF, firing approximately 20 rounds from the French fighter's 30mm gun. A deflection shot like this, from an aircraft moving at great speed is a great test of the pilot's skill and reactions.

In the Korean conflict, Bud Mahurin flew F-86's against MiG 15s. In *Honest John* he recalls "Gabby [Col. Francis Gabreski] and I had seen two wars and were familiar with the problem of combat fatigue. Thank God the doctors were also aware of the limits of human endurance and gave us a ration of combat whisky to be used at the completion of every mission. Had it not been for the whisky ration and rest leaves in Japan, we would have had frequent mental crack-ups. The strongest men usually saved up the whisky ration to use in Tokyo on leave. The weakest could be found opening up the bar at the officers' club at the end of the working day and closing it at the last possible minute. These were the men we watched, maintaining that no one could do an adequate job of combat flying when floating on Cloud Nine or suffering from a hangover. Gabby and I usually kept pretty close tabs on the men during our pre-mission briefings. We tried to make each briefing

he dived out of control and I followed him down to 6000 feet. There I watched him dive vertically into the calm sea... I opened my hood for a breath of fresh air."

As so often happens in an air fight, Simpson looked around and found that he was alone. When he climbed back up to the thin cloud layer, three Me 109s crossed in front of him. He fired on the last one and followed it into a twisting, ever-decreasing turn. As he fired, pieces of the German fighter's wings flew off and then black smoke began to trail it. The Englishman's ammunition was suddenly used up, and it was at this moment that he was engaged by the other two 109s. The three fighters were at 16,000 feet and roughly 8 miles from the English Channel coast. Simpson was in real trouble and knew it. He simply could not evade the skilful pair of German pilots on his tail. He felt the thudding impact of their bullets hitting the armour plating behind his back and watched

helplessly as massive, ragged strips were torn from his wings. His Merlin engine was hit and running roughly. Then he himself was hit, a searing pain in his left foot, while simultaneously his engine seized and acrid black smoke began to fill the cockpit. Almost mechanically he undid his Sutton harness, opened the hood of the ruined Hurricane and prepared to leave.

"The rushing slipstream did the rest. It felt like a hand lifting me from the cockpit, by my hair. I found myself in mid-air, beautifully cool and dropping. It seemed hours before I reminded myself to pull my rip-cord." There was a terrific jerk and Simpson was swinging like a pendulum on the end of his parachute. He vomited, and discovered that he was drifting toward the villas on the coast at Worthing.

And now one of the Messerschmitts began to circle him. "I was alarmed. He was near enough for me to see his face. I felt he would shoot me... but

different from its predecessor by bringing up any new point of tactics which might enable us to shoot down some MiGs. As a result the meetings were usually well attended, and I could generally count on an audience of 100 men every time I briefed. Out of that number I could pick, say, 18 who could actually be depended upon to mix it up with the enemy and perhaps do some shooting. Another 70 would fly into the combat zone, but for some strange reason would never see the enemy or fire a gun. The rest would inevitably develop some sort of mechanical, mental or physical difficulty sufficient to cause them to turn back home."

he behaved very well. The noise of his aircraft was terrific. He flew round me, then he suddenly waved to me." The German pilot dived for home.

Simpson had been lucky. Even "Stuffy" Dowding, Commander-in-Chief Fighter Command, thought that Germans descending over England by parachute were prospective prisoners and should therefore be immune from attack, while British pilots descending over England were still potential combatants and German pilots were therefore "perfectly entitled to fire on our defending airmen".

As Simpson drifted down towards the Worthing shore and across the beach, he noticed a number of soldiers looking up at him and was grateful that they had not raised their rifles toward him. "I must have looked English, even at 1000 feet." And then he thought he was going to end up being killed against the wall of a sea-side villa. The houses rushed up to meet him and "I hit the roof of a house... I was going through a garden fence backwards, and then

bang, into a cucumber frame." A woman at the house gave him a cup of tea and a policeman handed him a glass of whisky. He had survived.

"On 14th December 1944, while assigned to VF-11, Sun Downers, and flying an F6F-5 Hellcat from the aircraft carrier USS *Hornet* (CV-12), I was approaching the island of Luzon in the Philippines when we spotted a very large Japanese transport escorted by a destroyer and a destroyer escort. My division leader, Lieutenant Jim Swope, immediately signalled that we would make a run on the transport. We were all equipped with the normal six .50 caliber machine guns plus, on this flight, we had six 5-inch armor-piercing rockets under our wings. The usual procedure for rocket attacks was to divide the division into two two-plane sections and make a co-ordinated attack from different directions, and that's what we proceeded to do. As usual, you could not observe

What I expected was Thunder, fighting, / Long struggles with men / And climbing. / After continual straining / I should grow strong; / Then the rocks would shake / And I should rest long.
—by Stephen Spender

whether you had hit the target with your rockets, but as you retired from the attack you could observe whether they had caused any damage. It appeared that we had numerous hits and there were several fires on the ship.

"As I was recovering from the rocket run, my aircraft was hit by three 20mm or 40mm anti-aircraft projectiles. I was immediately aware that I had been hit, but it did not appear that my Hellcat had been damaged too much. When the division joined up after the rocket run, my wingman, Ensign Eddie Kearns, and Lieutenant Jim Swope both looked me over and, although they spotted some holes in the fuselage, it didn't look like there was much serious damage, and I decided to continue on the strike. One thing bothered me more than a little, though. The red 'beer can'-shaped WING LOCKED indicators (one in each wing) were both showing that my wings were unlocked. After the first panicky feeling, I figured out that just the cable that held the indicators down was cut, and that, since the actual locking pins were held in place by hydraulic pressure, there was no problem. In a few minutes, however, I noticed hydraulic fluid pouring over my starboard wing, and another moment of panic struck. Again, I analysed the situation and figured that the pins would require actual hydraulic pressure to unlock them and, as I didn't have any hydraulic pressure, I didn't have to worry.

"Our secondary mission on this flight was to seek and destroy any airborne enemy aircraft we found between Manila and Subic Bay. We flew down the Bataan Peninsula and did not spot any aircraft, and were returning to attack the transport by strafing.

"Just as we were leaving the Subic Bay area, I spotted a twin-engined Dinah aircraft and 'tallyhoed' it. In accordance with our division policy, I took the lead since I knew where the enemy plane was. I was in an excellent position to make a stern run on the Dinah and, since the enemy pilot took no evasive action, that's what I

did. As there was no reason to hurry the attack, I waited until I was very close and, after a short burst from my guns, the starboard engine flamed and, almost immediately, the plane exploded and went down.

"Following the attack, we rejoined on Jim Swope and proceeded to Manila, where we found the Japanese transport dead in the water, and other carrier aircraft attacking the other ships in the convoy. We all joined in and made strafing runs on the destroyer. After a couple of runs it was time for the strike to be over so we headed back to the Task Force.

"When we arrived over the *Hornet*, we made a break and went into a normal landing pattern. The first problem that occurred was when Jim Swope put his landing gear down. One gear went down and the other would not go anywhere but to the trail position. Next, my landing flaps would not go down. It took a few minutes to sort it out with the ship and, as I had a lot more fuel left than Swope, it was decided that he would land first. Everyone else in the recovery had landed by the time Jim went aboard. He made a good approach and landing. The crash crew quickly got his aircraft out of the arresting area, and it was my turn to land. It would be my first carrier landing with no flaps, but I felt it would be no problem. I made a good approach and got a 'Cut' from the landing signalman. I felt the hook engage a wire and, for an instant, felt relieved. But almost as soon as I felt the arrest, the plane began to accelerate again. My first thought was that I was going to flip over the side of the ship, but then I hit the first barrier and the prop wound up in the cables. The aircraft tried to go over on its back, but when the prop spinner hit the deck it stopped. The deck crew immediately climbed up on the plane, helped me unhook all my equipment, and assisted me out of the cockpit. Fortunately, I was unhurt and I went on down to the Ready Room for a debriefing.

"Shortly after I entered the Ready Room, a flight

deck crewman came to the door and asked for the pilot of the Hellcat that had just crashed. He came in and handed me the point of the arresting hook from my plane. When I landed without flaps, I was going a bit fast and the hook actually broke. He found the piece on the flight deck and thought I might like it as a souvenir. How right he was."
—Lieutenant Commander H.B. Moranville, USN (Ret)

Ivan Kojedub, Russia's highest-scoring ace of World War II, came from a poor peasant family in the Ukraine. He struggled in his studies but finally was accepted into a technical college and joined a state-sponsored flying club there. Early in 1940, he earned a pilot's licence and was accepted for flying training in the Red Air Force. He progressed quickly and, at an Operational Conversion Unit near Moscow, was introduced to the new Lavochkin La-5 radial-engined fighter, which he was to fly with amazing success against the best machine of the Luftwaffe, the Focke-Wulf Fw 190.
  On 15th February 1945, Kojedub was flying a lone reconnaissance patrol over the front when he spotted an unfamiliar low-flying shape against the snowy landscape. He closed rapidly to within a few hundred yards of the mottled Messerschmitt 262 jet fighter. As he approached it, the German pilot noticed him and applied full power to the twin turbines of the 262 in a futile attempt to outrun the Russian. Kojedub sent a stream of cannon shells into the German jet, which fell into a wood and became a fireball. It was Kojebub's fifty-seventh victory. He finished the war with a score of sixty-two.

Colonel Gidi Livni flew F-16s in the Israeli Air Force for fourteen years: "Great gunnery is a key factor in scoring fast kills while saving ammunition. The good shooter is able to snap-shot the enemy while he crosses the gunsight line.
  "During the Yom Kippur War [1973] two of my kills were achieved through snap-shooting at close range, low speed and a high-aspect angle.

"Gunnery today is much easier. All-aspect missiles can be launched at any angle. The missile 'eye' is slaved to various sensor sources such as radar, a helmet sight, etc. and the shooting envelope is calculated by computers. Nowadays, pilots are expected to be highly skilled and sensitive in order to operate the various switches and buttons on the stick and the throttle... switches that slave, release, lock or designate the radar and missile 'eyes', select weapon modes, and activate self-defence devices."

"The whole thing goes in a series of whooshes. There is no time to think. If you take time to think you will not have time to act. There are a number of things your mind is doing while you are fighting— seeing, measuring, guessing, remembering, adding up this and that and worrying about one thing and another and taking this into account and that into account and rejecting this notion and accepting that notion. But it doesn't feel like thinking.

"After the fight is over you can look back on all the things you did and didn't do and see the reason behind each move. But while the fight is on, your mind feels empty and feels as if the flesh of it is sitting in your head, bunched up like muscle and quivering there."
—Major Don S. Gentile, formerly with the 4th Fighter Group, 8 USAAF

Commander Randy H. "Duke" Cunningham, USN (Ret), flew F-4 Phantoms from the carrier *Constellation* during the Vietnam War. He relates his experience of 10th May 1972: "With the beginning of Operation Linebacker [a new and relatively unrestricted bombing offensive authorised by President Nixon against North Vietnam], and now the mining [of Haiphong harbour to deny it to Russian ships], apprehension dominated my thoughts. I suppose all fighter pilots like to think of themselves as indestructable, unbeatable, fearless... but my mind would wander back to home, my wife and child and the possibility that I might never see them again. I often fought back tears and a lump in my throat. This brooding had come over me the morning of the 10th, only more consuming. A few days earlier I had received a 'Dear John' letter from my wife. She wanted out of the marriage. The strain was almost unbearable. Just when I was feeling sorriest for myself, a voice bounced in... 'Hey, Duke! What you doin', eatin' more bullets?'

"Flying with backseater Commander Willie 'Irish' Driscoll, we were close enough to count on each other in times of trouble, though we had our arguments, both in and out of the cockpit. The moment of brooding introspection was gone. As time went on our friendship grew stronger, and later I was to find Willie a major support in keeping me up when personal problems became almost unbearable. The Irishman was always there.

"The target was the Haiphong railyard that served as a funnelling point for the Ban Kori, Mugia and Napi mountain passes leading to the Ho Chi Minh Trail. It was smack in the middle of several MiG fields—Phuc Yen, Kep and Yen Bai on the way in; Dong Suong, Bai Thuong, Thanh Hoa and Vinh on the way out. And the target itself was supposed to be heavily fortified with AAA ranging from 23mm to 120mm, not to mention SAMs along the flight path.

"The skipper looked over and smiled as he added our names to the strike roster as flak suppressors. Even though we'd be loaded with Rockeye bombs and would stay with the slower attack birds, once the bombs were away we still had four Sidewinder and two Sparrow stingers if the MiGs should want to play. It seemed so important for us to go, but then there were mixed feelings when our names were added, 'Maybe it's not such a good idea at that.' That old mixture of apprehension and aggressiveness.

"All strapped in, we waited for the 'start engines' call in the 100 per cent humidity. Word filtered down the line there might be a cancellation due to

In the wings of our planes was mounted a 16 mm movie camera, which started taking pictures as soon as the guns were fired. If no other pilot could verify your claim, the films would bear witness to your marksmanship. The films were rushed to Eighth Air Force Headquarters, where assessments were made; one was spliced together with an appropriate heading giving the pilot's name and claim, along with other movies taken from other pilots of the same date, and this was shown on the next day to the group. A movie room had been set up in back of the photo lab so that pilots could observe the previous day's shooting. I couldn't wait this long. That night I went to the photo officer's room to ask about my film. Did it show any strikes? His answer discouraged me: "Not a thing, Johnny. There wasn't even a picture of a German plane on the film."
—from *The Look of Eagles* by Major John T. Godfrey

Left above: Czech Air Force Generalmajor Frantisek Fajtl flew an La-5 in April 1945. He flew a Hurricane in the Battle of Britain and was grateful for its eight guns, reliable R/T system and its ability to take a lot of battle damage and still bring him back to his base. Left below: Generalleutnant a.D. Günther Rall, formerly with JG52, German Air Force, scored 275 victories in World War II.

The sunlight on the garden
Hardens and grows cold,
We cannot cage the minute
Within its nets of gold,
When all is told / We cannot
beg for pardon.

Our freedom as free lances
Advances towards its end;
The earth compels, upon it
Sonnets and birds descend;
And soon, my friend,
We shall have no time for
dances.
—from *The Sunlight on the
Garden*
by Louis Macneice

bad weather, making me fume, but the order soon came that the mission was a go.

"Turbines whined as they picked up speed and aircraft were rolling up to the cat. Jet blast deflectors went up and the first aircraft was off. One by one, each took his turn on one of the four catapults until it was our turn. Hooked on to the cat, we ran up to 100 per cent power, checked the instruments, lit the burners, saluted the cat officer and, WHAM...we were on our way, doing nearly 200 knots in just a few hundred feet.

"Brian and I were stepped up above the main strike force of A-6s and A-7s. Irish commented on what a shame such a beautiful country had to be bombed—winding waterways glistened through emerald green valleys as the sun reflected off the roofs of the populated wetlands.

"The first attack aircraft had demolished the primary target, so CAG directed the remainder of the strike force to secondary targets. Brian and I were sent to the large supply area adjacent to the railyard. We decided to close in tight to fighting wing formation and release simultaneously. We rolled over just as two SAMs were launched at us; failing to track, they came whizzing up past us. I looked back down at the target in time to see it disappear in a cloud of smoke and debris—A-7 1000-pounders had levelled it flat.

"We rolled over a bit more and I picked up a long, red-brick storage building. Dropping our bombs, we pulled off the target and I made the mistake of looking back over my right shoulder to see what we had done to the target. My head was down and locked when Brian, being the superb wingman he was, called, 'Duke, you have MiG-17s at your seven o'clock, shooting!'

"Two 17s flew right by Brian's F-4, about 500 feet away, and I was about 1000 feet in front! I popped my wing back down and reversed hard port in time to see a 17 pull in behind and start firing.

"My first instinct was to break into him. Then I thought, 'I did that two days ago and the guy

rendezvoused on me.' A quick glance at the MiG told me it was closing on me at high speed, meaning controls that were hard to move. I broke into him anyway.

"The MiG driver just didn't have the muscle to move that stick. He overshot the top of my two o'clock, but his wingman, who was back about 1500 feet, pitched up and did a vertical displacement roll out to my belly side. 'Duke,' Brian called, 'I'll take care of the guy at your six.' With utter confidence in Brian, I turned my attention back to the other MiG. When I squeezed off a Sidewinder, the enemy fighter was well within minimum range, but by the time the missile got to him he was about 2500 feet out in front of me... that's how fast he was going. The 'Winder blew him to pieces. That engagement lasted about fifteen seconds."

In the next few moments, Commander

Far left: US Marine Corps Colonel Bruce Porter flew with VMF-121 in World War II, achieving six victories, two of them at night. Left: A Royal Saudi Air Force F-15C Eagle moves in to re-fuel from a USAF KC-10 Extender during the Desert Shield build-up in 1990. An immensely powerful fighter, the F-15C has range, great acceleration and unique manoeuvrability, making it the most effective air-superiority fighter in the world. Above: Lugging a missile to its hardpoint on a USAF F-15 in Saudi Arabia during Operation Desert Storm.

The Battle of Britain was purely defensive. It was not fought to win a victory, but to avoid immediate and irretrievable defeat. When it was all over, very few people realised that a victory had been won at all, because another battle, the *night* attacks on our towns and factories was still raging.

What Hitler required was command of the air *by day* to enable his fleet of small craft to attempt the crossing from the Channel ports, so that he might have air cover during daylight. This he never attained, and so the attempt had to be abandoned. The night attacks could not be checked until new equipment in the shape of radar and aircraft was provided. A deficiency of aircraft was avoided owing to the genius of Lord Beaverbrook, and a deficiency of pilots through the co-operation of various Allied and friendly nations; it was a hard fought battle, fought with bravery and determination by both sides.
—Dowding

Cunningham and his backseater, Commander Driscoll, engaged and destroyed two additional enemy aircraft, including that of the North Vietnamese Air Force pilot known as 'Colonel Tomb', who is believed to have had thirteen American aircraft to his credit.

"I pitched off, broke and headed out again in burner. As we neared Nam Dinh I heard another SAM call. Glancing over to starboard I watched an SA-2 heading straight for us. Before I could manoeuvre, the SAM went off. The resultant concussion was not too violent but my head felt like it went down to my stomach. We had had closer SAM explosions than that and there appeared to be no damage. I immediately went to the gauges to check for systems malfunctions. Everything indicated normal so I continued to climb, watching for more SAMs. Irish couldn't understand how the thing got so close without our ECM gear's warning us. Neither could I.

"About forty-five seconds later the aircraft yawed violently to the left. 'What's the matter, Duke? You flying instruments again?' asked Irish. I steadied up and looked into the cockpit to see the PC-1 hydraulic system indicating zero, the PC-2 and utility systems fluctuating. Fear, that ever present companion, wanted to run the ship, 'What now, Cunningham?' raced through my mind.

"Thank God for sea stories, for somewhere out of my memory bank came the recollection that 'Duke' Hernandez, another Navy pilot, had rolled his aircraft to safety after losing his hydraulics. When an F-4 loses hydraulics the stabilator locks, forcing the aircraft's nose to pitch straight up. The stick has no effect on the controls, only rudder and power are available when this happens.

"Sure enough, when PC-2 went to zero, the nose went straight up! I pushed full right rudder, yawing the nose to the right and forcing the nose down. As the nose passed through the horizon I selected idle on the throttle and put out the speed brakes to prevent a power dive.

"I quickly transferred to left rudder, yawing the nose through the downswing to force it above the horizon. Full afterburner, retract speed brakes and the F-4 was in a climbing half roll. Just before the F-4 stalled at the top, the process was repeated.

"I rolled the Phantom 20 miles in this manner—I have no idea how many times, since all I cared about was making it to the water—beginning at 27,000 [feet] and working down to 17,000 by the time we reached the Red River Valley with wall-to-wall villages. The most fear I've ever known in my life was thinking that Irish and I were going to become POWs, especially if the Gomers [enemy captors] knew we had become the first American aces of the Vietnam War.

"The aircraft was burning just aft of Irish—I told him to reselect the ejection sequence handle so that if he decided to go, I wouldn't go with him. He asked why. I told him I wasn't about to spend nine or ten years in the Hanoi Hilton. 'Okay, Duke,' replied Irish. 'I'm staying with you until you give the word, but I'm placing the ejection handle so that we both go when I eject.'

"The next few seconds were full of fear—I even prayed, asking God to get me out of this. The aircraft rolled out, and I thought He didn't have anything to do with it. Then the F-4 rolled uncontrollably again, and I thought to myself, 'God, I didn't mean it!'

"An explosion ripped through the Phantom and I almost ejected, but we were still over land. The radio was full of screams from our buddies to punch out. They knew the burning F-4 could explode any second. A-7s and F-4s were all around us—I caught glimpses of them as we rolled up and down. Any MiG wandering within 10 miles of the area would have been sorry; a situation like this gets pilots hopping mad.

"Just as we crossed the coast we lost our last utility system and another violent explosion shook our fighter. A few seconds earlier and we would have been forced to come down in enemy territory.

Someone up there must have heard my prayer. At that moment I prayed the classic 'foxhole prayer' and pledged to myself that I would seek to understand and accept Jesus Christ if I made it.

"With the hydraulics gone, the rudder was useless. On the upswing I was unable to force the nose back down. The F-4 stalled and went into a spin.

"Each revolution I could see land, then ocean; incredible as it may seem, my fear kept me in the aircraft. I thought we were too close to the beach, and the winds normally blew landward. I told Irish to stay with me for two more turns as I attempted to break the spin and get some more water behind us. I deployed the drag chute with no effect—the controls were limp.

"Willie and I had often discussed what we would do should the need ever arise to leave our aircraft. I would say, 'Irish, eject, eject, eject,' and he would pull the cord on the third 'eject'.

" 'We are going to have to get out', finally left my mouth.

" 'Duke, the handle is set... when I go, you're going with me. Good luck.'

"I got out, 'Irish, e-...' and I heard his seat fire. There is only a split-second delay between the rear and front seats firing—if the front went out first the rocket motor would fry the guy in back—but I heard his canopy go and thought my seat had malfunctioned. As I started to reach for the ejection cord, my seat fired, driving me up the rail and away from Showtime 100.

"There was no pain from the G loading, then everything became quiet as I tumbled through space. I caught a glimpse of Willie's 'chute opening and, again, felt fear over the fact that something was not going to work and that I would not separate from my seat. But everything worked as advertised and I sailed away from the bulky seat.

"The 'chute lines rushed past me—I must have been going down head first—then the 'chute opened with a crack-the-whip jolt. Sharp pain ran through my back.

ORDE
29 Dec 1940

"SAILOR"

"Beautiful, a full canopy, but the first thing I looked for was land—was I drifting towards it? The choking fear of capture grabbed me again as I saw enemy patrol boats, a large freighter and some junks coming out of the Red River towards us. I just knew I had no taste for pumpkin soup.

"Totally fixated on the boats, I was startled by the intrusion of Corsairs and Phantoms rolling in on the enemy vessels. Hey, they hadn't left us—and I knew they were low on fuel, yet they pressed through AAA and SAMs to turn the boats around. I felt small and alone floating down in my 'chute until my buddies made their presence known. I find it hard even now to express the gratitude that flooded my senses.

"Then it dawned on me that I had a survival radio! I could talk! 'May Day, May Day! This is Showtime. 100 Alpha is okay.' (Willie was 100 Bravo.)

" 'Hang on, sailor, we're on our way,' replied the SAR team. Wow! In my joy I looked around for the first time. The biggest boost of the day was to see Irish a few hundred feet away waving like crazy to let me know he was okay. He flipped me the bird... no doubt about it, he was fine. I cordially returned the 'salute'.

"We were really coming down slow, plenty of time to go through all the procedures we'd been taught, but never had to use until now. Then, for some unknown reason, my thoughts shifted to home and the 'Dear John' letter from my wife. I seriously questioned if I would have what it takes to go through the camps if I were captured. We had been told the two major sustaining forces in captivity would be a strong faith in God and a loving wife. I was deficient in both areas.

"Thinking about my wife, I cried like a baby for a minute or so. My life was falling apart in great emotional upheaval. Again, I vowed to change my life for the better if I got out of this.

"My mind jolted back to the present difficulties when the wind caught my survival raft, hanging several feet below me on a tether. I started to swing back and forth like a pendulum. At the top of each swing the side of my 'chute would tuck under and, having never parachuted before, I thought it would fold up and let me fall. The para-riggers later told me it was perfectly safe, but it served admirably in taking my mind off personal problems.

"About 20 feet above the water I jettisoned the parachute while looking down at my raft. I went belly first into the warm, muddy water. Muddy? Struggling to the surface I found myself right in the mouth of the Red River! In scrambling for the tether attached to the raft I noticed something floating in the water next to me. A closer look revealed a rotting Vietnamese corpse, apparently washed down the river. For a second I thought it was Willie, but the body was too good looking. I swam for my raft with Olympic speed.

"We were in the water fifteen minutes pending fifteen years, when three Marine helos from USS *Okinawa* hovered over. As fighter pilots, we used to make jokes about those funny little machines with rotors that chugged along at just over 100 knots. My views changed radically at that moment.

"We were aboard in no time and on our way to the hospital ship. The President couldn't have been treated better. Everyone from the ship's cook to the CO came by to say hello and to ask if we needed anything. Doctors swarmed over us and we were checked for injuries. My back was stiff and out of place, but pronounced okay, so we boarded the helo again to get back to *Connie*.

"As we circled CVA-64, we could see the decks lined with waving, cheering men. As we gently set down, the cheers were audible above the chopper's roar. My back was throbbing, but damned if I was going to be carried aboard on a stretcher. Irish helped me out of the chopper. By the time I had my feet on *Connie*'s deck the tears were flowing—Irish, too. It was impossible to express our joy at being home and not under a Vietcong gun."

Left: Lieutenant-Colonel Francis S. Gabreski achieved twenty-eight aerial victories while serving with the 56th FG in England during World War II, and 6.5 additional victories in the Korean War.

After a strenuous combat mission / and the inevitable debriefing, / I would flop down on my bed / and try to unwind.

I was seldom successful because the many thoughts in my head / refused to go away... / about those who did not get back, / who might be struggling in enemy land.../ or lying dead in a frozen forest.

It was difficult to go to sleep at night / even though my body was drained / and my mind felt numb. / But I knew I must... / for there was tomorrow's mission.

When finally I drifted off to a fitful sleep / there were the dreams...horrible dreams...
always the dreams... / of another life I'd never known...
barbed wire, / machine-gun towers, / filthy living conditions, very little food...if it could be called that.

Then one day my dreams came true!
—*Horrible Dreams*
by Bert McDowell, Junior

"OCCASIONALLY, we'd have a party at the base. The prerequisite for this was that there'd be a group of young ladies who'd be willing to come to your base for a dance or a party. These young ladies would come out and make themselves available and we would have a party at the officer's club. Usually, we'd stock up pretty good on hooch and food. The British had a tough, tough time feeding their population and these young ladies enjoyed the opportunity to have butter, white bread and roast beef. There was a lot of drinking and horsing around. Sometimes it took two or three days to get the base cleaned up and get the gals out. But that's the facts of life."
—Captain William O'Brien, USAF (Ret), formerly with the 357th Fighter Group, 8 USAAF

Captain Grover C. Hall, Junior was Public Relations Officer of the 4th Fighter Group at Debden, Essex, during World War II. His war diaries formed the basis of the book *1000 Destroyed*, a history of the 4th in that war. In it, he referred to the group Commanding Officer, Colonel Don Blakeslee and his oft-quoted philosophy: "Fighter pilots and women don't mix." "He meant by that, that pilots had a way of getting cautious after cupid bit. It was a fetching quote. The press services pounced on it while Blakeslee was on leave in New York. The quote became a box insert on the front pages of papers from coast-to-coast.

"Almost immediately Blakeslee was deluged with letters from all over the country from young ladies who had fighter pilots for husbands, fiancés or friends, and had always understood that they were, far from a combat opiate, the sustaining inspiration to the pilot in his mortal struggles with the Axis monsters. And now this iconoclastic, outrageous 'fighter pilots and women don't mix', from this—whatsis name? Blakeslee. Blakeslee had clobbered the female vanity of America. Debden, when it saw the clipping, was one big belly laugh. 'Look who's talking!' they roared.

"Blakeslee returned to Debden. First thing he did was to make a flat-footed denial that he had ever really said 'fighter pilots and women don't mix'. He now said: 'You can't fight the war without 'em.' This was a laugh, as everyone could remember having heard him mouth the first statement until it was a Debden cliché. For example, a few days before Clark was to wed Lady Bridget-Elliot, daughter of a British earl, Blakeslee emitted an elaborate disquisition on just how the marriage would cause Clark to lose his vinegar. We assumed Blakeslee's disavowal of his favourite maxim grew out of his sobering experience with the wounded girls who wrote him the biting letters. Later we learned the reason why Blakeslee was so purposeful, if not systematic, in disowning authorship. In the States he had been secretly wed to his old hometown girl."

Bruce and Douglas Warren, identical twins, served together as Flight Commanders in No. 66 Squadron, RAF. Douglas recalls: "Our mother's birthday was on 21st of May, and ours was the 28th. I wrote my mother on the 21st after sending her a telegram. In the letter I pointed out that we would soon be twenty years old and said a year ago we were doing guard duty wishing we were pilots, and the year before that we were on the farm wishing we were pilots, and the year before that we were in school wishing we were pilots. We were very pleased that our wishes had come true.

"Occasionally we would meet Canadian friends whom we knew at school or whom we had met in training. At such times we would catch up on who had been killed or wounded, who had finished their tour, or transferred to another theatre, or married an English girl. Because of the nature of Air Force operations, far fewer RCAF men married while overseas than Canadian Army men, but many did. In the Air Force it was not unusual for a young woman to marry twice, or even three times, to Air Force aircrew. The woman would know her former

YOU CAN'T FIGHT THE WAR WITHOUT 'EM

Group-Captain A. G. "Sailor" Malan was married and had a son during World War II. Prime Minister Winston Churchill stood as godfather to the boy. When sitting for his portrait by Captain Cuthbert Orde, Malan told the artist that having a wife and son had been of the greatest moral help to him during the Battle of Britain, that it gave him an absolutely definite thing to fight for and defend, and that this was his constant thought.

Left: The chorus girls of London's Windmill Theatre, visiting the 4th Fighter Group at Debden, Essex, England during World War II.

another Air Evac, and a flight surgeon.

"We were just back from a mission, and I was turning around when she came in the door. I don't know what it was. She didn't look like any girl I ever went with, but in some way she looked like all of them.

"She was pretty good at it. She stood at the bar, looking like she was completely unaware she had stopped all normal activity in the room. She was just a little girl, and her nose turned up. She had green eyes and a soft tan and she was very lovely.

"The sergeant came in and yelled chow was on the table and I hung on to the last one. The three of them stood at the bar until everyone except me had left, and tagged on to the tail end.

"A captain, some friend of the flight surgeon, had squeezed in on the party, next to her.

"For some reason we sat down at the same table, and she was right across from me.

"When I passed her the gravy she smiled at me, and when I passed her the spinach I said, 'What are you?'

"I knew, but I had to say something.

" 'Air Evac,' she said. 'C-47s.'

" 'You evacuating us?'

" 'No. Just looking.'

"She had cagey eyes, pretty though. They were up here for a first-hand look at some human battle damage, so they'd know the score if they ever went to France.

"It wasn't a pretty thought.

"She wore brown nurse's slacks and they were made for her, and she was made for slacks. I closed my eyes and transported her into a white formal coming down the steps into the Cafe Rouge at the Pennsylvania. Glenn Miller would stop the band, and they'd all stand up. I'd sit there casually pouring down champagne until she got right to the table edge, then I'd ease to my feet and bow, and steer her into her chair. We'd have some more champagne. We'd dance.

"The illusion went away. They were talking about

husband's friends and they would come to see her. Both being young and under wartime pressure to enjoy the short time one might have, another marriage would take place. There were many wartime romances and marriages. Senior officers would often discourage pilots getting married because they had the idea it was 'distracting'. The pilot might be thinking of his wife, or impending marriage when he should be concentrating on the operation."

"The first time I saw her was just before chow in Number 2 Mess. She came in with another nurse,

I am sitting in a bus traveling narrow country roads bordered by green hedgerows. My husband sits beside me. We are in the part of England known as East Anglia, midmorning on a bright Saturday. I am one of fourteen wives on the bus, watching both the scenery outside and the unfolding drama inside.

Our husbands, some with thinning gray hair, some with slightly arthritic limbs, several with vials of heart medicine tucked handily in their pockets, lean forward in their seats, peering out the bus windows through the tops of their bifocals—excited and anxious as little boys. Each wears a specially ordered cap with *353rd Fighter Group, Eighth Air Force* printed on the front. They are looking for what's left of Raydon Airfield where they lived for two long, lonesome years during World War II.

"I say, it must be near here," says our travel agent in dignified British English. (The 1984 maps of England *continued* do not show old World War II airfields.)

"Look!" Suddenly, one of the men points across a flat field toward a bulky black shadow looming against a blue horizon. "That's a hangar!"

"That has to be Raydon," says another voice with a funny catch. Our visit had been carefully planned, even written up in the village newspaper. First we are to stop at the Peabody farm. Mr. Peabody now owns most of the land that was once Raydon Airfield.

"Welcome back to Raydon," Peabody says as he boards the bus. "As you can see, there is no longer an airfield here, but more of Raydon survives than most World War II airfields. I'd like to show you about."

The big bus pulls onto blacktop road and stops amid a cluster of metal Quonset-type buildings. These are the remaining buildings, now used by the government. And here, too, is the big black hangar.

The men fan out among the buildings. The three who were pilots head toward the hangar, those who were mechanics, armorers, and radiomen head toward other buildings. I follow my husband, who walks with his friend, Charley Graham, on the remains of the runway.

Weeds are growing through the cracks in the *continued*

wounds of the trunk.

"I passed her the lemon custard. 'Put some apple butter on it,' I said. I did, and it looked pretty, so she did.

" 'Mmmm,' she said.

"She was just about through.

" 'Look, I said, 'how would you like to wander tonight?'

"The captain jerked like he'd been stabbed in the brisket.

" 'All right... .' She was doubtful, but she was laughing.

" 'Who would I ask for?'

"She told me.

" 'Okay,' I said. 'Wonderful, we'll go surround a few bubbles.'

"It was pretty fast work for me, but it had to be that way. I gave the captain a blank look and checked out.

"After an afternoon in the sack I felt all right by night. I asked the other one for Sam, when I called her just before five.

" 'Where are we going?'

" 'We can throw darts, or wade in some ditch, or look at the moon, or just drink,' I said.

"We took a cab into town and found the King's Arms and drank.

"She came from Philadelphia and the uniform came from Bonwit Teller or Saks or somewhere hot.

"We talked about nothing much, about someone I knew in Philly, and someone she'd heard of in Denver.

"She was engaged to a Spitfire pilot. The diamond was tastefully enormous.

"When we didn't talk was the best. It was almost like being back in school, down in one of the joints, drinking during the week. She was out of the past, a sort of dream of other days, when there was woo in the moonlight, and laughter all the time.

"I closed my eyes and she was a girl named

Eleanor I took to the Senior Prom in high school. It was the first time I ever jacked myself into a Tux.

" 'I had a hell of a time,' I said.

" 'What?' she said.

" 'But it was wonderful.'

"I told her about it, but she couldn't understand it at all.

"After that we didn't talk much.

"I looked at her. Her hands were steady. She wasn't having a big time, but she was getting by. Her life was mostly plasma and bedpans now. She was over here to hold the shot-to-hell boys together till they could be flown out to the operating tables in the rear. Just her being there was pretty grim.

"But I could sit back and not look at her, and the flat English ale changed to a Zombie, and the smoky room became the Rainbow Room. If there had been music it would have been Goodman, and the GI over in the corner humming into his glass was really Sinatra.

"We went home after a while. The night was cool. The thank-you-we-had-a-swell-time was insincere. I knew I'd never be back.

"Walking home in the quiet dusk, the world sank pretty low. When I reacted like that to a dame, it was only because something big was completely lacking.

"She was pretty. She was built. She was American. So she was the past, and a halfway prayer for the future. I could see her in saddle shoes and a knocked-out sweater and skirt. I could see her sucking on a coke straw, and I could see her all ruffled up after a long ride home in a rumble seat.

"She was a symbol of something that was always there, in the back of the mind, or out bright in the foreground, a girl with slim brown shoulders, in a sheer white formal with a flower in her hair, dancing through the night."

—from *Serenade To The Big Bird* by Lieutenant Bert Stiles, formerly with the 91st Bomb Group (H) and 339th Fighter Group, 8 USAAF

Major James Goodson, USAF (Ret), formerly with the 4th Fighter Group at Debden, had his doubts about 'fighter pilots and women' in wartime: "Marriage tempered a man too much and the cautious pilot is doomed. I've never seen a fighter pilot get married and keep on the way he was. He gets careful, thinking about his wife. The first thing you know he's thinking about her and a Hun bounces his tail."

It was the girls in the services who figured most immediately in the lives of the Allied fighter pilots. Driver, plotter or nurse, the girls in uniform were often more than just that to the fliers. Friendships and romances flourished between the pilots and the girls working together on the same stations.

A portion of one of Major John T. Godfrey's combat reports sets the scene for an encounter on the evening of 21st March 1944. "VF-P—White Three—Fighter sweep into Bordeaux. Weather wasn't so hot so went under clouds at 20,000 feet all the way from Bordeaux to two aerodromes south of Rouen. We went down to strafe and I was hit by a 40 mm. Bad scare. Group destroyed twenty-one Jerries. Time—3:50.

"I climbed out of my Mustang and walked over to Larry, who was standing there gaping at the huge hole to the rear of the cockpit. We walked silently around the plane, and on the other side we saw where the shell had entered before exploding. Larry put his thumb by the hole and spread out his fingers; I knew what he meant. If the shell had entered 4 inches forward, instead of just in the back of my armour-plated seat, it would have exploded in the cockpit, and blown me to smithereens! He unscrewed the section which held the radio and, reaching in, brought out jagged pieces of metal. How lucky can a fellow get! Only one piece of the exploding shell had hit me. There was a small wound on my right knee, from which a small bit of shrapnel protruded—my only injury.

left: 1st Lieutenant Bert Stiles and Nancy, a friend from the American Red Cross. A young writer of great promise, he had completed his book *Serenade To The Big Bird* while finishing his tour as a B-17 copilot with the 91st Bomb Group (H) at Bassingbourn in Cambridgeshire. He then transferred to the 339th Fighter Group at nearby Fowlmere, to fly a tour in Mustangs. On 26th November 1944, he was killed as a result of aerial combat while on a bomber escort mission to Hannover, Germany, below: A dance at Debden, Essex for officers of the 4th Fighter Group in 1944.

old cement.

"Remember when we were standing right here when Colonel Ben's plane crashed," Charley says.

Slowly the men drift back toward the bus. I sense a sort of sadness, a letdown. Is this really Raydon? Are these few old buildings in the middle of a farm field all that's left to show for the years spent here? So long ago, the memories faint. Was it real—that war?

Reluctantly, they board the bus. Then, from a farm beyond the lane a woman calls to us. "Wait! Wait!" She runs toward the bus holding something in her hand.

She reaches the group breathless and laughing. "Forty years ago when you were here, I was a little girl living on my father's farm. One of you hit a baseball over the fence into our farmyard. I found it, but I didn't throw it back. I kept it all these years." She smiles sheepishly. "When I read you were coming, I thought you'd want to see it."

The men gather around her, laughing, each holding the old baseball for a moment, then passing it on. They need that baseball. Somehow it proves that Raydon was real, that the 353rd Fighter Group was here—and that the men were young and vital and strong enough to hit a baseball way over into that farmyard.

We thank her and climb back onto the bus. There *continued*

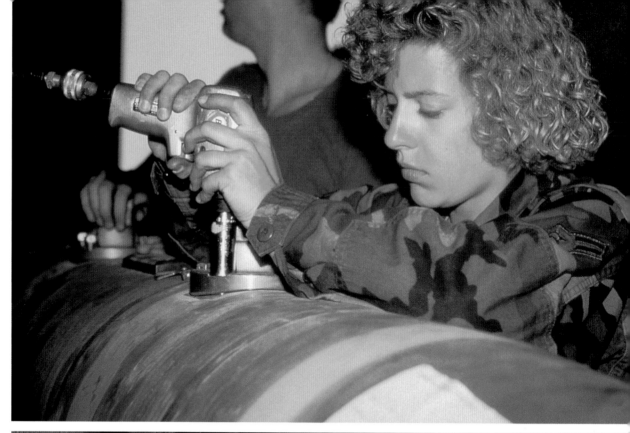

" 'Say, Doc, can you put a real big bandage around that little cut? I want to play a joke on someone.'

"The doctor had just removed some German steel from my knee, with tweezers. He now kept on bandaging until I had a knee as big as a football.

" 'Now will you call up the tent hospital and see if you can arrange for Lieutenant Charlotte Fredericks to change the dressing around, let's see, eight o'clock tonight?'

"The doc fixed me up, and at eight that evening I was limping horribly as Charlotte held me by the arm on our way to the dressing room.

" 'I don't know why they picked on me, but seeing you're here, don't expect any other treatment but medicinal.'

" 'Yes, ma'am.'

"I thought it was all a big joke, until I realized with embarrassment that I would have to take my pants down—the pant leg wouldn't pull up over the large bandage. I thought I caught a wry smile on her face when she held a white sheet in front of me as I dropped my trousers. I moaned horribly as I sat down and straightened my leg. I wanted to make this last, so I told her of the agonies I had suffered flying all the way from France with my mangled leg, weak from loss of the blood which nearly filled the cockpit.

"Very gently she started to unwrap and unwrap, until the floor was littered with the bandage. She didn't say a word when she came to the cut; she just took a Band-aid out of her pocket. Laughing in spite of herself, she said, 'Don't think you're so smart. The doctor's my friend, too. I was going to give you a hypo, but if you promise to behave yourself I just might let you buy me a drink.'

" 'Well, if you don't stand around gaping at me while I put my pants back on I just might do that.'

"I made progress that night—we held hands, but only after a few drinks."

In *Serenade To The Big Bird* Lieutenant Bert Stiles

recalled a woman of the wartime British capital. "There is a certain type of doll found in London called the Piccadilly Commando. A typical commando would be named Legion and her middle name would be Host and her last name would be Lots or Many or Thousands, and she'd probably be wearing a sable cape.

"When the dusk begins to grip the streets, the commandos come out of hiding and head for their respective theatres. The top operators wander along the edges of Hyde Park and past Grosvenor House. There are dark-eyed French girls in the eddies along Bond Street, but most of them are in and around Piccadilly.

"They ease along the avenues and they're always willing to talk, sometimes for quite a while, if business is flourishing and they think they won't lose anything by it.

"You couldn't pick a typical life story. She might have been born in the south of France, or maybe in a bower of heather in the Isle of Skye. About all you can say is she was born.

"Maybe her father drank flagons of ale and threw the empties at her. Maybe her mother made love with the ironmonger and didn't pull the shades. Maybe her sisters read unclean books.

"If she went to school it was probably casually, and she probably spent most of her time looking out of the window at the dandelions, or out behind the hedges with the little boys.

"She can see in the dark, and she can hear the casual white-feet of an MP a block away.

"She and her sisters come from every battered city in Europe, and she can whisper her sales talk in a dozen languages, including Braille and Indian Sign, but she is at her best in the tongue of the Yanqui.

"She is part of the night of London, part of the magic, part of the ugly loneliness. She fills in an hour or a stray ten minutes or any part of a night. She is someone, when all that is needed is someone. At least she is a human being.

A VALENTINE to one in the AIR CORPS

You've got them WINGS
And you can FLY
So please excuse this pun of mine—

But I am sure that you would make AN ANGEL OF A VALENTINE!

is a spirit of joy now.

On to town. Two hundred people live in Raydon. Most of them are here to celebrate the day with us. There are races and games in the schoolyard. Inside a potluck supper is waiting: chicken pies, Cornish pasties, potted shrimp. "You are the first group to come back," they tell us.

The next morning, we dress in our best clothes. The bus takes us to the tiny Anglican church built in the *continued*

Left above and below: USAF female personnel serving at a Saudi Arabian air base during the Gulf War Operation Desert Storm in 1991.

Below: Female guests being attended at a party on a USAAF fighter station in World War II England.

year 1200 and packed to capacity this Sunday morning. The Americans sit together in the front.

When the service ends, Charley Graham stands and asks to say a word.

"We have a gift for you." He holds *the* check, our collective gift. "We have 1,000 American dollars to be spent in any way you choose. We ask only one thing—that a little of it be spent for a plaque in this church remembering the *continued*

"She may be a hard-eyed bitch in the dawn, and she may put you away without pay for months, but when the mist is in your brain, and the war is yesterday and overhead and probably tomorrow, she is the princess of darkness.

"Some day the Yanks will go home, and the bit-of-love for five pounds will deflate like the barrage balloons, and her phase of Lend-Lease will unofficially terminate. Maybe she'll marry a shell-shocked tank driver who'll take her home to Detroit, or maybe a flak-happy bomb-aimer and go back to the Isle of Skye.

"She might make a dutiful mother and an excellent cook. And the past might fit into the past as merely an interlude, and grow over with time, and be almost forgotten in time.

"Or maybe one gentle spring morning the bobbies will fish her out of the river and no one will care whether her name was Legion or Host or Thousands, whether she plied her trade along Bond Street or in the soft shadows of Piccadilly."

"A Polish pilot, older than the rest of us, had been a pre-war regular officer in the Polish Air Force. He had fought in France and then joined the RAF after Dunkirk. There was a girl in Scotland, Margaret, who he was close friends with and with whom he spent his leave.

It fell to me one day to tell him he was to be sent on a rest tour. He protested at this, and I told him he had done his share and deserved a rest. I told him to go and visit Margaret, and that he was not as young as he once was. He thought about that and said: 'Perhaps so. I used to fly all day and sleep with girls all night. Now, when I fly all day and sleep with the girls all night, sometimes in the morning I feel a bit tired.' "

—Flight-Lieutenant Douglas "Duke" Warren, RCAF

(Ret), formerly with Nos. 66 and 165 Squadrons, RAF

The girls in the American airplane 'nose art' of World War II England were never dressed for the cold altitudes where the airplanes flew. Some were scantily clad, more were nudes but coyly posed, and some were front-view nudes, bold and biologically complete.

The girls most popular in barracks pin-up photos were Betty Grable, who had legs; Lana Turner, who was the 'Sweater Girl'; Dorothy Lamour, who wore sarongs; Mae West, after whose bulging balcony an inflatable life-jacket had been named; and Rita Hayworth, in a shot of her arising from bedcovers like Aphrodite from the ocean foam. The most desirable calendar art was the airbrush work of two artists named Petty and Vargas, whose nudes were shown in poses and proportions as seductive on paper as they would have been grotesque in life.

But the place of honour among these pin-ups was occupied by shots of the Girl Back Home, whose one-time reality was maintained only through correspondence. Much time was spent in writing long and often torrid letters to her. Letters from her were the highlight of mail call—unless one of them happened to be a 'Dear John', telling the crestfallen recipient he had been replaced in her affections, and causing him to suffer days of black depression usually accompanied by a monumental binge.

The American Red Cross girls ran the base Aero Club, which, but for its lack of a bar, was to enlisted men what the officers' club was to officers. Also, in a van called a 'clubmobile', the Red Cross girls took coffee and doughnuts to work crews around the base and to pilots at de-briefings. They were difficult to date, causing some enlisted men to complain that Red Cross girls had eyes only for officers. The problem, however, was simply that they were so few among thousands of men. Accordingly, most dating, by both enlisted men and officers, was with local girls, who were not difficult to date at all.

"They are loose as a goose," wrote one pilot in his diary, "and outspoken about what they will give you for gum or candy." He wrote those words, however, after only six days in England, and had not yet learned that in percentages of "loose as a goose", prim and proper, and somewhere in between, English girls were not too different from those in the States. The great influx of troops, though, did cause a sharp increase in English membership of the "oldest profession".

"A WAAF batwoman brought me some flowers for my room, and I reported this to my mother [in a letter]. 'First time a girl did that. They were wild flowers she had picked somewhere. I didn't even know her name.' "
—Flight-Lieutenant Douglas "Duke" Warren, RCAF (Ret), formerly with No. 66 and No. 165 Squadrons, RAF

When Mae West saw an item in a Los Angeles newspaper suggesting that the name "Mae West" for the RAF life-saving jacket might soon get into the dictionary, she wrote the following letter to *Tee Emm*, the wartime RAF magazine.

"Dear Boys of the RAF,

"I have just seen that the RAF flyers have a life-saving jacket they call a 'Mae West', because it bulges in all the 'right places'. Well, I consider it a swell honour to have such great guys wrapped up in you, know what I mean?

"Yes, it's kind of a nice thought to be flying all over with brave men... even if I'm only there by proxy in the form of a life-saving jacket, or a life-saving jacket in my form.

"I always thought that the best way to hold a man was in your arms—but I guess when you're up in the air a plane is safer. You've got to keep everything under control.

"Yeah, the jacket idea is all right, and I can't

men of the 353rd Fighter Group who served at Raydon—so that our grandchildren, when they come to visit, will know that we were here."

There is silence in the ancient church; the organ begins to play The Star Spangled Banner. I look down the rows and see tears on every cheek. How strange life is, I think: *An old baseball brought those long-ago days back to life, and a little plaque will keep them living.*

We walk from the cool stone church into the bright morning. We say goodbye and board the bus.
—by Eudora Seyfer, wife of George A. Seyfer—353rd Fighter Group armorer.

Men love war because it allows them to look serious. Because it is the one thing that stops women laughing at them.
—from *The Magus* by John Fowles

imagine anything better than to bring you boys of the RAF soft and happy landings. But what I'd like to know about that life-saving jacket is—has it got dangerous curves and soft shapely shoulders?

"You've heard of Helen of Troy, the dame with the face that launched a thousand ships... why not a shape that will stop thousands of tanks?

"If I do get in the dictionary—where you say you want to put me—how will they describe me? As a warm and clinging life-saving garment worn by aviators? Or an aviator's jacket that supplies the woman's touch while the boys are flying around nights? How would you describe me, boys?

"I've been in *Who's Who*, and I know what's what, but it'll be the first time I ever made the dictionary. "Sin-sationally,
"Mae West"

For the pilots of No. 238 Squadron, RAF, a favourite local was the Square Club at Andover, Hampshire. It was populated with groupies of the time who directed their attentions towards the 238 airmen. One of these ladies, known to the pilots as The Gypsy, had long black hair, wore full skirts and flaunted her curvy shape and excellent legs. During the Battle of Britain the average pilot's life expectancy was brief, but those the Gypsy favoured tended to last only a few days. Talk about fatal charms... more than once a pilot she slept with was shot down the next day. There was speculation that she was an enemy agent who doped the drinks of her pilot friends to foul their flying skills.

"I was tired and dirty when I arrived at the mess. In the bar I could hear sounds of merriment, but I was in no mood for jollity. I just needed bed. I should at least have washed, but I was too tired for that even. I went into the dining room. It was silent and in darkness, so I pushed through the swing doors into forbidden territory, the kitchens. My 'hello' produced an answer from amidst the ranges and sinks. It was a WAAF who answered me,

standing near a range with one shoe on. The other shoe was poised in her left hand. In her right she held a blacking brush.

"Obviously she was 'bulling up' her shoes. 'Who is the Duty Cook?' I questioned. 'Right here,' she replied 'Are you the Operational Breakfast?' My affirmative produced an immediate reaction. She dropped the shoe brush, pulled a mob cap over her upswept hair, and at the same time did a hop and a skip towards the hot range, pushing a large frying pan over the heat. She had her back to me and I was faintly amused at the girl. One shoe on and one shoe off, with wisps of mousy brown hair sticking out from the back of her cap. It was a stupid thing to do, as fraternisation between officers and WAAFs was frowned upon, but I pushed her loose hair back under her hat. She stiffened as I gazed at her slender white neck disappearing into a white overall. She wore no shirt. Round her neck was a gold chain with a small cross resting at the top of her bosom. She turned to look at me. I must have looked terrible, as an oxygen mask always left its outline of dirt around nose and mouth.

"She lifted her face and swung her arms around my neck, one hand still holding a black shoe. We kissed. It was a long warm kiss and I felt the blood run hot in my chest.

"Before I could repeat the operation, there was the sound of footsteps beyond the swing doors. We broke away from each other like naughty children. I turned towards the dining room and she to the frying pan. I was sitting in semi-darkness in the deserted dining room when she came in with a plate, which she put before me. 'That was nice,' I said. 'Lovely,' she replied, wrinkling her nose and turning away. I could hear distant laughter from the bar as I picked up a knife and fork. I glanced down at the plate. 'Oh good,' I thought. 'Two eggs!' That was the thing about WAAFs. Whatever the job, they never stopped being women."
—Pilot-Officer Nick Berryman, RAF (Ret), formerly with No. 276 Squadron

Left: "Jane" was a comic-strip cutie, the creation of cartoonist Norman Pett. She appeared every day in the London *Daily Mirror* during World War II, and her risqué adventures were eagerly followed by thousands of airmen and other servicemen. Throughout the Blitz a live "Jane" song-and-dance show was staged nightly featuring Chrystabel Leighton-Porter, Pett's real-life model for "Jane".

In late 1991 the United States Senate voted overwhelmingly to overturn a forty-three-year-old law that barred women from flying warplanes in combat. The measure was an amendment to the military budget bill for the 1992 fiscal year. It would permit, but would not require, the Air Force, the Navy, the Army and the Marine Corps to allow women to fly combat missions. The House had already approved similar legislation and Defense Secretary Dick Cheney indicated that he did not oppose the provision. The measure was sponsored by Sen. Bill Roth, R-Del., and Sen. Edward M. Kennedy, D-Mass. The action was a "victory for the women pilots who demonstrated in the Gulf their patriotism, courage and competence," Kennedy said.

A KEY ROLE of the Allied fighter pilot in World War II was to shepherd his 'big friends'—the bombers—to and from their targets in the various theaters of war. He did this with modest success for a while, but it was the advent of the ultra-long-range Mustang fighter that made the difference in the strategic bombing campaigns. One who flew the Mustang on the escort missions of the 357th Fighter Group was Captain William Overstreet, USAF (Ret): "It's funny how different a mission is after you have completed a few dozen. At first, everything is exciting—having the CQ wake you, eating your powdered eggs (usually green), going to the briefing room and seeing the tape across the map. So that's where we are going today. How many German planes will come up to intercept the bombers and us? How good are their flak gunners? Will we have a chance to go down and do some strafing? You make your notes to put on your knee pad so you have the vital information. When and where do we rendezvous with the bombers? What is the proper heading and how long will it take at X miles per hour? How strong is the wind and from what direction? I know some fellas who have been blown so far off course that they didn't have enough gas to get back to England.

"Now, let us get all of our equipment: mike, oxygen mask, Mae West, raft, parachute and all of the other things we may need. Climb on a weapons carrier for a ride out to my plane. It stops in front of my *Berlin Express* and I am greeted by Red Dodsworth and Whitey McKain. They are part of the crew who take care of my plane and make sure that everything is in the best shape possible. They have worked long and hard, and inform me that the plane runs smooth as a kitten. I hope it can be a real tiger as well.

"It is time to start the planes. As usual, the weather is so poor that they want a crew chief to ride the wing and help guide me while I taxi out to the runway. Whitey is sitting on my wing, and after the engine is running I leave the pad to follow

Andy's [Captain Clarence E. Anderson] plane. I get to fly Andy's wing today, so I know I will be with the best. He is already an ace and really helps all of the pilots gain confidence and be better in combat. I got to fly a lot with him while training in P-39s, and now in our best fighter—the P-51—no one can out-fly us.

"I have my canopy nearly closed to keep the snow out and feel sorry for Whitey out on the wing in the snowstorm. But, with his help, I make it to the end of the runway and pull up beside Andy's *Old Crow*. He is on the left side of the runway and I am on the right a few feet away and a few feet behind him. I wave for Whitey to leave and concentrate on Andy.

"Now I am in the air, climbing in the clouds, staying as close to Andy as I can because if I lose sight of him for an instant, I will be on my own in that cloud that I have to climb through before I can see anything or anybody again. I remember two friends who had a mid-air collision under these same circumstances and neither lived through it. That gives me enough incentive to stay close.

"Today we are lucky as we break out of the clouds at about 7000 feet, and soon the rest of the squadron is breaking out and forming up in flights of four. At full strength, each squadron would have four flights of four, and the group would have three squadrons. This time we don't have enough planes and pilots so we have only three flights and one spare from our squadron. This works out just right, as Irving Smith calls on the radio. 'Sorry fellas, my engine is too rough. I have to abort.' So the spare man, Ernest Tiede, moves up to take Smith's place. Now Irving has the fun of looking for our base in the heavy clouds, with a rough engine.

"We continue climbing and heading for Muritz Lake where we are to meet the bombers at 12.40. Andy has me for his wingman, with Joe Pierce and Bill Michaely as his element. We have all flown together for some time in P-39s and P-51s, so we

ESCORT SERVICE

During the first half of October 1943, VIII Bomber Command lost 166 heavies in six missions. This represented a loss rate that could not be sustained by any military force for any considerable length of time. In view of the fact that the Germans showed no inclination or probability of sudden capitulation, plus the fact that German fighter tactics appeared to be reaching perfection and fighter strength was being constantly reinforced, it is little wonder that responsible commanders were confronted with the necessity for an immediate re-evaluation of the American air position. This led to the realization that long-range missions deep in Germany must cease until long-range fighter escort could be provided en route and in the target area.
—Colonel Budd J. Peaslee, 8 USAAF

Left: B-17Gs of the 95th Bomb Group (H), 8 USAAF, stationed at Horham in Suffolk, England, are shepherded on a World War II mission to a German target by P-47 Thunderbolts.

settle in for nearly two hours of cold, uncomfortable sitting in the tight confines of our planes, on constant alert as the enemy could try to surprise us at any time. All he has to do is climb up into the sun and wait for a chance to pounce on us, as their radar gives them the information they need about where we are and what direction we are heading. That is why most missions are set in some general direction and then adjusted toward the specific target of the day. We try to keep them guessing if we can.

"We find the bombers just a few minutes late and in a somewhat loose formation. Our three squadrons take up their positions—one on the right—one on the left—and we are the high squadron for today. That means we stay above the bombers and, after checking to be sure the German fighters don't have a high cover to jump us, we can dive to get more speed and break up any enemy formations that try to attack the bombers. We gently weave at reduced speed so we can hold our positions with the bombers who are slower than us.

"Soon Andy calls, 'Bogies at twelve o'clock—get ready to drop tanks.' He has sighted enemy fighters straight ahead of us and we should turn our fuel switches from our wing tanks so we can drop them and prepare for combat. Now we really get apprehensive. All of our training, everything we know, is going to be put to the test. The Germans still have lots of good pilots and planes, and about forty of us are going to try to chase off about two hundred of them who are willing to do anything to keep our bombers from getting over their factories, refineries or any other prime targets in their homeland.

"We drop our wing tanks, give the planes more throttle, and head for the German formation. They are lined up in waves of about twenty abreast so that they can go through the bombers and use all their guns and cannon with plenty of targets for each of them.

"Andy picks out the one who seems to be their leader and goes after him. I ease back a little so I can watch behind Andy's plane and make sure that no one can get behind him. If a fighter can get behind another plane, his guns are much more accurate than at a wider deflection shot from other positions. That is why we always try to get on the enemy's tail, and try to avoid letting them get behind us. A good fighter group is a team. Each man has his job and if everyone does his job well, the team effort is successful. My job is to make sure that, while Andy is trying to get behind the enemy, none of them gets in position behind him.

"By now, the other squadrons have joined the attack. Try to imagine about forty P-51s and two hundred Me 109s and Fw 190s in a mad scramble with each pilot trying to shoot down any of the enemy planes he can get a shot at while making sure they are kept away from gaining position on our planes. Throttles are pushed forward for maximum power, and as fast as we can go we are in circles, climbing, diving, rolling... any possible manoeuvre to get a shot at them while they are trying to do the same to us. I see Andy get hits on several of them and I get a burst at a 109 that got too close to getting behind Andy. When he felt my .50 caliber rounds hit his tail, he dove for the deck to get away from us.

"The scramble is really getting wild. All our planes are chasing German fighters and breaking away when they get in position behind us. That means making a fast turn to keep him from having a good shot at us. It seems that the sky is full of planes in every conceivable position, frequently inverted, and I am firing whenever I think I am in position to get some hits.

"We have succeeded in diverting most of the enemy but a few have got through and hit the bombers. By now, a lot of planes are smoking— some of our bombers and some of their fighters— and parachutes are blossoming below us as people leave their crippled planes.

An "Order of the Führer" arrived in the evening. Our combat successes had, it seemed, been too few. Four-engined bombers were now no longer to be attacked from right ahead on opposite courses, but from positions astern. Only we knew what that meant. A single attack would now last thirty seconds, and not three as formerly. The concentrated fire of the *continued*

Left: *Queenie*, a B-17G of the 490th Bomb Group (H) based at Eye, Suffolk, England in WWII. Above: On 6th January 1944, Lieutenant-General James H. Doolittle took command of the Eighth US Army Air Force at High Wycombe, Buckinghamshire, England.

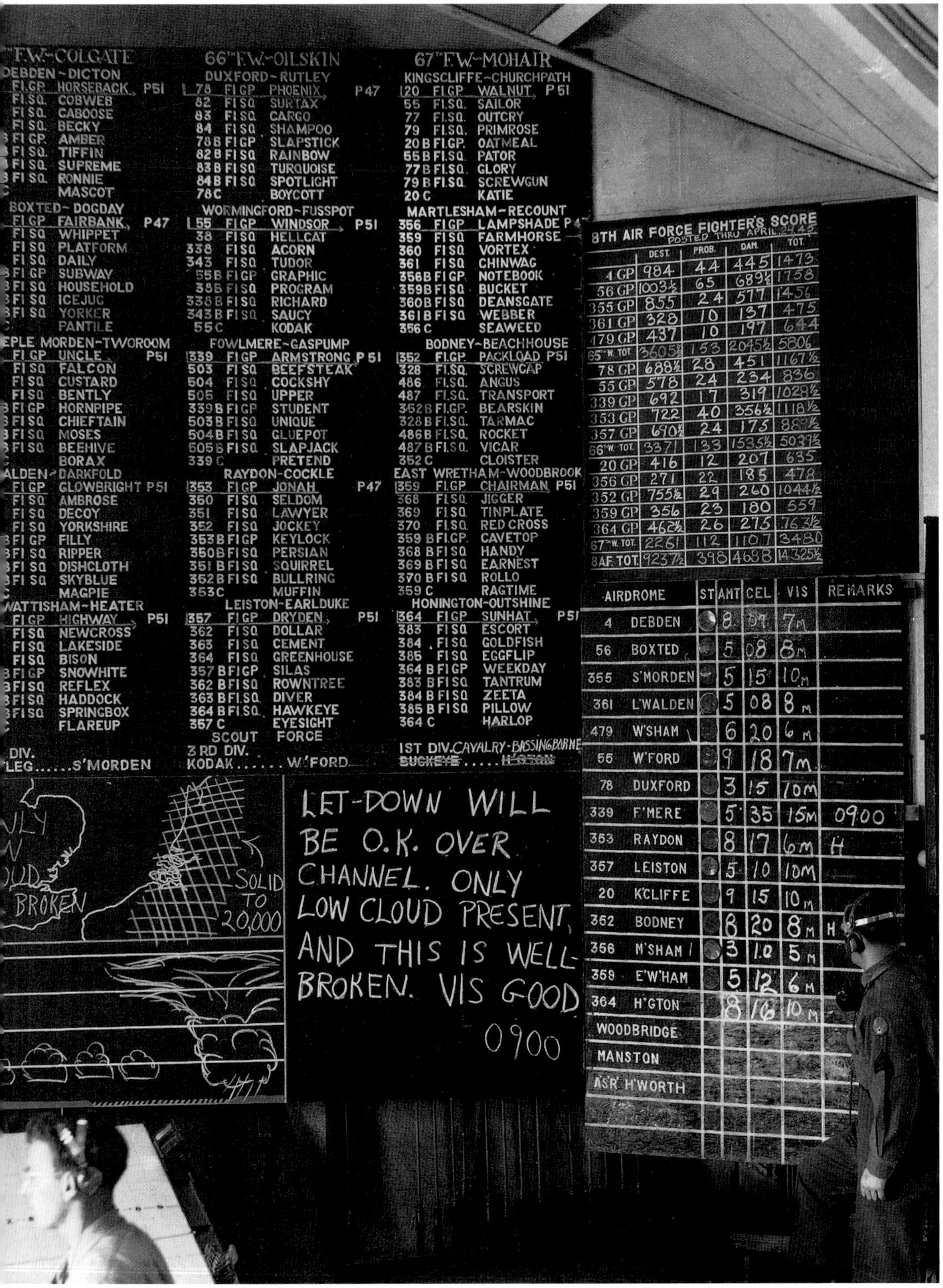

"After what seems an eternity, but is actually only about five or ten minutes, the remaining bombers are still heading for their target and our fighters are now chasing any German fighters that haven't dived for the deck to get out of the fight. While most of our planes are scattered, Andy and I are still together and the element, Joe and Bill, is still nearby. Andy sees some German fighters getting ready to hit the bombers again, so we head for them. Andy comes up below and behind a 109 and closes to within a few hundred yards. I keep thinking he can fire but he waits until he is about 100 yards out and pulls the trigger. There is an explosion, the right wing falls off and the enemy pilot decides he had better walk home. He leaves the plane with his parachute while I fire at his wingman. Sparkles light up on the fuselage and tail. He flips over and dives for the deck. Joe has convinced another German to leave his plane by setting his engine on fire.

"Now targets aren't as plentiful, but we see ten German fighters still trying to get to the bombers. They see us coming and decide to head for home. We decide to go after them. We follow them in a power dive, pushing the airspeed indicator to the red line. When you go from 25,000 feet to the deck in a hurry, you are fighting trim tabs, rudders and everything else to keep flying straight. We all manage and Andy is closing on one of their planes when it pulls back on the stick and tries to lose us by climbing. Andy stays right with him and I stay with Andy just a little later. The German starts every evasive tactic he can, but when he and Andy are upside down, Andy gets a burst into the German's engine and that is that. With his engine on fire, he also elects to walk home.

"Now we are a few thousand feet over Germany, the German planes are scattered in all directions, and when we followed them our group was spread all over the map. A decision has to be made—do we go back up to see if we can help any bombers who may have lost engines and can't

---

F.W.-COLGATE

DEBDEN~DICTON
- FI.GP. HORSEBACK, P51
- FI SQ. COBWEB
- FI SQ. CABOOSE
- B FI GP. AMBER
- FI SQ. TIFFIN
- FI SQ. SUPREME
- FI SQ. RONNIE
- MASCOT

BOXTED~DOGDAY
- FI GP. FAIRBANK, P47
- FI SQ. WHIPPET
- FI SQ. PLATFORM
- FI SQ. DAILY
- B FI GP. SUBWAY
- FI SQ. HOUSEHOLD
- FI SQ. ICEJUG
- FI SQ. YORKER
- PANTILE

EPLE MORDEN~TWOROOM
- FI GP. UNCLE P51
- FI SQ. FALCON
- FI SQ. CUSTARD
- FI SQ. BENTLY
- B FI GP. HORNPIPE
- FI SQ. CHIEFTAIN
- FI SQ. MOSES
- FI SQ. BEEHIVE
- BORAX

ALDEN~DARKFOLD
- FI GP. GLOWBRIGHT P51
- FI SQ. AMBROSE
- FI SQ. DECOY
- FI SQ. YORKSHIRE
- B FI GP. FILLY
- FI SQ. RIPPER
- FI SQ. DISHCLOTH
- FI SQ. SKYBLUE
- MAGPIE

WATTISHAM~HEATER
- FI GP. HIGHWAY P51
- FI SQ. NEWCROSS
- FI SQ. LAKESIDE
- FI SQ. BISON
- B FI GP. SNOWHITE
- B FI SQ. REFLEX
- B FI SQ. HADDOCK
- B FI SQ. SPRINGBOX
- FLAREUP

DIV.
LEG......S'MORDEN

66"F.W.-OILSKIN

DUXFORD~RUTLEY
- L 78 FI GP. PHOENIX, P47
- 82 FI SQ. SURTAX
- 83 FI SQ. CARGO
- 84 FI SQ. SHAMPOO
- 78B FI GP. SLAPSTICK
- 82B FI SQ. RAINBOW
- 83B FI SQ. TURQUOISE
- 84B FI SQ. SPOTLIGHT
- 78C BOYCOTT

WORMINGFORD~FUSSPOT
- L 55 FI GP. WINDSOR, P51
- 38 FI SQ. HELLCAT
- 338 FI SQ. ACORN
- 343 FI SQ. TUDOR
- 55B FI GP. GRAPHIC
- 38B FI SQ. PROGRAM
- 338B FI SQ. RICHARD
- 343B FI SQ. SAUCY
- 55C KODAK

FOWLMERE~GASPUMP
- 339 FI GP. ARMSTRONG P51
- 503 FI SQ. BEEFSTEAK
- 504 FI SQ. COCKSHY
- 505 FI SQ. UPPER
- 339B FI GP. STUDENT
- 503B FI SQ. UNIQUE
- 504B FI SQ. GLUEPOT
- 505B FI SQ. SLAPJACK
- 339 C PRETEND

RAYDON-COCKLE
- 353 FI GP. JONAH P47
- 360 FI SQ. SELDOM
- 351 FI SQ. LAWYER
- 352 FI SQ. JOCKEY
- 353B FI SQ. KEYLOCK
- 350B FI SQ. PERSIAN
- 351B FI SQ. SQUIRREL
- 352B FI SQ. BULLRING
- 353C MUFFIN

LEISTON-EARLDUKE
- 357 FI GP. DRYDEN, P51
- 362 FI SQ. DOLLAR
- 363 FI SQ. CEMENT
- 364 FI SQ. GREENHOUSE
- 357B FI GP. SILAS
- 362B FI SQ. ROWNTREE
- 363B FI SQ. DIVER
- 364B FI SQ. HAWKEYE
- 357 C EYESIGHT

SCOUT FORCE
3 RD DIV.
KODAK......W'FORD

67"F.W.-MOHAIR

KINGSCLIFFE~CHURCHPATH
- 120 FI GP. WALNUT, P51
- 55 FI SQ. SAILOR
- 77 FI SQ. OUTCRY
- 79 FI SQ. PRIMROSE
- 20 B FI GP. OATMEAL
- 55B FI SQ. PATOR
- 77B FI SQ. GLORY
- 79B FI SQ. SCREWGUN
- 20 C KATIE

MARTLESHAM~RECOUNT
- 356 FI GP. LAMPSHADE P4
- 359 FI SQ. FARMHORSE
- 360 FI SQ. VORTEX
- 361 FI SQ. CHINWAG
- 356B FI GP. NOTEBOOK
- 359B FI SQ. BUCKET
- 360B FI SQ. DEANSGATE
- 361B FI SQ. WEBBER
- 356 C SEAWEED

BODNEY~BEACHHOUSE
- 352 FI GP. PACKLOAD P51
- 328 FI SQ. SCREWCAP
- 486 FI SQ. ANGUS
- 487 FI SQ. TRANSPORT
- 352B FI GP. BEARSKIN
- 328B FI SQ. TARMAC
- 486B FI SQ. ROCKET
- 487B FI SQ. VICAR
- 352 C CLOISTER

EAST WRETHAM~WOODBROOK
- 359 FI GP. CHAIRMAN, P51
- 368 FI SQ. JIGGER
- 369 FI SQ. TINPLATE
- 370 FI SQ. RED CROSS
- 359B FI GP. CAVETOP
- 368B FI SQ. HANDY
- 369B FI SQ. EARNEST
- 370B FI SQ. ROLLO
- 359 C RAGTIME

HONINGTON-OUTSHINE
- 364 FI GP. SUNHAT, P51
- 383 FI SQ. ESCORT
- 384 FI SQ. GOLDFISH
- 385 FI SQ. EGGFLIP
- 364 B FI GP. WEEKDAY
- 383 B FI SQ. TANTRUM
- 384 B FI SQ. ZEETA
- 385 B FI SQ. PILLOW
- 364 C HARLOP

1ST DIV.CAVALRY-BASSINGBORNE
BUCKEYE.....H'GTON

8TH AIR FORCE FIGHTERS SCORE
POSTED THRU APRIL 24 45

	DEST.	PROB.	DAM.	TOT.
4 GP	984	44	445	1473
56 GP	1003½	65	689½	1758
355 GP	855	24	577	1456
361 GP	328	10	137	475
479 GP	437	10	197	644
65"W. TOT.	3605½	153	2045½	5806
78 GP	688½	28	451	1167½
55 GP	578	24	234	836
339 GP	692	17	319	1028½
353 GP	722	40	356½	1118½
357 GP	690	24	175	889½
66"W. TOT.	3371	133	1535½	5037½
20 GP	416	12	207	635
356 GP	271	22	185	478
352 GP	755½	29	260	1044½
359 GP	356	23	180	559
364 GP	462½	26	275	763½
67"W. TOT.	2261	112	1107	3480
8AF TOT.	9237½	398	4688	14325½

AIRDROME		ST	AMT	CEL	VIS	REMARKS
4	DEBDEN	8	0?		7m	
56	BOXTED	5	08		8m	
355	S'MORDEN	5	15		10m	
361	L'WALDEN	5	08		8m	
479	W'SHAM	6	20		6m	
55	W'FORD	9	18		7m	
78	DUXFORD	3	15		10m	
339	F'MERE	5	35		15m	0900
353	RAYDON	8	17		6m	H
357	LEISTON	5	10		10m	
20	K'CLIFFE	9	15		10m	
362	BODNEY	8	20		8m	H
356	M'SHAM	3	10		5m	
369	E'W'HAM	5	12		6m	
364	H'GTON	8	18		10m	
	WOODBRIDGE					
	MANSTON					
	ASR H'WORTH					

LET-DOWN WILL BE O.K. OVER CHANNEL. ONLY LOW CLOUD PRESENT, AND THIS IS WELL-BROKEN. VIS GOOD 0900

SOLID TO 20,000

BROKEN

keep up with their formation? They are sitting ducks for enemy fighters, so some P-51s escorting them could make the difference to their survival. Or shall we stay on the deck and look for trains, barges, ammunition dumps or military convoys?

"As we are low on ammunition, we start climbing. Soon, Joe and Bill join us, and after all of the action, our flight is together to start back to England, offering assistance to any 'wounded' bombers we see as long as our fuel holds out. We try to avoid the areas of heavy flak. In some places German gunners can turn the sky black with exploding bursts.

"We stay with a bomber who has lost two engines until we approach the English Channel and we feel they can make it. We have just enough fuel to get back. There are still a lot of clouds over England, but now the ceiling is almost 100 feet so we have no trouble getting to our base and landing.

"There is no way anyone could count the planes we shot at, or who shot at us, or the number of ground gunners with good radar firing at us. How many times did we have an enemy plane in our sights, but had to break it off because an enemy plane was closing behind us? How many times did we have to break off to chase one who was closing in on one of our teammates? A dogfight is almost a blur because of the fast and furious action. Today went in the books as a mission of a little over five hours, with us destroying sixteen German planes, while one of our pilots had to bail out over Germany. I am awfully glad to be back."

"On 11th September 1944, we were escorting B-17s to Ruhland and were approaching the rendezvous point at 25,000 feet when I had to use the relief tube. In order to use the tube (which is vented overboard), it was necessary to unbuckle the lap belt and shoulder harness as well as the leg straps of the parachute and slide well forward on the seat. I was in this position when a voice came over the radio shouting, 'Me 109s, here they come.' I looked up and saw about fifty Me 109s diving through our formation and firing. One crossed in front of me in a 45-degree dive and was firing at a P-51 below and to my left. This was the first time I had ever seen an enemy aircraft and with a case of 'buck fever' I peeled off and went after him. He saw me chasing him and steepened his dive to vertical. I was also headed straight down with full power. Both of us descended from 25,000 feet at extremely high speeds. Being completely unstrapped, I was a free floating object in the cockpit and heading straight down my body was at zero Gs. The slightest movement of the stick would cause me to leave the seat and hit the canopy. The airplane was very touchy at this speed and at times I felt like a basketball being dribbled down the court.

"We both started to pull out at about 8000 feet. I glanced at my airspeed indicator which, at that moment, was showing 600 miles per hour, 95 miles per hour over the red line speed. The Me 109 had only completed about 45 degrees of his pull up when his right wing came off through the wheel well area. He spun into the ground in a few seconds with no time to bail out. Even though no one else saw this victory, nor did I have any of it on the gun camera film, I still got credit for it due to the fact that one of the other pilots had counted the fires on the ground after the huge fifteen minute dogfight and reported to the debriefing officer that he counted thirty fires. There were claims of twenty-eight Me 109s shot down with a loss of two P-51s. After landing, when I had stepped out on to the wing, my crew chief remarked, 'Better zip up your pants before you go in for de-briefing.' "
—Major Walter J. Konantz, USAF (Ret), formerly with the 55th Fighter Group, 8 USAAF

"The worst escort I had to fly was against England in June 1940, from Coquelles near Calais. The order was a direct escort for Ju 87s, the dive-enemy would spray us for half a minute with bullets, for which period we would be without protection or concealment—a long time, probably too long, for us to have a chance of emerging alive. Instead of approaching our target at 250 metres per second, we would have to overhaul the enemy gradually from astern, as the bombers flew only a little more slowly than ourselves. The enemy pilots would no longer have to look down our gun-barrels, but we, on the other hand, would have to make our approach under the eyes of the rear-gunners and in the face of hundreds of weapons for long enough for them to shoot us down before we could even fire our first burst. Well, we had taken an oath, which made it easier to carry out our new instructions.
—from *Heaven Next Stop* by Gunther Bloemertz

Left: The Operations Room of the 65th Fighter Wing at Saffron Walden, Essex, England in World War II was located in a disused school building. There radio control of all VIII Fighter Command groups was maintained. The nerve centre was the plotting room manned by the duty controller and assistants. The 65th Fighter Wing also operated the Air/Sea Rescue radio fixer service from this facility beginning in July 1943.

bomber, heavy, slow and unmanoeuvrable. So, [we] gave up all our advantages and the Spitfires just waited for us upstairs. We had big losses and the tactics were changed. Certainly escort is a primary mission for a fighter, but he has to have the freedom of moving and selecting his position in the air."
—Generalleutnant a. D. Günther Rall, German Air Force (Ret)

Oberleutnant Dirk Wiegmann has been a Navigator/Weapons System Officer with 1/AG51 of the German Air Force, flying Tornados since early 1995. "On our recce missions, we try to protect ourselves with our weapons, but we have our escort... our own fighters flying with us, and we pretty much count on them. They try to keep us free from enemy fighters, and if this doesn't work we try to run away. That's our actual role in the Tornado. We can't really fight with the aircraft. It's not built for that. It's built for taking pictures or delivering bombs, not to fight against a third-generation fighter. There is no chance. In that situation, we just drop everything and run away, if possible."

Debden-based Major John T. Godfrey recalled his first combat mission, 27th September 1943. On that day the 4th Fighter Group, 8 USAAF, was assigned to support four boxes of B-17s in the target area of Essen, in the Ruhr Valley. Godfrey's squadron, the 336th, was due to rendezvous with the bombers in the target area at 08.30 hours. He was flying as wingman to Major Don Gentile and, as they approached the Channel *en route*, Gentile motioned for Godfrey to spread out from him into battle formation. "A peculiar whine suddenly started in my earphones. The Germans were jamming our frequencies. (But this interference was never effective enough to disrupt our communications.) We were now approaching enemy territory, and for the first time I saw flak. It looked harmless, like little puffs of black smoke. As the puffs grew thicker the weaving of the planes became more erratic. There was no such thing as dodging these puffs, but weaving made the individual pilot feel more secure, even though there was still just as good a chance of flying into an exploding shell. The 335th was through the black puff, and now our squadron entered it. What had looked so harmless up ahead was now appearing all around me. The crunch of the explosions could be heard even above the noise of the motors. Unconsciously, I veered my plane to the left as one exploded right ahead of me. My rear end was tightening in a peculiar fashion, such as I had never felt before; along with this I seemed to be gulping oxygen, trying to fill my lungs, but never quite able to because my breathing was so rapid. Everything was happening so damned fast that I had no recollections of our advancing on the bombers that we were to escort. They just materialized below us. *I mustn't lose Don*, I kept

repeating to myself, and moved in close to him. I expected any minute to see a million Jerries appear out of the air, every one of them shooting at me. There was no question of my being scared stiff, but along with this, a strange exhilaration was filling me."

Captain Jack Ilfrey, USAF (Ret), formerly with the 20th Fighter Group, 8 USAAF, based at Kings Cliffe, Northamptonshire, England, has vivid memories of a day in May 1944 when his group was escorting B-24 Liberators of the 2nd Air Division on a bombing mission. "Shortly after the bombers— what was left of them—were leaving the target, as we were weaving around protecting them, I counted fourteen of them from the cockpit of my P-38, going down. White parachutes (and some brown German ones) everywhere. I thought, 'My God, more than 140 men right here in front of my eyes. What in the hell is this all about? Why are we doing this—all this wanton destruction—havoc,

Far left above: A remaining T-2 hangar and Nissen huts at Raydon, Suffolk, England, World War II home of the 353rd Fighter Group, 8 USAAF. Far left below: Warming up an Fw 190 on a German airfield in World War II. The 190 was nicknamed "Butcher-bird" by German airmen. The RAF first encountered the Fw 190 over France in early 1941 and found its Spitfire V thoroughly outclassed by the new German fighter. The 190 was faster than any Allied fighter of the time and had heavier armament. It was powerful, highly manoeuvrable and offered extremely good visibility. In 1944 a new, long-nosed version, the Ta 152 entered production and proved an awesome, truly formidable dogfighter.

WE KNOW IT'S A MAN
                SIZE JOB,
AND NEEDS NO END
                    OF PLUCK,
SO HERE ARE OUR
        BEST WISHES, LAD,
        AND ALL THE BEST
                    OF LUCK!

603

mayhem. Are we crazy idiots? Why in the hell is God letting this happen? Or is there even a God anymore?' I was a long time getting over this scene. It still remains vivid in my memory."

"In my first tour we did a lot of escort work, which was frustrating as we were flying the Spitfire Mk Vs which were no match for the Fw 190s. [It was] really difficult to keep position on the slower bombers. Free-ranging area escort, with good ground control, is more effective. My opinion is that it is better to fly fighters than bombers. We saw our share of bombers brought down by flak and couldn't do anything about it."
—Flight-Lieutenant Douglas "Duke" Warren, RCAF (Ret), formerly with No. 66 and No. 165 Squadrons, RAF

2nd Lieutenant Robert N. Jensen was a P-38 pilot with the 55th Fighter Group, 8 USAAF based at Nuthampstead, Hertfordshire, England. On 13th November 1943 he was shot down while on an escort mission to Bremen. "I had about 175 hours in the P-38, none of it in preparation for high-altitude bomber escort. A few hours' transition time in our new planes in England and we went into combat. I have no excuse for being shot down on my 12th mission, but I do feel we had far too little training and were rushed into combat because we had planes capable of long-range missions, something sorely needed at that time.

"On 13th November 1943, the mission was bomber escort, target Bremen, Germany. Before we caught up with the bombers I lost the left engine and dropped out of the flight. I was attacked by a twin-engined German fighter but managed to avoid significant damage and may have destroyed him as he went into the clouds smoking. I tried to head for England in the clouds but broke out with an Me 109 on my tail. He set my plane on fire and I bailed out.

"I was burned about the face and neck and had

shrapnel wounds in my left leg and arm before I bailed out. The 'chute was damaged by burning bits of my clothing after it opened but I landed relatively softly, a few kilometres inside Germany straight east of Amsterdam.

"I was picked up by German civilians immediately since I could not walk or run. I was taken to a rural schoolhouse where I was picked up that night by German soldiers in a truck. I was taken to a prison in Lingen, where a French prisoner doctor treated me. While I was at the prison, the only Red Cross medical parcel ever received there came in. It contained some type of sulpha powder. The French doctor used part of the sulpha on the infected leg of an American navigator and part on my face, which had become infected. I suspect that my life was saved by that Red Cross medical parcel. After about two months I was able to travel and six of us American prisoners were taken to the interrogation centre near Frankfurt."

"Early in June 1942 our squadron, No. 312 (Czech) RAF, was transferred from Harrowbeer to Kenley. From there, together with Nos. 310 and 313 Squadrons, we were detailed to escort some Boston bombers to a target south-west of Cherbourg, France. On our way back to England we were attacked by a large number of Focke-Wulfs and several of our pilots were shot down. I was attacked by four of the Germans and I pushed my plane into a steep dive, hoping they would pass over me. They did, but then I had another problem. We had been instructed that if our Spitfire Vs ever reached 500 mph in a dive the ailerons would go to a certain position and the aircraft would become very hard to handle. At this point I noticed the Isle of Wight in the distance and decided that if my plane started to break up I would bail out and maybe be picked up soon by a boat. Finally, I was able to pull out of the dive, but in doing so I blacked out. As I recovered, I found that I was flying straight up and there, right above

me, was one of the German fighters. He flew into my sights, and after a few short bursts of my machine guns and cannon he went down."
—Generalmajor Frantisek Perina, formerly with No. 312 (Czech) Squadron, RAF

Carroll "Red" McColpin was born in Buffalo, New York. A pilot since 1928, he volunteered for the Royal Air Force in November 1940 and was the only American to fly in combat with all three Eagle Squadrons. He commanded No. 133 Eagle Squadron until it transferred to the Eighth USAAF in September 1942, becoming part of the 4th Fighter Group at Debden, Essex. Red McColpin is officially credited with 11.5 kills, four probably destroyed, twelve damaged (all aerial) plus numerous aircraft, tanks, trucks and boats destroyed. He holds twenty-nine decorations from five governments and two Presidential Unit Citations. He retired from the US Air Force in 1968 with the rank of Major General.

"We met them over England... thirty-six B-26s, and they went on over Belgium in bright sunlight. We were all around them. They went in and there was Liège and the river there, and the bridges across the Rhine. They were to bomb these particular bridges. We were sitting up there, looking at the sky and [at] them too, and pretty soon it got down to the point where I said, 'You know, you're getting awfully close to your target. It's just ahead of you to the left.' No answer. Then, finally, someone in the formation said, 'We know where we're goin.' And they flew by their IP [Initial Point in bombing run to target]. Well, with no IP, they don't know how to bomb... so they go all the way around and all this time, with flak all over the place. They go all the way back out to Brussels and they turn south again... got on course again to hit the IP to make another run. This time they got up to the IP and then turned (I guess they thought they didn't see the right bridge). I thought, 'Jesus, they've got it this time'...

Left above: The briefing room of the 353rd Fighter Group at Raydon, Suffolk, England in World War II. Left below: Lieutenant Harold Konantz, brother of Major Walter Konantz, both World War II pilots with the 55th fighter Group at Wormingford, Essex, England. Harold arrived at Wormingford as a replacement pilot in March 1945 and took over *Saturday Night*, the P-51 Mustang of his elder brother, who had just completed his own operational tour of duty. Harold was shot down by "friendly fire" from a B-17 that he was escorting on a bombing raid over Germany on 7th April 1945. He then became a prisoner-of-war.

When Major-General Jimmy Doolittle arrived at High Wycombe to take over as commander of the Eighth Air Force early in 1944, he noticed a sign on the wall of his office, which had been occupied by the man he was replacing, General Ira Eaker. The sign read: THE JOB OF THE FIGHTERS IS TO PROTECT THE BOMBERS. Doolittle ordered that the sign be taken down and replaced with one which read: THE JOB OF THE FIGHTERS IS TO DESTROY ENEMY FIGHTERS. For the rest of the war, however, he made certain that the bomber formations of the Eighth Air Force were always well protected by their little friends.

Right: Shipboard and ground-based jet aircraft directors and handlers during the Gulf War in 1991. Their jobs were difficult and demanding, preparing and directing aircraft like F-14 Tomcats for strike escort missions in which they accompanied bombers, usually A-10A Fairchild Thunderbolt IIs on attacks deep into Iraq.

MARSHALL ISLANDS

Me 262A-1a Schwalbe

MARSHALL ISLANDS

F9F-2 Panther

MARSHALL ISLANDS

F-86 Sabre

and they flew right past it... and all the way out to Brussels again and in again. And this time I said, 'I don't know what your problem is, but if you'll just continue on that course for three minutes or so, turn left and there are the bridges.' And the guy says, 'Stop trying to talk us into the target.' And I said, 'It's your target, dammit.' And they missed it again. They go all the way back out and this time, on the way to Brussels, I said, 'I'm real sorry, but I've got fifty-two guys here and we don't have enough fuel for you to do this again, 'cause if you do it one more time and then we're jumped at that point, we ain't gonna get home. So, I suggest you figure out something else 'cause we're leaving you when we get to the coast.' And they said, 'Well, we're on our way home anyway.' And they went out over the coast ten or fifteen miles off of Brussels... and all of them jettisoned their bombs and went on home."

"Escorting our bomber formations always seemed to be an evolving process, as we gradually learned what to do and what not to do. Initially, our leaders seemed to believe that the mere presence of fighter aircraft would deter enemy attackers. This was most certainly not the case. Our orders directed us to remain with the bomber stream and this was probably generated by the bomber pilots, who liked to see the fighters around them. However, it became apparent that just going along with the stream would not keep enemy aircraft away. Our group usually stationed one squadron in front and a squadron to either side of the lead box of bombers in a stream. We had to weave back and forth to remain slow enough to equal the bombers' speed. Often the Germans would assemble and then direct formations of fifty to over one hundred fighters against the lead box, and there was no way to divert this sort of attack. It was always necessary to seek out the enemy before he had an opportunity to assemble a large formation and then to attack to break up his

formations before they reached our bombers. It was also necessary to chase the enemy aircraft to keep them from reforming and making another attack. I have seen fifty-plus German fighters make an attack on the lead box of bombers by attacking from one o'clock level [and] passing through the bomber boxes while firing at aircraft in the bomber formation. On one occasion, I saw twelve B-17s shot down quickly from the lead box way before we could get into position to attack and ward off the Germans."
—Colonel Walker M. Mahurin, USAF (Ret), formerly with the 56th Fighter Group, 8 USAAF

Lieutenant Ray Mull had only twenty hours flying time in the P-51 when he was shot down over the German-occupied Netherlands on 9th September 1944. His squadron was the 343rd, of the 55th Fighter Group out of Wormingford, Essex, England. They had been returning late that morning from an escort mission when they were contacted by their controller. They were told that any Mustangs with ample fuel remaining were to turn back and head eastwards to look for enemy troops reported retreating from France. Mull's flight answered the call and, after twenty minutes of fruitless searching, turned west again for England.

The P-51s came under fire from a flak battery and Mull's fighter was hit. His cockpit quickly filled with coolant vapor and the engine lost power. He left the airplane and parachuted down among some small farms where he was promptly picked up by German Army personnel. There followed a rail journey to Oberursel, near Frankfurt, where he was questioned by Hanns Scharff, the well-known interrogator of Allied fighter pilots.

Mull was soon sent to Stalag Luft I at Barth near the Baltic Sea, where he finished the war as a guest of the Germans. The Barth prisoner-of-war camp was liberated on 1st May 1945 by the advancing Russian Army. After a few weeks of negotiation between the US Army Air Force and the Russians, it was finally agreed that American planes would be allowed to transport the prisoners from behind the Russian lines to Camp Lucky Strike, a US staging facility near Le Havre, and from there on to England.

Raydon Army Air Force Station 157 was located in Suffolk, near the eastern coast of England in 1944. The Ready Room bulletin board of the 351st Fighter Squadron, 353rd Fighter Group, showed Lieutenant Robert Strobell and his fellow pilots the names of those who would fly in combat each day. "If your name was not on the combat board, you could be sure that you would be assigned to other flying chores such as 'slow-timing' an airplane that had had a new engine installed, much like breaking in a new car engine. Or you might be assigned to a plane that was having turbo supercharger problems and a test flight had to be made to 30,000 feet to test the adjustment or repair. Or you might be asked to take a plane to the depot inland for major repairs, train a new replacement [pilot] on instruments, dive bombing, rat races, navigation, or simply test hop a plane that had been running rough before repairs or adjustments [had been done]. It was in the Ready Room that you got these assignments.

"The room was set up theatre-style facing a very large map of most of England, the English Channel and most of western Europe. I recall that the map was almost always covered when we entered the room for a briefing—I assume for security purposes. The map always had two coloured lines on it, one for the bombers and another colour for our route and support, showing where we would rendezvous with the bombers and stay with them, either going in or coming out, when the mission was to escort bombers. Whenever the mission lines showed deep penetration into Germany, you could hear some muttering and cussing among the pilots as soon as the curtain went up. Off to one side of the map there was a bulletin board with large letters and numbers on it, readable

"While sleeping in the Nissen [hut], you didn't have to be concerned about waking at a specific hour. You simply went to sleep knowing that an orderly would come through and wake you and tell you the time that you were due in the Ready Room. You jumped out of bed, hit the latrine, dressed, and walked to the Ready Room. There you would find your assignment for the day posted on the board. If it was a combat mission you would attend the briefing right after breakfast. Following the briefing, most of us hit the latrine again, some in panic and others out of necessity. Then you picked up your parachute and went outside where there was a personnel-type truck with a canvas cover and bench seats on each side to take you [and the other pilots] out to the revetments, dropping pilots at their airplanes as it proceeded around the perimeter of the field. There you would find your crew chief waiting. He had been alerted many hours before as to the time of the flight and which planes would be flying that day. This was done on the telephone, conference-style, to all squadrons, so that the orders for the day only had to be read once. The crew chief briefed you on the status of the plane, usually 'ready' for combat, and warned you about the minor glitches such as a tail wheel shimmy. Then he helped you climb up on the wing, don your parachute (some did this on the ground), and settle into the cockpit. He helped you with the shoulder harnesss and seat belt. If it was a combat mission, you usually sat in the airplane for a few minutes, or even a half hour, waiting for a signal to start your engine. Since you already knew what your position was in the flight, and on whose wing you were flying, you taxied out to the taxi strip in that position when your leader came by, and you would both take off, side by side, on each side of the runway. Then it was off into the wild blue, complete the mission, come home and taxi back to the same revetment. You would tell your crew chief what you did on that mission, and most

Above: A Thunderbolt of Hub Zemke's 56th Fighter Group, the Wolf Pack, on escort duty with an Eighth Air Force B-17 group in World War II. Despite their long-range belly fuel tanks, Thunderbolts did not have the range to accompany the bombers all the way to most of their targets, and back to England.

from the back of the room. This board had the time of take-off, the combat altitude that we would fly, the compass heading to rendezvous, the time that we would stay on escort with the bombers, and the compass heading for the return portion of the mission. We were briefed on the weather over the mission area and the forecast for the base upon our return, the bomber's mission, enemy movements if any, and sometimes a brief comment on what some of the other squadrons had done the day before. It was obvious that a lot of time and effort went into the planning and presentation of these briefings.

importantly, what the airplane did or did not do, and what needed to be repaired, or if you had any battle damage, bullet holes or flak hits... that is, if you knew about them... some pilots didn't know they had been hit. Then you hopped into a jeep or truck that took you back to the Ready Room. If you had fired your guns on the mission, the Intelligence Officer wanted to see you for a debriefing, particularly on enemy encounters, in which you had fired on an enemy aircraft in the air or on the ground. Then you were free to return to the Ready Room. The whole process, from beginning to end, took from four to as much as eight hours, depending on the length of the mission and the complexity of the operation. Back in the Ready Room you learned if you were scheduled to fly another mission, the second of the day. During my six months [at Raydon] I flew two combat missions in one day ten times."

Robert Strobell remembers again: "There were physical problems for some of the pilots. The most painful was the sinus block from head colds. No problem climbing up to altitude. But on the way back to base, over the Channel as you let down, if your sinuses blocked up it felt like someone hit you in the forehead with a sledgehammer. The only choice you had was to climb back up high enough to relieve the pain and start blowing and praying that it wouldn't block again on the way down. On one long flight into Germany, I had a hip joint pop out. Not particularly painful, and my flight leader wondered why I was flopping around in the formation. This was caused by the seat belt putting pressure on my hip on a long flight. So physical problems could add a measure of stress to combat flying.

"Most pilots were uncomfortable in the cockpit because of the dinghy that they had to sit on. There was no way to pack a one-man dinghy so it would make a comfortable seat. The heavy rubber dinghy was packed in a square and mounted as

the seat of the parachute pack. When you put on the parachute pack you had the dinghy next to your buns, with the parachute below it. It was far from [being] a cushion, and on a long flight it became almost unbearable. The dinghy was cussed by pilots, and you shifted and squirmed in the cockpit to relieve the butt numbness. The dinghy was appreciated only by those who went down in the sea. For everyone else, the discomfort added to the stress of flying.

"One might think that, with a year of training in navigation, cross-country flights, and weather studies, a replacement pilot would arrive at the squadron with confidence in his ability to fly over Europe in any kind of weather and find his way back to the base. Not so. Flying in heavy, solid, soggy weather was avoided in the States for safety reasons. I received more weather training from the 'old boys' after I got to the squadron than I did at any other station. You had to use your head in navigation, as well as your maps. Combining navigation and weather flying on the same flight demanded a bit of skill. Some pilots didn't have it, and it became a stressful situation for those who became separated from the squadron and had to make their own way home.

"On a number of combat missions time and distance became a matter of grave concern. Deep penetrations into Germany extended the P-47 to its maximum range. When you were in enemy territory and you knew you had reached the half-way point of the flight, you started to pray that you would not see or engage any enemy fighters. To do so meant opening up the throttle and burning off large amounts of gasoline rapidly in a dogfight, leaving you without enough fuel to make it back to England.

"Much to my disappointment, the majority of combat missions during my tour were uneventful, because enemy aircraft were seldom encountered. Bomber escort missions were dull, as were the area support flights in France during the invasion,

At year's end [1943] the P-51, a fighter pilot's dream, finally became available. This great machine actually made possible the successful prosecution of the air war that led to the ultimate victory of the Allies. Commonly called the Mustang, this single-engine fighter mounting six .50-caliber machine guns in the wings, and equipped with long-range droppable fuel tanks under each wing, was capable of escort work to any part of Germany. It was the Mustangs that took the heart out of Hermann Göring when he saw them shooting down his best fighter pilots over Berlin. The advent of the "51" made possible a system of escort that allowed continuous coverage of bomber formations from the Channel coast to the most distant targets in East Prussia and Poland. As the bomber formations proceeded along their route, the escort of fighters—first the P-47s, the the P-38s, and finally the P-51s—arose from their English bases in successive waves to intercept the bomber stream at designated points *en route* both to and from the target city. As the Germans came up to meet the invaders, great air battles were fought and famous American fighter aces earned their glory in the cold thin air over the Continent.
—Colonel Budd J. Peaslee, 8 USAAF

Right: A Spitfire at Booker,
Buckinghamshire, England.
Below: Mustangs of the 357th
Fighter Group from Leiston led
by Captain Harvey Mace in
Sweet Helen in World War II.

On 6th March 1944,
Hermann Göring looked
up in the sky over Berlin
and saw P-51 Mustangs
escorting the American
bombers and said, "The
war is lost."

although I did get two air victories during this period. Combat flying is a lot of hard work, and there is certainly a stress factor.

"There is no sight more spectacular and impressive than the sun [shining] on the condensation trails of hundreds of fighters and bombers cross-hatching the sky. The bombers fly in a straight line for the most part, while the fighters hover over them, looping back and forth to stay with them at their slower speed. At altitude, 25,000 feet or more, these contrails may stretch clear across the Channel into Europe. It is a beautiful phenomenon, so large and changing each minute in shade and design... brilliant in the setting sun.

"Another thrilling sight, and sound, was that moment when all the group's Thunderbolts assembled on the taxi strip awaiting take-off. Each is cocked off the strip at a 45-degree angle. The engines are run up to 1900 rpm, the magnetos checked, and the planes are shuddering with power. The roar of the engines fills the air, the cockpit canopies are open and you feel the vibrations... all that power in check and waiting to be released for the mission. It was an awesome sight and sound... a memorable moment when we were filled with anticipation and excitement, looking forward to the adventures of the day."

Carroll 'Red' McColpin knew that Morlaix, a big mission, was coming up. "...But I'd been ordered to transfer to the USAAF. *Ordered.* I kept delaying it week after week. We were down at Biggin Hill, but 133 was being moved up to Great Sampford, near Debden. The mission was being laid on... then off... then on again. I decided I wouldn't go and leave the outfit until the mission was over with. I was gonna lead that mission. Then, General 'Monk' Hunter called up from Fighter Command Headquarters of the Eighth Air Force and said, 'I understand you haven't transferred,' and I said, 'Yes sir.' He just said, 'Well, you get your butt in

there and transfer, right now!' To which I came back, 'Sir, I'm waiting for this Morlaix mission and I'm trying to keep enough boys in here to run it, 'cause it's a big one.' 'To heck with that... you get in there and transfer,' Hunter replied. 'Well, sir,' I said, 'you understand that I'm in the Royal Air Force, sir, and I have an ops instruction here which says we are going to Morlaix when they lay it on. I'm the CO here, and I've got my squadron on the line.' With that he snorted and hung up. About an hour later I got a call from an air marshal in the group. 'McColpin, do you take orders from me?' I said, 'I certainly do, sir.' That's how I came to transfer over."

The Morlaix raid, when it came, was a disaster, and proved a sad way for the Eagle Squadrons to bow out of the RAF. Gordon Brettell, a British pilot, was placed in command of 133 Squadron, and led the mission on 26th September 1942 in Red McColpin's place.

The Morlaix raid required the Eagles to escort American B-17 bombers hitting the Brest Peninsula, flying out across the widest part of the Channel, over a heavily defended area, and back again. By this time 133 Squadron was at Great Sampford in Essex, waiting to be absorbed into the USAAF... but still was to fly the mission. The unit was sent to Bolt Head, a forward base located between Dartmouth and Plymouth in Devon. Here its pilots were to refuel, be briefed for the mission, and join the other two squadrons flying it, 401 and 412 (Canadian). On the flight down to Bolt Head, the weather was bad and getting worse, threatening the impending mission.

Without McColpin's discipline, the pilots of 133 Squadron were over casual in preparing for Morlaix. Most did not bother to attend the briefing. Only Brettell and one other pilot were briefed for the raid. In it the Met officer gave a tragically erroneous piece of information—a predicted 35-knot headwind at the mission height of 28,000 feet. Further, no one knew precisely

Overleaf: An oil refinery near Hamburg under attack by bombers of the 8 USAAF during World War II. While the bombing accuracy and results achieved by the crews of Eighth Bomber Command were often spectacular, so too were their losses, which were reduced significantly with the arrival in early 1944 of the long-range P-51 Mustang on the US fighter squadrons in England. Their great range, coupled with their many performance advantages, provided US bomber crews the cover they desperately needed on their deep-penetration raids to targets in Germany and greatly improved their chances of returning safely to their English bases and surviving their tours of duty.

15th March 1944
Dear Sis Eleanor,

To give you an idea of what nice living quarters we have I'll just describe my room. I have a room to myself which I like. I like privacy occasionally—for instance I can write a much better letter when there is no one around to bother me. About my room—I have a very comfortable bed with a thick mattress and sheets, etc. I have a dresser with a large mirror and plenty of drawers. I also have a wall closet with more room than necessary for my clothes. I have a nice writing desk and a wash basin with a mirror above it also. The room has steam heat and carpeting on the floor. Just across the hall is a complete bathroom. A civilian caretaker, called a "batman" comes in and keeps the place clean. He gently wakes us up in the morning and shines our shoes, makes the bed up, etc. This applies only to officers' quarters of course but the enlisted men have nice brick barracks to live in which is a heck of a lot better than the "Nissen huts" and tents that most of our men over here have to live in. Outside of the fact that we are in combat, to say that we have it nice would be putting it mildly.

You know it seems as if I've been getting the "breaks" ever since I got in the army. With God's help let's hope I still keep getting them!
Love,
Donald

when the bombers were to take off, or their precise rendezvous time with the fighters. The pilots lounged under the wings of their Spitfires and waited. McColpin's key word—planning— certainly did not apply. The take-off was a mess. There were near-collisions; pilots did not get proper instructions about radio channels; some even left maps and escape kits behind.

Flying with auxiliary fuel tanks, thirty-six Spitfires headed out to meet the bombers. There was no sign of them, and the fighters continued on course and called by radio for news of the big friends. The predicted 35-knot headwind had been a major miscalculation. Both bombers and fighters—miles apart—were being whisked along by a 100-knot tailwind. One of the pilots later commented: "It all added up to a streaking catastrophe." Miles ahead of the fighters, the bombers had unknowingly crossed the Bay of Biscay above a blanket of cloud and, on reaching the Pyrenees, discovered their problem, dumped their bombs and swung back to the north on a reciprocal course, meeting the Spitfires head-on. The fighters turned north as well. By this time, all the aircraft had vanished from the radar plots in England, and communications between bombers, fighters and their various bases was a shambles. Having been airborne for two hours and fifteen minutes, the Spitfire pilots believed they were near home again and began to let down through the cloud cover. A coastline appeared which they assumed to be England. It was, in fact, the French coast, and they passed over Brest harbour and through a massive flak barrage. In moments, ten Spitfires were lost, four pilots killed, and six downed and captured, among them the CO, Gordon Brettell. Two other Spitfires failed to return to Bolt Head. Morlaix was a most unfortunate final mission for the Eagles.

"On 13th October 1944, we were on escort duty with the air group dive bombers and torpedo bombers. One of the targets was a dam up in the mountains south of Taipeh, the capital of Formosa. Our division drew the assignment to escort the photo-reconnaissance plane that was to take pictures of the strike damage on the dam.

"The squadron's photo pilot was a colourful little guy named John Hutto. The standing joke was 'Photo by Hutto'. Hut always seemed to be in a state of wide-eyed amazement. Everyone loved the guy because he had a way of turning the most common-place thing into a dramatic event. His photo plane was equipped with several aerial cameras, but it carried the standard Hellcat armament as well.

"Before we left the ready room to go on this flight Hut came up to Bill Masoner, our division leader, and said, 'Mase, all the guys in your division have shot down some airplanes and I don't have any. So, if we see anything today, how about letting me get it?' Mase was very democratic and quickly agreed to the deal. He looked directly into the eyes of the other three members of his division to make sure we understood. We all nodded.

"The strike went off as planned and Hut got his pictures of the damage. We were heading back to the ship when we spotted a twin-engine Betty bomber about 3 to 4000 feet below us at a distance of about two miles. Mase picked up the mike and said, 'He's all yours, Hut. Go get him.'

"Hutto lined up and made a classic high side run on the unsuspecting bomber. As he came into firing range he let loose a long burst which set the port engine of the Betty on fire. The bomber nosed down and started into a spiral towards the ground, leaving a heavy trail of black smoke. Hut pulled up and banked over to keep an eye on the stricken bomber. Suddenly Hut came on the air with a frantic call, 'Mase, Mase, get him, he's climbing.' There was a long pause, then Mase drawled, 'Roll over Hut, you're on your back.' "
—Commander William E. Copeland, USN (Ret), formerly with VF-19

IDENTICAL TWIN BOYS were born in Canada on 28th May 1922 to Marie and Earl Warren of Nanton, Alberta. The twins, Bruce and Douglas, grew up on their parents' grain farm and had already started their first year of school in 1928 when their father decided to go into mixed farming and moved the family to Wetaskiwin, about half way between Red Deer and Edmonton.

As they grew, the boys became interested in flying and enjoyed reading *Flight* and *Aeroplane*, the pre-eminent aviation magazines of the day, in the local library. In 1938, when they were sixteen years old the family moved to a new farm some 18 miles west of Ponoka on the Battle River. In early September 1939, when conflict broke out in Europe and Canada declared war against Germany, the twins decided to join the Air Force. They had to wait until the following May, when they turned eighteen, to enlist, and their distressed parents were very much against their decision. Their father, an unswerving isolationist, was often heard to say, "Let them fight amongst themselves, don't send our men to be killed over there." In March 1940, they received their notice to report to Edmonton for a medical exam. When they showed the message to their father, his by now usual comment was: "We shouldn't be sending our young men overseas; let the Europeans fight their own wars."

The twins passed their medical, were sworn in to His Majesty's Royal Canadian Air Force and given service numbers R93529 (Douglas) and R93530 (Bruce), as well as train and meal tickets and instructions to be on the eastbound train departing Edmonton that evening.

Following six weeks of preliminary training at the No. 2 Manning Pool, Brandon, the Warrens were sent to Mossbank, Saskatchewan... to do guard duty. It was there that they first flew, cadging rides in an obsolete Fairey Battle during test hops. In June 1941, they were posted to Initial Training School [ITS]at Regina in western Canada, where they underwent sessions in the theory of flight, navigation, radio, engines and, briefly, the Link trainer, as well as mathematics, science and Morse code.

The twins enjoyed their time at ITS and, through a constant flow of letters, kept their parents informed of such vital facts about their training experience as "a brick of ice cream here costs 17 cents". They wrote often to their mother and father. "We felt by writing frequently and assuring them that we were in good health and happy it would lessen their anxiety."

At Regina the boys' pay was very low, and some of the men training there were always short of cash. Bruce Warren decided to augment his income by pressing clothes for his fellow trainees, and received 10 cents for doing trousers and 25 cents for tunics. The better-off men were those whose families sent them additional funds, or whose previous employers were making up the difference between their service pay and what they had earned as civilians.

RCAF aircrew selection in those days was made at ITS. Most of the men, of course, wanted to be pilots, but other aircrew were needed too, including wireless operators, observers and air gunners, and, in time, navigators, bomb aimers and flight engineers. Selection depended heavily on the subjective opinions of the training staff, as well as exam results, and the particular needs of the training schools. However, they did try to accomodate the wishes of the trainees as much as possible. Happily for the Warren twins, they were both selected for pilot training at No. 5 Elementary Flying Training School, High River, Alberta.

As Douglas recollects, "Now we were allowed to wear the coveted 'white flash' or 'wedgie' in our service caps, indicating that we were under training for aircrew duties in the RCAF. We were also promoted to the rank of Leading Aircraftman or LAC, increasing our daily pay to $1.50 plus 75 cents flying pay. We were rich!

"We were to receive fifty hours flying time in forty-nine days. I began flying at High River on 18th July with my assigned instructor, a small, dark-complexioned American from Los Angeles named Dusenbury who got a surprise when he learned that he was to instruct Warren, B. and Warren, D. He just couldn't tell us apart, and he was never able to tell us apart all the time we were at High River.

"For most of our young lives we had had this overpowering wish to fly. Now we were on the way and we were terribly enthusiastic, about the thrill of flying... actually learning to handle the controls, and becoming confident that we would qualify as pilots.

"The routine at High River was half the day at ground school, and the other half flying. The Tiger Moth aircraft was one of the basic training aircraft of the British Commonwealth Air Training Plan (BCATP). The Moth had a top speed of 110 mph and the RCAF had an inventory of more than 1500 of them. High River is located in an area of strong winds, and often these winds, at ground level or a few hundred feet up, would exceed the stalling speed of the Tiger Moth. Occasionally an aircraft would appear in the circuit and, when flying directly into the wind, would stay in one spot relative to the ground if the pilot adjusted the power to give an airspeed equal to the windspeed. Another problem, in summer, was severe turbulence encountered as a result of surface heating at mid-day. Consequently, flying was scheduled in the early morning and would sometimes be shut down for a few hours during the most turbulent time of the day. Sudden thunderstorms or hail were also a menace—the latter particularly so, for the Tiger Moth wings and part of the fuselage were fabric-covered and hail stones could do a lot of damage. If a hailstorm was thought to be likely, all aircraft on the ground were pushed into the hangar. Those in the air would stay away till the storm passed, or divert to

Left: A tattered windsock on the airfield at Kirton-in-Lindsay, Lincolnshire, England. Above: Mr and Mrs Earl Warren, parents of the twins, Bruce and Douglas.

"Don't you ever cry, don't ever shed a tear. / Don't you ever cry after I'm gone." There seemed nothing melancholy in those lilting words and the catchy little tune seemed suited to our mood. Some of us would die within the next few days. That was inevitable. But you did not believe it would be you. Death was always present, and we knew it for what it was. If we had to die we would be alone, smashed to pieces, burnt alive, or drowned. Some strange protecting veil kept the nightmare thought from our minds, as it did the loss of our friends. Their disappearance struck us as less a solid blow than a dark shadow which chilled our hearts and passed on. We seemed already to be living in another world, separate and exalted, where the gulf between life and death had closed and was no longer forbidding.
—Group-Captain Peter Townsend, formerly with Nos. 43 and 85 Squadrons, RAF

another base. The decision to divert would have to be made by the pilot, as there were no radios fitted to the Tiger Moths. Indeed, there was no electrical communication between student and instructor. Gosport tubes had been fitted. This was a simple system developed at Gosport aerodrome, England, in World War I. It consisted of tubes, rather like a garden hose, between the cockpits and stethoscope-like fittings plugged into it. There were earpieces on one's head so that the student could hear the instructor's shouts. Most of the conversation was instructor to student, and only infrequently student to instructor.

"Parachutes were carried on all flights, and we students were told they cost $450 each, and that if we carelessly damaged one we would be charged.

"Dusenbury tried to keep all his students at about the same level, and at the end of the week of 27th July my twin and I had each flown about seven and a half hours and our instructor was satisfied with our progress. We knew that if the weather remained good we would most likely be sent solo the following week. Being sent solo is a 'high point' in every pilot's life, and the occasion is never forgotten"...

At the end of August, the Warrens' training at High River was finished. Bruce logged a total flying time of 60:55 hours and Douglas a total of 57:45 hours. They were posted to No. 34 Service Training Flying School at Medicine Hat.

As they approached the start of flying training at Medicine Hat, the twins were thrilled to learn that they were to be taught to fly the North American Harvard. Those who were trained on the Harvard generally went on to fly fighters, which was the dream of the Warrens, even though it meant yet another new ground school course. The Harvard was an excellent advanced trainer with a top speed of 212 mph and was a handful for most trainees. It was said that, if you could fly a Harvard, you could fly anything.

"We were allotted to Flying Officer Cherrington,

a taciturn RAF officer who was bitter about being selected to instruct in Canada rather than remaining in the UK on operations. He seemed to discourage any conversation other than the strictly necessary. When Cherrington realized that we were twins, and identical twins looking very much alike, there was some discussion as to whether we should be 'split up' and one of us sent to another instructor. In the end, we were both kept as students of Cherrington, and, as it was customary to use only the last name, he called my twin 'Warren Mark I' and I was 'Warren Mark II'.

"It was quite a big step to go from the relatively light Tiger Moth to the Harvard, which weighed three times as much, with about four times the horsepower and twice the speed. The cockpit was big and roomy, compared with the Moth, and a decided change was having the instructor behind you rather than in front. The centre of gravity in the Moth was such that if flown solo, it was flown from the back seat. To get the students used to this, we always flew in the back cockpit, dual or solo.

"Our new instructor had a habit which we found most annoying. Later on, when we ourselves were experienced and took an instructors' course, we discovered that it was a dangerous habit as well. At times, if Cherrington became impatient with what the student was doing, he would grab the control column and thrash it about hitting one's knees. Since the importance of transferring control of the aircraft by the words 'You have control' and the response 'I have control' had been drilled into us, when Cherrington did this we were never sure who had control at the moment. Sometimes control would be transferred in the normal manner, but other days it was seldom done in the approved way. Much later, when overseas, we met one of the RAF officers who had instructed at Medicine Hat. When we brought up the subject of Cherrington and his habits, we were told that not only was he bitter about the task of instructing, but he also was suffering from a severe stomach ulcer. This made us feel sorry for him, but he had caused us some worrisome moments.

"On 16th December, after a check ride with the Flight Commander, we were put up for our wings test with the Chief Flying Instructor. We qualified for our pilots' wings, and on the evening of the 18th there was a party in the airmen's mess. Our instructor, Flying-Officer Cherrington, approached us during the evening and told us we had both received an above average mark on our Wings test. He congratulated us and then said: 'I have a question: why do you both have the same nickname?' This went back to our schooldays when we had a teacher who explained to the class that we were duplicates of each other. The other youngsters began calling us 'Dupes' and, not caring for this rather unflattering nickname, we changed it to Duke, and it stuck." Bruce was Duke Mark I and Douglas was Duke Mark II.

"On 19th December our Wings Parade was held. Coupled with the joy of graduating as pilots, there was some 'bad news.'" Of the thirty-seven graduates in their class, Bruce stood eighth and Douglas ninth. The first eight students were granted commissions, so Bruce became Pilot Officer Warren and Douglas became Sergeant Warren. "We were ordered to report to Halifax on 5th January 1942 for embarkation and decided to see what could be done to reverse the decision, which would cause us to be split up. We went to RCAF Headquarters at Calgary and, not knowing the administrative organization, asked to see the padre. The gist of our argument was that our academic marks and the results of our flying tests were remarkably close, and that the arbitrary 'cut-off' would not have resulted in this problem had we not been twins. Furthermore, we argued, if it was not possible to rectify the situation by granting me a commission, we would be satisfied if the RCAF would cancel my brother's appointment and make him a sergeant. The padre

listened intently and was sympathetic. He told us that there was an army regulation that allowed an older brother to 'claim' a younger brother, and asked us who was the older. We had never really thought about it, but my brother quickly said he was the older, and if necessary would claim me. This meant that we would have to be together and would not be divided by his commission. The padre made several phone calls and we then were granted a series of interviews, the final one being with a group-captain who assured us that our case would be looked at closely and, if our air and ground marks were as close as we stated, very sympathetic consideration would be given to commissioning me. But nothing could be done until our records arrived and by then we would probably be on our way to Halifax. We left feeling confident.

"From our first awareness of the world around us, there always existed an 'us and them' feeling... the special feeling that identical twins have for each other. My twin was always of paramount importance in my life, and others were secondary. I know that he felt the same.

"We arrived at Halifax and here started the physical separation of my brother and me, for he was allocated a room in the officers' quarters and I in the NCOs' quarters. On 8th January, we marched to the ship and in a few hours were bound for England."

The Warrens were sent to Bournemouth, a resort town on the south coast where, as arriving air crew from overseas, they were to be held until assigned to an Advanced Flying Unit (AFU) or an Operational Training Unit (OTU). There they had a lot of free time and spent much of it together. "We enjoyed Bournemouth but we were impatient 'to get on with the job'. In mid-February, some postings came in for men who had arrived about the same time we had. My commission had not yet been decided, but we were told that the details of our training had been forwarded to

Ottawa and that it looked favourable for us. Bruce and I discussed what our best course of action would be if we were split up. We knew that it was not likely that we would be on the same draft for further training at an Advanced Flying Unit or Operational Training Unit. There the training was on higher performance aircraft and one also became familiar with flying conditions in England. The often cloudy weather, frequent fog and the numerous railways going in all directions, could easily confuse a young pilot for the first few hours.

"We decided to make no effort to go to the same AFU, but would, of course, be happy if we were sent together. However, when we finished our OTU, we would see what squadrons we were sent to, and then 'decide who was the oldest' and which of us would 'claim' his younger brother. My brother was sent to No. 8 AFU at Hullavington in Wiltshire, and I to a unit at Hastings, Sussex. Then, about three weeks after I arrived in Hastings, a message came through that I had been granted a commission dated from 19th December 1941. This gave me the same seniority as Bruce. I was ordered to report back to Bournemouth. Time went slowly as I waited for a posting to an AFU. I was concerned that my brother would get so far ahead of me in training that we might be separated for that reason. This was really the first time in our lives that we had been apart for more than a few days. I missed him and frequently thought of him, but not in a manner which would be called 'worrying about him'. I was always confident that he was OK and I know he felt the same about me.

"Eventually, I was posted to No. 17 AFU at Watton, Norfolk, where, having not flown for nearly four months, I was given one and a half hours instruction on a Miles Master Mk II and sent solo. I enjoyed flying at Watton AFU, a necessary step before going on to an Operational Training Unit where I would be flying either Hurricanes or Spitfires. In the meantime, I was learning about flying in English conditions—reduced visibility, instrument flying and map reading, which often presented problems with so much detail and so many railway tracks, as compared with flying in Alberta. I left Watton having flown a little over seventeen hours in the Master aircraft. My posting was to No. 57 OTU, a Spitfire outfit at Hawarden, Cheshire. I was very pleased with my good fortune. In April, my twin had been posted to No. 52 OTU, also a Spitfire unit, at Aston Down, Gloucestershire. Our luck held. We were both training to be operational on the same type of aircraft.

"Toward the middle of June, Duke (we both called each other Duke) phoned to say how pleased he was with the squadron he had been posted to—No. 165 RAF at Heathfield, near Ayr in Scotland. He said that his Flight Commander, Squadron-Leader Archie Winskill, had promised to try to arrange with Fighter Command personnel that I be posted there.

"The course finished and my posting came in—to No. 403 (RCAF) Squadron at Digby in Lincolnshire. I left for my new squadron with mixed feelings, glad to be going operational but sorry it was not north to Scotland. My new Squadron commander at Digby was Squadron-Leader Al Deere, a renowned Battle of Britain pilot who had bailed out so many times, he was nicknamed 'the man with nine lives'. A New Zealander who had joined the RAF, he was an exceptional leader and was highly respected by all fighter pilots in England. He was rather a quiet man, whose sense of humour showed through a small smile. I liked him immediately. But my stay at Digby was very short. In two days, a message arrived changing my posting from 403 Squadron to 165 RAF at Heathfield. Squadron-Leader Winskill had carried through his promise to try to get me sent to his squadron and, of course, I was delighted. I had not mentioned my desire to join 165 Squadron to Squadron-Leader Deere, but when I happened to meet him just before my departure I explained why I was so pleased about the change. He said very little, but seemed quite understanding, and wished me luck.

Among certain pilots in the Royal Air Force during and after the Battle of Britain, it was trendy to wear a German life jacket instead of the standard RAF issue type. It was an affectation that sometimes proved unwise for, unlike the British Mae West, which was kapok-filled and automatically held a pilot up in the sea, the German model had to be blown up manually; not an option if one happened to be unconscious.

Left above: The rear cockpit of a DeHavilland DH-82 Tiger Moth, the aircraft used by the Warren twins for their basic flying instruction at the Elementary Flying Training School, High River, Alberta, Canada. Left below: The Warrens in front of a Tiger Moth during their flying training in World War II. In addition to their training role, Tiger Moths were used during the War by the RAF in so-called "Scarecrow" patrols to frighten German submarines. The planes were unarmed.

I stuck my toothbrush in my left breast pocket, took my sponge bag, and made for the bathroom. The Duke of Kent, brother of the King, was expected at 10 a.m. Halfway to the bathroom, the alarm went. No. 85 Squadron, scramble! A few minutes later I was climbing away from Croydon at the head of six Hurricanes. "One hundred plus" from Fliegerkorps II were heading for Dover. By the time we arrived they were on their way home. Sergeant Sam Allard, our finest pilot, sent a stray Me 109 into the sea. Back at Croydon, Tim Maloney—Adjutant of 85, its friend, father, and managing director—told me to hurry. The Duke was waiting. "Get the pilots lined up, he wants to meet them," Tim told me. "Flight-Lieutenant Hamilton from Canada," I introduced Hammy, who to my consternation seemed to be squinting at me and doing his best not to laugh. I retreated a pace and glanced down the front of my tunic. On my left breast, beside my wings and a solitary DFC ribbon, a gleaming white toothbrush stuck out of my pocket. I had taken it into battle with me. The Duke refrained from comment.
—Group-Captain Peter Townsend, formerly with Nos. 43 and 85 Squadrons, RAF

"On my arrival at Heathfield I was sent to the officers' quarters where I was shown Duke's room and I stowed my kit. Duke knew I was coming, but no exact time had been given; nor was it possible to do so with train travel the way it was then. For that reason he was carrying on a normal day of duty, and was down on the flight line. It was a great thrill for both of us when I arrived at 'A' Flight to find him there, for this was the culmination of all our hopes of the past eighteen months, to be on a fighter squadron together, and, equally important, here we were... physically together again, a wonderful feeling which is hard to understand if you are not a twin.

"I was interviewed by Squadron Leader Winskill and expressed my gratitude for what he had done for us. I liked him at once, and not just because he had brought us together. He was the sort of officer everyone liked—a very handsome man, who we later found often had calls from the Windmill girls (of the famous London theatre). He never took himself too seriously and was an excellent leader. He told me that he was placing me in 'A' Flight along with Duke, and was confident that we would be a credit to the squadron.

"After a short time on the squadron, and after I had been assessed in the air, Duke and I became a more or less permanent section of two. This was the smallest fighting section of a squadron; a flight might be four aircraft, two sections of two, or sometimes six, three sections of two. Generally, the squadron put up twelve aircraft, in three flights... red, yellow and blue. Often it happened we flew as Yellow Three and Four. Duke was considered the more experienced since he had arrived first on the squadron, so he flew as Yellow Three and I as Four.

"In August there were rumours of a move south to 11 Group, Fighter Command, which covered the south-east portion of England. This was the area where most fighter operations took place at this time, and corresponded roughly to the area where the Battle of Britain had been fought two years before. In effect we were going into battle. One night Duke and I had a serious talk about the future and what it might bring. We knew casualties occurred among fighter pilots everywhere, but were far more likely to happen in the south where air-to-air fighting took place. We recognized that

200

one or both of us might be injured in a crash, wounded or killed, and reading the intelligence reports we recognized this was more than likely, or at least a 50-50 chance. We were not distressed by our conversation. Our main concern was the likely reaction of our parents. We were well aware of our parents strong reaction against our joining up because of the potential danger. Even before leaving Canada we had witnessed the reaction of parents and families who had lost a member due to a flying accident or some other tragic event. We had a Christian belief that everything was in the hands of the Lord, and He would make the decisions. We agreed on one thing, and cautioned each other not to 'go crazy' if one of us should see the other shot down, or crash...and go against impossible odds in a fit of rage. Looking back now, perhaps we were being overconfident in our ability to maintain self-control under those circumstances, but luckily, we were never put to the test. Soon we flew south to Eastchurch to become part of 11 Group, Fighter Command, and the famous Biggin Hill wing.

"165 was considered a 'new squadron' in that it had not operated in the south before, and further training was thought to be needed. We did two training flights and a sweep toward Le Touquet on 17th and 18th August. Pilots taking part in the combined Dieppe operation on the 19th knew it was a 'big show'. Only later did we learn how big it was. The RAF had flown almost 3000 sorties, the Luftwaffe 945. At the time, it was thought losses were about equal, 100 aircraft on each side, but it was later found that the Germans had only lost fifty, whereas the Allies lost 106.

"Shortly after Dieppe, the squadron left Eastchurch and relocated to Gravesend, where the officers were quartered in a beautiful old English home, Cobham Hall. Just prior to coming south, our CO, Squadron-Leader Winskill, was posted and his replacement was Squadron-Leader Jim Hallowes, an older man who had been a pre-

war Sergeant Pilot and was a 'Halton Brat' (a person who had joined the RAF as a boy apprentice and been sent to Halton for technical training). Squadron-Leader Hallowes had distinguished himself flying at Dunkirk and in the Battle of Britain. He was rather more reserved than Squadron-Leader Winskill, but was respected by everyone, and we had great confidence in him as our leader.

"The squadron took part in many sweeps over France. Sometimes we escorted bombers, Blenheims, Venturas, or Bostons.

"Whenever possible, we went up to London. The train service was frequent and took about forty-five minutes to 'the Big Smoke', as it was called by some then. We went to museums, shows and cinemas. We didn't drink and seldom went to pubs unless we were with other pilots on some special occasion.

"Fighter Command had a policy of rotating squadrons through its various stations, and in early November 165 was moved down to Tangmere, near Chichester, on the south coast. We were sorry to leave Gravesend with its proximity to London and the friends we had made there, but Tangmere was a much better location for the winter, for it had permanent runways. It was also a famous fighter station that had played a prominent part in the Battle of Britain. At Tangmere we trained in night flying and during the period from mid-November 1942 to mid-February 1943, I flew sixteen night sorties and twenty-three operations, while Duke flew twelve night sorties and twenty ops. Most of these night sorties were in co-operation with searchlight practice. The searchlights would try to illuminate the aircraft as if they were enemy aircraft. When caught by a searchlight I would lower my seat, turn the cockpit lights as bright as I could, and fly instruments till the exercise was over."

For the Warrens at Tangmere, a combination of night and day flying continued until the last week of March, when the squadron was moved north

These treasured days will come and go / At swifter pace...but this I know...I have no fear...I have no dread / Of that marked day that lies ahead. / My flesh will turn to ash and clay But I'll be here... somehow... some way.
—*Somehow*
by Don Blanding

Katharine Brush for Cosmopolitan Magazine reported about Captain Sam Gevorkian, 338th Fighter Squadron, finding himself engaged in solitary battle with a whole flock of German fighters, who called happily over the radio to squadron mates flying high above him, "Hey fellows, come on down here! I've got ten Focke-Wulfs surrounded."
—from *Double Nickel–Double Trouble*
by R.M. Littlefield

Below: The RAF Tangmere station sign. Right above: The control tower at the former RAF Tangmere in Sussex, England. Right below: An RAF aircraft mechanic's World War II Air Ministry tool kit. The station sign and tool kit are in the collections of the Tangmere Military Aviation Museum.

A rumour was circulating in Britain during the summer of 1940 that RAF Biggin Hill had set up a dummy aerodrome complete with flare path etc., and the Germans had supposedly dropped a dummy plywood bomb on it with the word BANG! painted on it. In Germany, a story made the rounds then about a the Germans having built a dummy airfield that had been hit by a British dummy bomb.

again, this time to Peterhead near Aberdeen. "On a training flight a new Aussie pilot collided with Duke and chopped off part of his tail. Both pilots landed safely, the Aussie's aircraft with a much shorter prop. When he brought his parachute into the crew room, Duke was ready to really tear a strip off the Aussie. But the Aussie never came into the crew room. He was so embarrassed, ashamed and sorry for what he had done, he wouldn't leave his aircraft. It ended with Duke going out to tell him "Don't worry, it could happen to anyone."

No. 165 Squadron was moved again as the year advanced, to Exeter and then to Kenley, another famous Battle of Britain station and part of the Biggin Hill wing. Prior to this move, in August, Bruce Warren was assigned to, and completed, the Fighter Leaders' course for prospective Flight Commanders, at RAF Charmy Down near Bath in Somerset.

"Duke and I roomed together in the old pre-war officers' mess which was luxurious in comparison with other quarters we had been in. We had a nice room, and the ablutions were just down the hall. This gave rise to a funny situation which, at first, we didn't know about. A few days after the squadron arrived at Kenley, the station commander, a Group-Captain, came to the flight to meet the pilots. He was introduced and said how pleased he was to meet us, for he thought the squadron had a lunatic pilot. Each morning he would be in the washroom shaving, when a Canadian officer would come in, say 'Good Morning, sir,' wash and leave. A few minutes later the same man would return, say 'Good Morning, sir', wash and leave. He couldn't understand what was going on with this chap. The reason this was our morning drill was that we had only one electric razor between us, which we shared. Whoever shaved first went and washed up while the other one shaved and then washed up. Since the Group Captain didn't realize there was a set of identical

twins on the squadron, to him it was just a crazy pilot."

In mid-September, No. 165 moved again, this time to RAF Church Stanton near Taunton, Somerset. "Finally, our fervent wishes and prayers were answered. For sixteen months we had suffered under the Fw 190s while flying Spitfire Vs. Now we were issued Spitfire Mk IXs and what a wonderful change! The Mk IX maximum speed was 416 mph at 27,500 feet. It had a ceiling of 45,000 feet and a vastly superior rate of climb...at 22,000 feet and above, we had the edge on any German fighter at the time." Bruce Warren said of the change: "165 finally equipped. It's about time we got rid of these trash heaps." "One of the good things about the new aircraft was that all the instruments and controls were exactly the same as on the Spit V, so it was easy to feel at home in the cockpit. The big difference was the power, rate of climb, and the ceiling. We were often at 40,000 feet, and with no pressurization and no heat. So we were issued submariners' big wool sweaters and socks. Later we received electric bootees to keep our feet warm, but we found them prone to short circuits and burning if they were worn very long. When this happened the pilot had to struggle in the cockpit to pull the heating plug out."

In January 1944, after eighteen months of operational flying, the Warren twins were sent on a rest leave. At that point in the war, RCAF aircrew in England were given the option of taking leave in Canada but many declined the opportunity for a month at home for various reasons, not least the long, unpleasant sea journey. The Warrens chose not to return home because of the emotional trauma their mother and father had experienced when they had left for the war. They knew how upset their parents would be when the time came for them to return to England and decided not to tell their parents about their leave.

Once again the boys were posted, to No. 58 OTU at Grangemouth in Scotland, and Bruce left for their new station. Prior to the move, Douglas was sent to the Fighter Leaders' course at Aston Down. When he arrived at Grangemouth, Douglas was immediately moved to a satellite field called Balado Bridge where he lived in a cold and miserable Nissen hut in the Scottish winter. "The Nissen hut we lived in had a small pot-bellied coal stove which would have been OK except the coal was so poor in quality that to get it to burn we used to bring back a partly used oxygen bottle from the flight line and, with a bit of wood and paper and the oxygen, we could get a good basic fire going."

The twins were shuffled around some more as 1944 wore on, doing a stint in bomber affiliation work. In July, they were posted to No. 66 Squadron, which was part of 132 Royal Norwegian Wing RAF. In August, the squadron moved across the Channel to airfield B16 in France. "The Battle of Falaise stretched over several days as the Canadian and British armies fought down the road from Trun to Chambois. American forces were met on 21st August and the gap was closed. At this time our aircraft were armed with two 20mm cannon and two .5 Browning machine guns. They could be fired independently or all together. It was an armament that we especially liked because the pilot had an option as to what to use on various targets. Furthermore, if we did not carry drop tanks, we could put a 500 lb bomb under the fuselage and a 250 lb bomb under each wing.

"All accounts of the battle give great credit to the work of the fighter-bombers. Among these, the Typhoons played the major role. They were armed with four 20mm cannon, bombs and rockets, and were especially effective against the German tanks. We Spitfire pilots ensured air superiority as well as doing armed recce and fighter-bomber attacks. Losses were heavy, both in the Typhoon squadrons and the Spitfire squadrons doing fighter-bomber work. The flak was plentiful and accurate. By their nature low-level attacks are

203

Below: The Warrens with the 165 Squadron Spitfire *Duke II* at Gravesend, Kent, England in 1942. Douglas is on the left, Bruce on the right.

dangerous, and when a plane is hit low down there is very little time to bail out.

"We attacked horse-drawn transport along with staff cars and trucks. The German soldiers would hold the horses' bridles as the horses reared in fright and pain. Duke and I, having grown up on a farm with an intimate knowledge of horses, felt especially sorry for the animals because they could not understand what was happening to them.

"B16 was located near a small village, Villons les Buissons, and was what we called a 'tar paper strip'. This was a method of laying down a heavy, black, treated paper in an attempt to control the dust during take-off and landing. The dust was very damaging to the motors... Typhoons especially because of the sleeve valves in the 24-cylinder Napier Sabre engines. They experienced more engine failures, as the Merlin could eat dust better than the Sabre engine.

"Operations continued. The Germans had left pockets of men in Le Havre, Calais, Boulogne, Ostend and other places. Now the Canadian Army was fighting to get them out. We continued to support them with low-level attacks and bombing. We seldom saw a German fighter, as they were being held back to intercept bombers or defend against the British Army. What we were doing was dangerous, for all these places had lots of anti-aircraft guns, and the gunners had been practising with live targets since 1940 and were accurate. So we lost pilots all the while. One of the puzzles we thought about for some time was why pilots didn't bail out when they lost a wing. This was a fairly common occurrence. If the wing was hit by flak it would be seriously weakened and break off when the G forces built up in the pull out. The aircraft appeared to fall quite slowly, with seemingly gentle rotation. Following a number of these incidents, the medical officers found that when the wing broke off the initial rotation was so fast it flung the pilot's head sideways and broke his neck.

"On my 44th operational sortie I almost 'bought it'. The squadron had been detailed to bomb heavy artillery sites at Calais. We approached at about 15,000 feet and I trimmed for the dive. Then there was a loud explosion under the aircraft and sunlight came through a hole in the left side of the cockpit. An 88mm flak gun had exploded a shell just under my left wing—a piece passing through drove the trim wheel into my leg, carried on up bending my parachute D ring as it passed, and ended up in a small tin box in my upper left breast pocket. One might ask why a fighter pilot would be flying with a small tin box in his pocket. This was a special box used as part of an escape kit. If a person was shot down and trying to evade and hide from the enemy, it was difficult to get safe drinking water. In the small box was a large rubber balloon which you filled with water from a ditch or dirty pond. You popped in a tablet, shook it up well, and in fifteen minutes you could drink it. It tasted like water from a ditch, but all the bugs in it were killed. The fragment of shell had pierced the tin box deeply, but had the box not been there it would have pierced my body and perhaps my heart.

"Since I had been trimmed for the dive in level flight at normal speed, the aircraft was difficult, but not impossible, to control. Duke realized I had been hit, but he could tell I still had control, and so proceeded with the attack while I returned to base. I could smell something burning, but was not aware of where it was coming from, which was rather a worry. After landing I found the red-hot fragment had ignited the kapok in my Mae West and it was smouldering. I kept the fragment, D ring and tin box for souvenirs.

"In late fall, Paul Gibbs, who commanded B Flight, finished his tour and I took over as his replacement. This was a great occasion for Duke and me, now both flight commanders in the same squadron. Every senior officer we spoke to said that they had never known such a situation

William Henry 'Buster' Prout / Stopped some flak and, baling out, / Landed safe but somewhat shaken North of Schnitzel-unter-Laken.

With what courage he could muster / The aforesaid William 'Buster' Faced and even cracked a joke / With the untersucher bloke.

(In case you do not Sprechen Deutsch, / He's the guy whose soothing voice / Interrogates the P.O.W.— / Here's hoping that he'll never trouble you).

Well, anyway, our hero found / Himself with several such around. Good types, they seemed,— quite decent chaps, / Who gave him fags and lots of Schnaps.

They didn't seem to ask him much, / Just "How are all at home?" and such. Gin followed brandy, then came port. / Our Buster talked—without a thought.

He didn't tell 'em much, it's true /—Just all he knew. All this was noted in a file. (He'd underrated Jerry's guile.)

Results: Some things were added to / The store of stuff that Jerry knew. / And (Buster being such a duffer) *His* pals will be the ones to suffer.

205

before. Further, the fact that we were Canadians and identical twins at that level in the Royal Air Force was quite unique. It really went smoothly, for we had roomed with Paul Gibbs so we knew all the ins and outs of B Flight as well as A Flight. There were many in the squadron who didn't even try to tell us apart, because there was really no need. We were recognized by our rank and position and the pilots followed the orders that came down. One thing was not so good. We often flew separately with a small section, so that cut down on our operations together. However, on a squadron show we would both be flying.

On 22nd December 1944 the Wing moved to Woensdrecht, in the Netherlands. "The Germans had been pushed back, increasing the range to London for their V-weapons. Now most of these were targeted at Antwerp. We were now on the main flight path of the pilotless aircraft. The pulse jet made a Br-r-r-r noise as it went along, till the timer cut the motor and deflected the elevators. The weapon then dived steeply and exploded when it hit the ground. As long as the Br-r-r-r was heard, it could be ignored, but if the noise suddenly cut out, most people took shelter. All prudent people did. V-1s could be shot down by aircraft, and they were, both on the Continent and in the UK. The V-2 was a rocket and could only be destroyed by an aircraft if caught on the firing stand before launch. Some people, both service and civilian, found the V-1 attacks very trying, and some suffered nervous breakdowns. One of the more serious of these was a Norwegian military policeman who suddenly began shooting at anything that moved, including pilots on the ground."

In mid-December a signal arrived awarding the DFC to both Douglas and Bruce Warren. The citations read:

"Flight-Lieutenant Douglas Warren: Flight-Lieutenant Warren during two tours of operational duties has shown outstanding skill and courage. His determination to engage and destroy the enemy in the air and on the ground is worthy of high praise. He has completed numerous missions on heavily defended ground targets and enemy shipping. He has participated in the destruction by cannon fire of twenty enemy vehicles and the explosion of the magazine of a large enemy strong point. By accurate bombing he has destroyed one enemy aircraft and shared in the destruction of another. On another occasion his accurate bombing severed an important rail link in Germany."

"Flight-Lieutenant Bruce Warren: This officer has led his flight with such skill and determination in attacks on ground targets that more than twenty vehicles have been damaged and many probably destroyed. During his numerous sorties, he has destroyed two enemy fighters and participated in the destruction of a hostile bomber. His fine fighting spirit and zeal have set an excellent example to all."

In mid-February their commanding officer told the Warrens that he was trying to find replacements for them as they were nearly tour-expired, and that both No. 127 and No. 66 Squadrons were being sent to a practice gunnery camp at Fairwood Common in Wales. While there, Bruce and Douglas were taken off the squadron. On 13th February, both Warrens flew their final operational flights.

On 27th February, a farewell party for the two Dukes was given in the officers' mess. A great concession was made by the mess in allowing their squadron NCOs to attend. This was seldom done, and the twins were honoured by the way it was carried out. The Warrens regretted leaving the squadron, a close bond having developed among the men who had shared a common danger and had depended on each other for survival.

"A message arrived telling us that we were to attend an investiture at Buckingham Palace on

20th March. The reason we were selected to attend at the Palace was because we were doing nothing but waiting to go home. Men awarded the DFC and still flying operationally on a squadron were not sent to London for an investiture. Most often the award was presented at squadron level by a senior RAF officer. On the day of the investiture, when our turn came, Duke received his DFC from the King, and marched off. When I appeared before him, looking the same, with the same surname, the King looked rather bewildered and said: 'I don't think I have ever done anything like this before,' meaning awarding similar decorations to a pair of twins.

"On 14th April, we boarded the USS *Mount Vernon*, a converted passenger liner, for the trip home. The *Mount Vernon* arrived at Newport News, Virginia, on the 23rd, and on the night of the 25th we got on a train in Montreal for the trip west and our return home after three and a half years overseas. We arrived in Ponoka on Sunday the 28th, and went to our parents' farm. They were thrilled to see us, and our mother seemed quite hysterical. We knew it had been a terrible strain on them while we had been on operations overseas. They told us how especially worried they had been at the time of Dieppe when it was reported that some 100 Allied planes had been lost, and how relieved they were when they got mail from us after the Battle.

"Duke became engaged to Lois Burroughs, a beautiful and charming girl we had gone to school with. Duke had had an understanding with her while we were overseas. On 11th June, they were married. I was best man and had invited a special person for me, Melba Bennett from Edmonton, who would later become my wife."

The Warrens were determined to remain in the Royal Canadian Air Force and obtain permanent commissions. They steadfastly refused to take release from the service when ordered to do so. They were threatened with appointment as flying instructors, which in fact happened. Their new careers as instructors continued, along with a sprinkling of 'odd jobs' and assignments until, in October 1946, their persistence paid off and they were both granted commissions in the RCAF Permanent Force. They retained their rank and seniority.

In the immediate post-war years, Douglas's role in the Air Force included a posting as Chief Flying Instructor at the Sabre OTU at RCAF Chatham. Bruce left the service to become a test pilot with Avro in the early days of the CF-100 program. On 5th April 1951, he was killed in the crash of the second prototype.

Of the Warren twins, Hugh A. S. Johnston, who had been their squadron commander in both No. 165 and No. 66 Squadrons, wrote in his book *Tattered Battlements*: "They were of the same height to an eighth of an inch, the same weight to a couple of pounds, always dressed alike and, though different in characters, were as similar physically as two peas in a pod. Everything they did they did together, and everything they had they shared, even their bank balance was common to both. As pilots they had the right mixture of determination, discretion and dash to be successful and formidable. On the ground, while not overburdened with academic learning— indeed they often made heavy weather in the pronunciation of unfamiliar words—they both had vigorous, inquiring minds and little patience with tradition-bound methods or ways of thought. They had remained together throughout their careers in the service and liked to say that if only one of them had joined up they could have worked alternate weeks. They were typical of their trade in never taking exercise, but unusual in that they neither smoked nor drank; photography was their main preoccupation and delight. They represented the New World at its best. And each, with an impartiality and detachment which was sometimes puzzling, called the other 'Duke'. "

Far left: The Royal Air Force badge. Above: Douglas Warren in the uniform of the post-war Royal Canadian Air Force. He retired from the RCAF as a Wing-Commander.

RED STARS

IN MARCH 1943, Tamara Pamyatnikh and Raya Surnachevskaya, members of the all-female Soviet 586th Fighter Air Regiment, were assigned as duty fighters to patrol the airspace over Kastornaya. The rest of their air regiment had been scrambled to repel an air raid against Liski.

Large formations of German bombers had been sent to attack installations near the Kastornaya railway junction and the nearby bridge across the Don river. The other fighters of the regiment quickly destroyed two German bombers and dispersed the remainder. The fighters returned to their base to learn that Pamyatnikh and Surnachevskaya were long overdue. A search was launched and the wreckage of a Yak fighter was spotted. There was no sign of life near the wreck,

and no sign of the other missing fighter. The remaining members of the 586th were depressed at the apparent loss of two of their most experienced pilots.

Tamara Pamyatnikh describes their mission that spring day. "We were going toward the assigned grid square at an altitude of 4000 metres. I saw some black dots to the south-east. I thought they were birds. But no—they were flying too high and too evenly. I had orders to attack. I waggled my wings at Raya to say 'follow me' and flew towards them.

"The ground controller, Lieutenant Slovokhotova, heard me say, 'I see the enemy aircraft!' The written report by our squadron commander, Captain Agniya Polyantseva, states that Raya added, 'There are a lot of them!', and that our chief of staff,

Captain Aleksandra Makunina, ordered 'Attack!' But our communications soon broke down and we heard nothing. We knew we had orders to defend Kastornaya, where the trains were already loaded with troops and ammunition. We also knew that the rest of the regiment was fighting in another area. We were alone, but the sun was behind us, so we could surprise them. I saw one large group of enemy bombers and, farther back, another group of heavy bombers. [It is believed that there were at least forty-two Junkers Ju 88s and Dornier Do 215s in the German formations.]

"We had an opportunity to break up the formation with a surprise attack—they might think there were more of us if we flew down at them boldly. We had to try to prevent the bomb drop. So we both went into a steep dive and opened fire at the bombers flying in the centre of the group. We pulled up into a chandelle and saw two burning aircraft falling. The explosions went up from the ground. The bomber group scattered. Then we went towards the next group, which was approaching in tight formation.

"They were bristling with machine guns. We attacked from behind and from the sides. The enemy directed concentrated fire at us. I saw the machine guns and a gunner's head. I could even discern the features of his face. Suddenly, my aircraft shuddered and then sharply turned over and started falling. I tried to open the cockpit canopy, but a powerful force pressed me into the seat. I could not lift my arms, and the ground kept coming closer with each second. The canopy finally broke off with a crack; I undid my safety harness with difficulty, and got out. My right hand instinctively pulled the rip-cord ring. I felt the jolt from the opening parachute, and in an instant my feet touched the ground. My aircraft was burning beside me. My neck and face were bloody. I looked up at the sky. The enemy had turned and was going in a westerly direction with Raya still attacking. We had saved the station!

"Raya saw my airplane burning and falling. She told me that she was in despair at losing me and became so careless that she forgot all the air-combat rules and fired point-blank into the nearest Junkers. It went down abruptly, covered with black smoke... but so close that her plane was damaged [by explosion or debris] and she had to make a forced landing. She belly-landed the crippled plane, and a funny thing happened. People came running towards her armed with pitchforks, sticks and rifles, thinking she was the enemy. They were amazed when they saw Raya and her red star emblem.

"The regiment heard that we were safe the next day, and Captain Olga Yamshchikova came to get us. She flew us very low over our battle site and the station. The locomotives were busy pulling out the trains loaded with troops. It made us happy, although we were in pain.

"Our great leader, Marina Raskova, chose the most experienced pilots she could find. The first came from military units. It was very difficult for a woman to be a military pilot. One had to enter as ground personnel and work up. Very few did. There again, there were not many civilian pilots with enough experience. When Raskova was placed in command of the all-female 125th Air Group [actually an air corps consisting of the 586th, 587th and 588th regiments], we were sent to Engels, many kilometres south-west of Moscow, for training. We crammed a three-year course into a few months. The mechanics had to work in bad weather for long hours, the navigators studied all the time, and the pilots had to get 500 hours. We were equipped with Yak-1s, Yak-7Bs and Yak-9s. Operations started over Saratov, then to Stalingrad for the great battle from September to November 1942, and after that came the air battle over Kastornaya in early 1943. We had many other missions and covered important centres from east and west. We made about 5000 sorties, were in 125 air battles, damaged forty-two enemy planes and destroyed thirty-eight."

Far left above: Ekaterina Budanova. Far left below: Russian aces Lily Litvak, Ekaterina Budanova and Maria Kuznetsova. Below: Lily Litvak leaving the cockpit of her 586th Fighter Squadron Yak-1. Litvak was the highest-scoring Soviet woman ace with twelve confirmed victories. Budanova was second with eleven.

ASK ANY WORLD WAR II fighter pilot what the most dangerous part of the job was. Odds are he will say that it was ground attack and low-level strafing. The practice claimed hundreds of men who fell victim to the ever-increasing numbers of flak guns defending enemy concentrations, airfields, barges, trains and supply dumps. If he flew close to the ground in the combat zone too long, his chances of survival diminished to zero. To do this most dangerous job took guts and determination—essential attributes of the effective fighter pilot.

2nd Lieutenant William Laubner, who was born in Ludwigshafen, Germany, on 23rd November 1919, was flying a P-38J of the 55th Fighter Group on the first all-fighter sweep scheduled by the American Eighth Air Force on 15th April 1944. The 55th was attacking an airfield south-west of Berlin. His flight was supposed to provide top cover for the other P-38s of the group, but after a time his flight leader took the fighters down to 'join in the fun'. Lieutenant Laubner located and strafed a locomotive, some power lines and, finally, a Rhine dry dock surrounded by flak towers. His Lightning was hit, the left engine damaged, and the left fuel tank set ablaze. Laubner was able to crash-land the plane near a German anti-aircraft camp and was immediately captured. In the landing impact, his nose was broken when his head hit the gunsight. His knees were badly cut as he hastened to leave the burning aircraft, and his shoulder felt as if it had been hit by a hammer. He later discovered a right-angle tear in the left shoulder of his flight jacket and surmised that a round must have penetrated the armour plate behind his seat, piercing his parachute backpack and lacerating his jacket. His injuries were mainly minor and he did not require hospitalization.

Laubner understood enough German to realize that a heated rivalry was being played out before him by two German anti-aircraft officers, both of whom were trying to claim credit for having shot the American pilot down. One of the Germans commanded an 88mm gun crew and the other had charge of the flak towers. Soon a German major arrived to pick up the American prisoner and, as they left, the two German officers were still arguing intensely about which of them was going to claim the "victory".

At the Oberursel interrogation centre near Frankfurt, Lieutenant Laubner was interviewed by an interrogator who told Laubner more about the 55th Fighter Group than the lieutenant knew himself. The interrogator named the American's commanding officer, his base name and location, wing number, wing commander, their Red Cross girls' names, etc. Laubner was then transported to Stalag Luft III near Sagan in Silesia. There, he recalls: "We called them [the guards] ferrets. Since the barracks were built with a crawl space, the ferrets would crawl under them in order to pick up bits of information. They could speak and understand English. The floors had cracks between the flooring and when we heard them underneath we would get water, buckets and brooms to clean the floor. We could hear them scramble out and, of course, that tickled hell out of us. They could not chastise us because keeping our room clean was SOP [Standard Operating Procedure].

"I was not mistreated, because I was captured by the military. I did see some POWs that were man-handled by civilians before being turned over to the authorities. I also saw the Gestapo come into the camp and take out three POWs. We heard that their gun cameras showed they were shooting civilians and other non-military targets. We never saw them again."

In the winter of 1945, Laubner and the other prisoners were marched for three days to Spremburg, and in March they were made to walk to Moosburg. The treks by these exhausted, poorly clothed and under-nourished airmen took a deadly toll. Finally, on 29th April, General George Patton arrived to liberate the Moosburg camp. His tank

He is with me still.
The years have cast up and drifted out again; / And the memories, dried on the shore, / Have been bundled and stored / For this time, For this quiet time while I am alone.
—from *War Widow* by J.B. Warr

Left: A Thunderbolt pilot of the 56th Fighter Group at Boxted, Suffolk, England, photographed by Major Mark H. Brown, 3rd Air Division, 8 USAAF in World War II. In the first five months of 1945, Thunderbolts flying ground attack missions in the European Theater of Operations destroyed or damaged 9000 locomotives, 86,000 pieces of railway rolling stock, 68,000 trucks, 6000 armored vehicles and tanks and more than 50,000 horse-drawn vehicles. The big, sturdy P-47s took a lot of hits and absorbed punishment better than other Allied fighters operating in the ground attack mode, saving the lives of many US and British fighter pilots.

Slowly, gently, I close my
eyes and let out a deep
sigh...
bits of scenes from long
ago begin to come into
focus.

England, winter, flying low
through a snowstorm...
trying to find our field—
any field—fuel gauge
bouncing on empty.

Germany, winter, hiding
out in the cold woods,
walking by night...trying to
get back to friendly
territory.

Germany, spring,
marching all day and all
night too...
in a steady rain... / enemy
guards and dogs on each
side of our column miles
long.

Hearing the bombs
screaming down on us...
a wartime mistake...
ungodly loud explosions
all around— / dust, debris,
and bodies flying
everywhere / in the chaos...
the panic...of those few
minutes / which seemed
an eternity.

Burned indelibly in my
mind... forever.
—*Burned Indelibly*
by Bert McDowell, Junior

rammed through the front gate and he climbed
out and, standing there with his pearl-handled six-
gun, polished boots and helmet, asked, 'Did any
of these bastards mistreat you?' I believe he would
have shot them on the spot."

"The most dangerous job we flew in Hellcats was
strafing missions. We flew three strafing missions
to one bombing strike sweep and to four CAPs
[Combat Air Patrols over the fleet or around a
wide circle of the fleet]. The pilots we lost were
due to ground-fire. VF32, USS *Langley*, lost no
pilots in air-to-air combat."
—Commander Richard H. May, USNR (Ret),
formerly with VF32

Ten little fighter boys taking off in line/ One was in
coarse pitch, then there were nine. / Nine little
fighter boys climbing through the gate / One's
petrol wasn't on, then there were eight. / Eight
little fighter boys scrambling up to heaven / One
weaver didn't, then there were seven. / Seven little
fighter boys up to all the tricks / One had a
hangover, then there were six. / Six little fighter
boys milling over Hythe / One's pressure wasn't
up, then there were five. / Five little fighter boys
over France's shore / One flew reciprocal, then
there were four. / Four little fighter boys joining in
the spree / One's sight wasn't on, then there were
three. / Three little fighter boys high up in the
blue / One's rubber pipe was loose, then there
were two. / Two little fighter boys homing out of
sun / Flew straight and level, then there was one.
One little fighter boy happy to be home / Beat up
dispersal and then there were none. / Ten little
Spitfires nothing have achieved / AOC at Group is
very peeved. / 'Fifty thousand Smackers thrown
down the drains / 'Cause ten silly baskets didn't
use their brains.' "
—from *Tee Emm*, January 1942

Captain Alan J. Leahy, RN (Ret), a former Royal

Navy Flight Commander and Air Weapons
Instructor, suspects the tactical wisdom of some
fighter pilots in the ground attack role: "Quite
often, I believe, they [the pilots] were the victims
of their own poor tactics and their own weapons.
Wartime camera gun films often show low, flat
attacks with the pilot 'hosepiping' along a row of
targets, often up to a target. Very impressive, but it
is not the most effective way to hit a target. The
flat attack along a line target means that Nos. 2, 3
and 4 cannot attack at the same time for fear of
zapping their leader. If they leave a gap for him to
get clear, the opposition have time to fire at each
individual. Carrying out ground attack, an aircraft
can shoot itself down by flying through its own
weapon effect—in my opinion, all too common an
occurrence. Tactically, one heard too often how
repeat attacks were made on "juicy" targets.
Having wakened up the [enemy] gun crews, why
come straight back and let them have another
crack at shooting you down?"

"Thank God I was taught by the RAF the art of
flying on the deck. I was, perhaps, the only one in
No. 71 (Eagle) Squadron and later in the 4th
Fighter Group who had attended this RAF-Army
Co-operation college at Old Sarum near Salisbury.
It was there where I flew the P-40 and the P-51A,
the low-altitude model.

"While attending the Army Co-op (41 OTU) I was
taught the proper and only way to fly on the deck.
The RAF always believed that low flying was to be
conducted below tree-top level; below the height
of a two-storey building.

"First, I was taught the most essential part of low
flying—learning by heart the complete layout of
the cockpit of the aircraft. My instructor at Old
Sarum was an old-timer in the RAF, a fellow of
extremely good nature and a master in low-level
flying. He insisted that we learn the exact location
of all the buttons, switches and levers in the P-51A
cockpit, not visually, but by touch alone. When

I asked him why, he told me that when you are travelling on the deck at more than 400 mph you have neither time nor opportunity to look for a switch or a button in the cockpit. You have to learn to identify these gadgets by the touch of your fingers, without taking your eyes away from the outside environment.

"One day my instructor and I went out on a low-level training flight to do some firing at a ground target on the Salisbury Plain. After we took off and flew away from the aerodrome, we dropped down to the deck. I was travelling at an extremely high speed just above tree-top level, which I thought was low enough. My instructor cut in on the radio, while he was flying line abreast and a little above my level. He said, 'You bloody fool, you are too high. Get down on the deck.' Was I scared? You bet I was. But, as the training in flying down on the deck progressed, I began to realize what that fine Englishman was driving at [the closer to the ground you fly, the harder you make it for the enemy to shoot you down].

"After OTU, when I was posted to an Army Co-operation fighter squadron flying Rhubarbs [RAF name for low-level nuisance raids on the European continent in World War II] inside the Dutch coast, shooting trains and targets of opportunity, my thoughts were always with my instructor in 41 OTU.

"Later on in the war, I did considerable strafing over France with the RAF as well as with the USAAF, and I can honestly say that I owe my survival to the training I received at the RAF–Army Co-operation OTU."
—Colonel Steve Pisanos, USAF (Ret), formerly with the 4th Fighter Group, 8 USAAF

"The toughest job was ground attack. We did our share on our second tour. I must confess that I was 'shook-up and really twitchy' on more than one occasion. Most fighter pilots were leery of flak. It seemed so impersonal. When fighting

Still let my tyrants know,
I am not doomed to wear
Year after year in gloom,
and desolate despair; / A
messenger of Hope comes
every night to me, / And
offers for short life, eternal
liberty.
—from *The Prisoner*
by Emily Brontë

Above: Lieutenant William J. Laubner and, below: Lieutenant Tunis J. Lyon, both of the 55th Fighter Group which was based at Wormingford, Essex, England in World War II. Both Laubner and Lyon flew P-38 Lightnings and both fell to ground fire from flak towers in Germany and were captured.

213

FIGHTER ACES
Of World War Two

Locomotive destroyed

Dive-bombing mission

Umbrella: Target-area support

Top Hat: Bomber escort, penetration/withdrawl support

Broom: Low level strafing "sweep"

HAPPY JACK, AZ
MAY 24 1986 PM
86024

San Jacinto 1836
Republic of Texas

North American P-51D "Mustang" of 79th Fighter Sq., 20th Fighter Group, Eighth Air Force, King's Cliffe. England. Sept. '44. Note mission symbols on cowl.

Cpt. Jack M. Ilfrey, USAAF
8th and 12th AIR FORCES
Victories-8

Jack Ilfrey
Signature used with permission

Lockheed P-38F "Lightning", 94th Ftr.Sq., First Ftr. Grp., Youks-le-Bains, North Africa. Nov. '42, in which he scored first victory.

another aircraft in a dogfight one can think that it's another man in there and am I as good or better than him? But flak was just there, and many good pilots were downed by it. At first you could only see small black puffs. When they were closer, the puffs were bigger; and when they were really close, the puffs were big with red centres—and when you could hear the big black puffs with the red centres explode with a loud bang, you knew your time was limited if you didn't get out of there.
—Flight-Lieutenant Douglas "Duke" Warren, RCAF (Ret), formerly with No. 66 and No. 165 Squadrons, RAF

"I got chewed out by General Arnold when I came back to the States to help train and form up other groups to take over. He asked me, 'What is the best bomber we have?' I looked him in the eye and said, 'Sir, I think the P-38 is the best bomber we have.' God, he got mad! 'Why do you say that?' he said. I said, 'Well, it's got two engines instead of four. It carries two 1000-pounders, has only got one guy in it instead of ten, so, if you lose one, it's a lot cheaper on people. Also, when you send the fighter pilot in a P-38 in to bomb something, he can probably hit the target most of the time, and the bombers can't'."
—Major-General Carroll W. McColpin, USAF (Ret)

"On 1st September 1943, we were launched pre-dawn from about 150 miles north of Marcus Island, about 700 miles from Tokyo. A pre-dawn launch from a completely blacked-out carrier is an incredible experience. You take off into the pitch black night with no running lights on any of the planes or other ships in the task force. You climb up toward the rendezvous point and finally see the exhaust flames from a slightly darker blob ahead. You join up, not knowing who it is since you cannot see the numbers on the other plane. When it finally gets light enough to see numbers you shuffle around to your proper place. That

214

morning, after we had gotten all of the strike force assembled, some idiot towards the rear of the group accidentally fired all six of his .50 caliber machine guns, sending an arc of huge red tracers over the strike force. In the dim light, a .50 caliber tracer looked about the size of a basketball, and more than a few planes took violent evasive action!"
—Commander Hamilton McWhorter, USN (Ret), formerly with VF12

2nd Lieutenant Tunis J. Lyon was flying a P-38J as part of the 338th Fighter Squadron, 55th Fighter Group on 15th April 1944. His group was on a strafing mission in western Germany and, flying at extremely low altitude, he came upon a flak tower in the centre of an airfield. His plane was hit and both engines were severely damaged. Lyon's only choice was a dead-stick landing in the clearest area he could find. Unfortunately, the Lightning struck some trees, lost both wings, and burst into flame when the fuel tanks exploded.

Badly burnt about the face, head and hands, Lyon managed to walk to a small town where he was denied assistance by all but one elderly man and his daughter, who provided him with water and some bread. He was then turned over to the Home Guard who, in turn, put him in the hands of the military.

Lieutenant Lyon was interrogated and ointment was applied to his burns. By now he had lost his sight. After a few agonizing days riding in the back of a truck, he arrived at a small hospital. There, a French doctor, supervised by a roving German doctor, saw to his treatment. After a month and a half, his sight was partially restored. His left hand, which had been burnt to the tendons, was treated by the German doctor and, thanks to him, Lyon has full use of the hand today.

In time, Lyon was transferred to a larger hospital near Frankfurt-am-Main. During the journey, Lyon, his guard and two other prisoners were caught in an air raid and taken into a shelter with many other

people. The civilians became angry as they noticed the presence of the three Allied prisoners, and the German guard didn't know how to handle the ugly situation. They were saved by a German woman who moved to shield the prisoners with her baby carriage in a corner of the shelter until the raid ended and Lyon and the others returned to their train.

At Frankfurt, the flesh on Lyon's forehead was cauterized where it had not been healing properly. Later, he was sent to Bad Soden, Salmunster, a mineral springs town. A hospital there, staffed by Catholic sisters and run by a British medical unit, provided more specialized care for Lyon's injuries.

Liberated on 31st March 1945, Lieutenant Lyon was taken to Paris, and on to Valley Forge General Hospital in Pennsylvania. While a prisoner in Germany, he had been operated on by a doctor from New Zealand who repaired his face and provided him with a new pair of eyelids. The doctor had never performed the procedure before and did it by following instructions from a book by an American, a Dr Brown. Brown later met Lyon at the Valley Forge hospital, and there performed the remaining work on Lyon's face. He was amused when Lyon related the story of how the New Zealand doctor had done his eyelid procedure.

On 21st October 1944, US Navy Lieutenant Elvin Lindsay shot down his first enemy aircraft, a

Left: Captain Jack Ilfrey of the 20th Fighter Group which was based at Kings Cliffe, Northamptonshire, England in World War II. Ilfrey's group became known as the "Loco Bunch" because they had shot up so many German trains late in the War. Above: German Air Force Oberstleutnant Stephan Stritter and Hauptmann Markus Isphording of 1/AG 51, and their Tornado, are based at Schleswig-Jagel north of Hamburg.

Helen Gardiner, RAF Tornado F3 fighter pilot: "We think of ground attack as far as GR1, a bomber, a mud-mover... not a fighter as such. We are now doing strafe, and are now a lot more aware of what happens on the ground. They can shoot back just as much as what's airborne. People go back one too many times because they want to get the bombs away or they want to strafe whatever target they've got. This happened in Bosnia. It happened all over the place, with people coming in, missing for whatever reason, whether it be technical or an error of their part, and going back around and trying again. The pressure to get the job done, if the bombs don't come off—whatever—they will plan to go back, but not from the same direction the second time around. People will try their best. If you don't succeed the first time, you're gonna go back again."

Boys are the cash of war. Whoever said / we're not free-spenders doesn't know our likes.
—John Ciardi

Japanese Kate torpedo bomber. On that same day, he sank two fast torpedo boats and became the first Allied pilot of World War II to observe the Japanese-held airfield at Lipa in the Philippine Islands. The grass airstrip located about 60 miles south-east of Manila had revetments sheltering many single-engine aircraft, and at least thirty twin-engine Betty bombers were lined up along the runway. The four F6F-5 Hellcats of Lieutenant Lindsay, his wingman, his section leader Lieutenant Bus Rossi and his wingman began a systematic strafing attack on the airfield, initially concentrating on the Bettys. They quickly realized that they were facing no resistance from anti-aircraft fire, and continued their attack, leaving at least twenty enemy bombers burning on the Lipa base, along with several fighters and buildings on the site. When Lindsay returned to his carrier, the USS *Lexington*, he was asked to meet Admiral Marc Mitscher, who wanted a full report on the Lipa airfield, which the Admiral's staff considered a major threat to the pending Allied landing on Leyte Island. After receiving Lindsay's report, Mitscher ordered a large-scale air attack on the airfield. It was quite an achievement and contribution on the part of the young Navy pilot who had scored his first aerial victory that day.

Lieutenant Bruce Carr finished his World War II service in the USAAF with fourteen confirmed victories and the Distinguished Service Cross. Carr flew P-51 Mustangs with the 354th Fighter Group which, in October 1944, was based in France. On a mission over Czechoslovakia he was shot down by German flak and spent days attempting to evade capture. Finally, near physical exhaustion, cold and hungry, he became convinced that it was best to give himself up—he hoped—to the German Air Force, which he knew, from observing local air activity, was operating in his area. Carr somehow found his way to the enemy airfield and for the rest of that day hid in the woods at the edge of the field.

Near his hiding place was a fighter revetment and in it sat a Fw 190 which was being serviced and fuelled by its ground crew. Lieutenant Carr watched this procedure, and as he did he began to reconsider his planned surrender. Here was a wonderfully available front-line enemy fighter plane, apparently full of fuel and begging to be "borrowed". He decided to do just that and fly back to his base in France, rather than spend the rest of the war in a German prison camp. He planned to wait until late in the day, when he hoped he would get a chance to get to the fighter unobserved. He knew that if he were caught at the plane, anything might happen to him, and probably nothing good. As soon as dusk fell, he quietly made his way through the perimeter fence to the plane. His luck held. It was unguarded and he climbed into the cockpit and, in the failing light, hurriedly tried to work out the unfamiliar German instrument panel. He planned to spend the night in the plane and be ready to take off at first light.

Having (he hoped) located the correct switches for the landing gear and flaps, he was ready when the dawn came. He had located a handle to the right of the seat, which he thought must relate to starting the engine. He noticed the first signs and sounds of ground crew activity on the airfield and knew that he had no time to experiment with the various cockpit gadgets. Gambling, he pulled the handle, and nothing happened. Next, he tried pushing the handle and this time fortune smiled on him. He heard the sound of the inertia starter winding and he opened the throttle a bit. The starter continued to wind, he pulled and the engine caught and roared to life.

Now, without a parachute, helmet or the use of a radio, Carr taxied the powerful fighter through the woods towards the field ahead. His luck continued and he made it on to the grass field without any reaction from the airbase personnel.

He gunned the big BMW engine and roared across the field taking off and holding the sleek

Focke-Wulf at tree-top level. As far as he could tell, no one was coming after him. He adjusted to flying the 190 with relative ease and aimed it in the direction of the Allied lines. From the moment he reached Allied territory he came under intense ground fire. He could not take evasive action as he felt that his only chance was to keep the German fighter right down among the tree tops. Fortunately, he incurred no hits. His next problem was how to avoid being shot down by his own airfield defences when he arrived over the base in France. Without the ability to contact his field by radio, he had no way of letting them know that he was, in fact, a "friendly". His best and only bet, he thought, was to slam the 190 on the ground at his base as fast as possible. As he approached the American field at a high rate of speed, he pulled up sharply, rolled, and activated what he hoped were the gear and flaps as he continued through a short approach. Since he had not heard a "thump" [of the landing gear locking into position], he prepared to go around for another try, but in doing so he noticed anti-aircraft crews at their guns on the field and, rather than subject himself to another round of flak, elected to bring the bird in wheels up. He managed to belly-land the plane with no injury to himself and was relieved to be safely back among his own, until he found himself surrounded by MPs, who were not in the least sympathetic on hearing him explain why he had arrived by German fighter plane.

Lieutenant Carr's group commander, Colonel George Bickell, arrived at the plane where Carr still sat in the cockpit, and his first words to the young lieutenant were: "Where the hell have you been?"

In the afternoon of 20th November 1944, Captain Jack Ilfrey led five P-51D Mustangs of his 20th Fighter Group to a rendezvous with two F5As (P-38 photo reconnaissance aircraft) to cover them while they photographed Berlin and the surrounding areas.

The weather was reasonably good with 7/10 cloud cover, and the flak had been light thus far. When the F5s finished photographing in and around Berlin they headed south-west along the Autobahn towards Magdeburg, taking more photos and attracting more intense flak as they went.

The mission then required them to proceed to the Bonn area, where American bombers had attacked airfields and synthetic oil facilities earlier in the day. Before arriving at Bonn, however, the F5s radioed that they were low on fuel and film, and were going to head for home. The overcast was becoming solid, with only an occasional glimpse of the earth appearing.

After an escort mission, it had become standard

Below: This ruined aircraft hangar at Villacoublay aerodrome, France, resulted from an attack by Allied fighters.

No coward soul is mine,
No trembler in the world's
storm-troubled sphere:
I see Heaven's glories shine,
And faith shines equal,
arming me from fear.
—from *Last Lines*
by Emily Brontë

practice for the Mustang pilots of the 20th to drop down on the deck and shoot up targets of opportunity on the way back to Kings Cliffe. They had cut their teeth on the P-38 Lightning and were completely sold on the plane. Many of them resented having to convert to the P-51, but now, after several months with the Mustangs, they had come to appreciate this finest of American fighters. "The P-51s made us feel like hunters in the skies over Germany. Our morale was high during ground strafing, chasing, or evading their fighters, during dogfights or just firing the guns. We also got an adrenalin high."

They all spiralled down through a hole in the cloud cover and found an abundance of trucks, tanks and other equipment heading for the front lines. The fighters were heading in west and continued under the massive weather front, busying themselves by shooting the various opportune targets. At one point, Ilfrey realized that he did not know quite where they were. He told the other pilots to form on him and they would head for home. They had expended a lot of ammunition and most of their fuel. It was a little after 4 p.m. and it got dark early in that part of northern Europe in November. Ilfrey set a course for England but figured that, with very little fuel remaining, they might have to land in Belgium or France. He decided they would stay low, below the weather front, as a stream of bombers might still be heading home through the overcast. He recalled an earlier day when, flying a P-38 with one engine out, in the overcast above Hamburg, the clouds were suddenly illuminated with dozens of terrifying red flak bursts. Captain Ilfrey describes the events of that November afternoon: "We were in a good, tight formation and I was still trying to get my bearings when we came up on Maastricht, the Netherlands, which was still in German hands, and those hands began firing at us. We were headed north-west, so I veered right to get away from the city and all that ack-ack, but we were still picking up heavy fire, so we turned

right again [east] to get away from all that ground action. At that point, my wingman, Duane Kelso, radioed that he had been hit and was losing power. We were at around 700 or 800 feet in poor visibility. I happened to see a clear stretch which appeared to be a small emergency strip surrounded by trees. There were a few bombed-out buildings and a few wrecked aircraft scattered around. I pointed out the strip and told Kelso to try for it, and that I would try to cover him. Knowing we were almost out of ammunition and very low on fuel, I told the other pilots that they were on their own. They all made it OK to Belgium."

Ilfrey then instructed Kelso to use his own judgement about whether to try a wheels-down landing and, if he did decide to do so and thought that Ilfrey could make it in there as well, to give him a "thumbs-up" signal as he circled the strip. All the while, both Ilfrey and Kelso were being fired on from the ground. Under heavy ground fire, Kelso approached the short strip and made a rather hairy landing with wheels down, stopping near the edge of the trees. Kelso quickly left the Mustang, observed by Ilfrey, who also continued to attract ground fire. As Ilfrey came around in a circle above the trees, Kelso flashed a wide grin and gave his leader the thumbs-up signal.

Ilfrey recalls the moment: "I must have been out of my mind, but the thought of not going in never occurred to me. He was a good pilot, an excellent wingman, and would have followed me anywhere, and I couldn't help feeling very close to him at that moment. Flashing through my mind was how Art Heiden and Jesse Carpenter had tried to pick me up when I had been shot down on June 13th, but couldn't because of the trees and the glider barriers where I had come down, and of their thoughts when they had to leave me there deep in enemy-occupied territory. Friendships forged in combat are never forgotten."

Impetuously, Jack Ilfrey lowered his wheels and flaps and took his Mustang, *Happy Jack's Go-*

Buggy, in for an equally hairy landing on the little strip. The Germans in the area were now firing on Kelso's plane and Kelso quickly put 100 yards between himself and his former mount. He ran to the end of the strip where he believed Ilfrey would stop and turn around, ready for an immediate take-off, regardless of wind direction.

"God, what a hairy landing, dodging holes, muddy as hell, but the *Go-Buggy* made it. I taxied a short distance up to Kelso, set the brakes, and jumped out on the wing. I took off my 'chute and dinghy and threw them away. Kelso got in and sat in what now was just a bucket seat lowered all the way down. We immediately discovered that four legs were not going to fit in the space and allow me full rudder control, so I stood up and he crossed his legs under him and I sat down on them. There was no time to try other positions or adjust the seat and shoulder harness. I nearly scalped myself trying to close the canopy. Thank God it was a 'D'. So, there I was... head and neck bent down, knees almost up to my chin. As I closed the canopy and turned the P-51 around to start the take-off roll, we were well aware that ground troops were firing at us and we were very tense. I yelled back at Kelso, 'Don't get an erection or it'll push me out of here.' "

Ilfrey thought they were not going to clear the trees. He threw down more flaps and the Mustang just pulled up over them. Fortunately, she had been light in fuel and ammunition. They made the short flight to Brussels and yet another wild and difficult landing. That night they celebrated.

The next morning, hung over and still without a parachute and dinghy, Ilfrey brought *Go-Buggy* back to Kings Cliffe, and Kelso arrived a few days later by transport. At Kings Cliffe, Colonel Rau, the group CO, gave Ilfrey hell for "pulling a trick like that", jeopardizing himself and his aircraft.

In all the ensuing years, Jack Ilfrey has not seen or heard of Duane Kelso.

"On one occasion, I very nearly shot myself down.

I was strafing a target when there was a loud explosion which blew a large hole in the port wing through which I could see the ground. Additionally, the aircraft was shaking violently, and looking in the rear-view mirror, I could see the rudder and tailplane waving at me as they had been hit by bits of wing flying back. Reducing speed, I crept out over the sea with my wingman telling me—in order to boost my morale, I presume—that he thought the back of the aircraft was going to fall off. We eventually reached the island of Paengyong-do. The island was in friendly hands and had a small maintenance unit to receive and look after crippled aircraft which landed on one of the island's magnificent beaches. I was able to land the aircraft without further damage. I later discovered that a high-explosive shell had gone down the barrel and met up with a solid round which had stuck there."
—Captain Alan J. Leahy, RN (Ret), formerly with No. 801 Squadron

Flying from his Raydon base in 1944, Thunderbolt pilot Robert Strobell remembers that nothing was more stressful than strafing surface targets. "The 88s came up by the dozens, while the 20mm came up by the hundreds. These 20mm were usually located around airports, bridges and marshalling yards. They were manned by a gunner who was looking right through his gunsight at you, and they were well concealed. While we silenced one or two of them around an airport, it was the job I hated most of all in combat flying because it meant that you had to go in gun barrel to gun barrel. Those passes at a 20mm gun position were the most tense flying that I did.

"Battle damage to your plane deep inside Germany or France will set your brain to working overtime. It makes you wonder what systems will or won't work, like hydraulics, electrical circuits, fuel cells and lines, control mechanisms. So you start wiggling the stick to check it out. The rest must wait until you attempt to land. I took a flak

Below and bottom: The patches of the 376th Fighter Squadron, 361st Fighter Group and the 367th Fighter Squadron, 358th Fighter Group, respectively.

hit in the engine. It was so bad I had to leave the squadron inside Germany and head for home. There is safety flying with the squadron, but a lone plane flying straight and level across enemy territory is in danger from both flak and fighters. You watch your tail all the time while milking the best you can get out of a sick engine. I was convinced that it wouldn't last long enough to get to the Channel, but it did. Then, out of enemy territory, I started to plan what to do if the engine quit over water. Tension all the way back to base.

"Then there are those times in combat when you must ask the plane for maximum performance, shoving the throttle to the firewall, hoping that it has the stamina and durability to take the abuse. You have to red-line the rpms and the manifold pressure to get its best. It turns your tension up a few notches.

"Strafing is exciting to a fighter pilot, and we had many missions that were specifically strafing operations. While we may have been sent off to beat up an airport, for example, it was also a game where you looked for targets of opportunity. It was exciting to let those eight .50 caliber machine guns open up on an airplane parked on the field. It required considerable flying skill to dive in and get off a burst of gunfire on the target without ploughing into buildings, trees and power lines in the process. A strafing pass usually put you right down under 50 feet when you pulled off the target. It was the sight of the bullets hitting the ground and the target that made it exciting. It was visual evidence that you had let awesome power loose with those guns. The guns roar, the plane vibrates, a billow of dust comes up off the ground in front of you, and you are through it in a second. Strafing was gratifying because you could immediately see the results of your fire power."

"The loss rates were very high and the work most dangerous. After all, firing guns and rockets from an aircraft that is moving and changing both

220

direction and altitude is a lot different from firing back from a firmly fixed platform on the ground. From the combat films we see on TV, it looks like a lot of fun to shoot up a train or attack vehicles moving along a road, but it was often a killer. I know of one occasion when one of the squadrons of the 56th Fighter Group went out to support a parachute drop with orders not to shoot at anti-aircraft guns unless they fired first. The squadron went out with sixteen aircraft and only two got back. Imagine what that kind of a loss rate will do to morale."
—Colonel Walker M. Mahurin, USAF (Ret), formerly with the 56th Fighter Group, 8 USAAF

"The USAAF had issued a directive stating that all German planes destroyed on the ground would be given as credits to a pilot's score. I often think, now, that they were wrong in doing this, for due to strafing, the Air Force lost the cream of its pilots. Skill was not necessary and often blind luck was the principal factor in a successful strafing. The 20mm and 40mm fire of the Germans who were protecting their airdromes was deadly. Against these insuperable odds we continued at every opportunity to attack the airdromes. Yet I suppose the risk could be justified at Air Force headquarters; after all, if we could destroy a plane on the ground, that would be one less to meet our bombers on the next raid. There was only one fighter pilot's life at stake compared to ten men in a Fortress. The ruling was like throwing a bone to a pack of hungry dogs. The Air Force threw us the bait, and when the German fighters were not in the skies we went down on the ground to look for them.

"Up ahead I suddenly saw an enemy airfield. And there they were—eight juicy fat Ju 52's, sitting peacefully at the edge of the field. One pass, I promised myself; there's no harm in that. Down I went, building up speed in my dive to the ground. One Ju 52 loomed bigger and bigger in my ring

sight. *Now*, I said, and pressed the tit to watch the fat Ju 52 wither in a shroud of machine-gun fire. Pulling up, I waited; no flak. Then—down again, this time joined by my wingman. Another Ju 52 melted into the ground.

"Again, again, again—five passes and each time my bullets hit home. But now the flak was all around us. And the ground was alive with gunners of every kind, all of whom were firing at us.

"Why didn't I leave now? What was I trying to prove?

"I heard the crunch of a shell as it exploded near my wing. But down again I flew, to assure the destruction of the last two planes on the field. The light tattoo of a machine-gun fire raked my plane from the hub of the propeller to the tail assembly. Not one struck the cockpit. My motor was suddenly sluggish, but there was that one last plane—and I dove once more for my final kill.

"But there was no fast pull up now. As I flew over the burning wreck, my engine began to falter badly, but my momentum carried my up to 1500 feet before the twelve hundred horses gave their last gasp. I aimed the nose of the plane at a small clearing I could see ahead. And as my plane started its downward plunge, I felt a strange sense of relief—there were no flashbacks of my life, no self-pity for what was happening. For I was tired, dead tired of the struggle. As I pulled back on the stick to ease the crash, I felt the plane slide into the soft earth. My head shot forward and hit the gun sight as the plane crunched to a stop."
—from *The Look of Eagles* by Major John T. Godfrey, formerly with the 4th Fighter Group, 8 USAAF

"I did my operational flying on Spitfires I, II and V, in England. In Russia, I flew the Lavotchkin V and VII. More than half of my ops were convoy patrols and escorts. We did some strafing, some Rhubarbs of airfields and bombing, mostly in Slovakia. At the end of the Slovakian campaign it started raining and our grass field got quite soft in some places.

Left above: An RAF pilot scrambles to his Typhoon fighter-bomber in Normandy, late July 1944. Left below: Ninth Air Force Lieutenant George W. Wicks is helped from his damaged Mustang, having crash-landed in the Normandy region in 1944.

Only those / who have lost their freedom... / can appreciate—truly appreciate—how terribly vital it is.

I have looked / through barbed wire / at machine gun towers... / and longed with all my being / to be free again.

My body was imprisoned... but never my mind... / my thoughts...my soul.

Since my liberation / I have treasured my freedom... and will never forget those terrible, torturous months when I was hungry and dirty and cold... / but most of all... when I was enslaved.
—*Freedom*
by Bert McDowell, Junior

Flight-Lieutenants Roy Macintyre (top) and Martin Harris (above) both of No. 43 Squadron, RAF, at Leuchars, Scotland, fly the Tornado F3 in a variety of missions. In the Gulf War twelve F3 Tornados were based at Dhahran, Saudi Arabia. F3s were the first RAF aircraft sent to the Gulf to defend the Saudi oil fields. RAF Tornado F3s shared the 4-hour combat air patrol task 24 hours a day with RSAF Tornados, RSAF and USAF F-15 Eagles in Desert Storm.

One of our pilots came in to land after a bombing sortie and his brakes were U/S [unserviceable; in need of repairs]. While still at high speed he ran into the soft turf, and his plane tipped and then did a funny loop for about 30 metres. It turned over and disintegrated. All of the mechanics ran to the wreck and, after some effort, managed to pull the pilot out. The chief mechanic came over and said, 'It is the end.' They dragged the pilot out without his boots and socks, and his feet were very blue. Just then there was a scramble and I had to take off. We made no contact with the enemy and after thirty minutes I returned and landed. At the dispersal, to my surprise, was this "dead" pilot. He was smoking a cigarette and had one small bandage on his face. He was smiling. I said, 'You should be dead... your feet are all blue.' He said, 'There is no hot water in our billet.' "
—Colonel Antonin Vendl, formerly with No. 313 (Czech) Squadron, RAF

RAF Flight-Lieutenant Helen Gardiner flies the Panavia Tornado F3 interceptor. Here she describes the plane's ground-attack role: "We've got the gun which we use air-to-air and we now also use it air-to-ground. We started using it air-to-ground for the helicopter threat in Bosnia. Basically, the easiest way to shoot a helicopter when it is stationary on the ground is to treat it like a ground target, and the only thing we've got on this jet to actually do that is the gun. So, we now practise air-to-ground strafe as if we were to go up against a helicopter. Obviously, if it is moving quite fast, we can chase it down and use the missiles we've got, but sometimes that gets very difficult. He might hide behind a hill and stay stationary, or get very low, and then comes the only real weapon we've got against him. We still, basically, think of it as a mud-mover's job rather than a fighter pilot's job."

According to Oberstleutnant Stephan Stritter, the primary role of his German Air Force Tornado squadron, 1/AG51, based at Schleswig-Jagel in northern Germany, is tactical air reconnaissance. "We are supposed to fly low level and take pictures to do battle damage assessment of what our bombers did—did they manage to fulfill their mission or not? We do recce–attack interface— we fly to a certain area where, for example, we've been told that a group of enemy tanks are located. We check their exact location and use a special matrix co-ordinates system to transfer via voice the exact co-ordinates of the target to our bombers. We do target assessment photography so our photo section can interpret how to destroy targets.

"We are trained to do a lot things. Although our main role is recce, we can also use our Tornado as a bomber. We just put away the reconnaissance pod, put some bombs under the wings, and go bomb the bridge in the afternoon that we photographed in the morning.

"We also do basic fighter manoeuvres in our training areas for self-defence, and do low-level evasive manoeuvres which are more tactical. We fly in a two-ship, three-ship or four-ship flight, and there is one other Tornado who knows where we are. We fly a special route and he comes after us as a fighter and tries to shoot us down. We learn to watch out; to interpret what he is doing and react to it. We try to draw him down and prevent his shooting us. Against a fighter like an F-16 though, for example, we have no chance. The limits of the F-16 are different. It can pull 9 Gs and still accelerate. When I pull 5 Gs in the Tornado for ten seconds, I don't have any airspeed left. The F-16 doesn't even have to use a missile and I am falling down. But what we do in the basic fighter manoeuvres is to get a sense of the geometry of the fight. We try to get an advantage out of a mistake by the enemy fighter and, as we are generally two or more Tornados, the point is just to survive as long as possible so that your buddy can come in and shoot the fighter.

"A fighter today loses his 'situational awareness' [SA] very quickly. When he flies high and has a good radar picture, everything is fine, but then he comes down to try a shot, and if this doesn't work, usually he goes back up again and tries to get a new SA. While he is down tangling with one of us, he doesn't know how many more of us are around. He might then get shot down by a Tornado because he isn't paying attention to the situation. It's like his focus is entirely 'I want to shoot this guy', and that's when the other Tornado comes up behind him.

"Modern missiles are sophisticated. They can 'lock' from the front or the rear. If the enemy fighter comes at me from the front, I pull my throttles to idle; then the engines are too cold and he can't lock. Then, he'll probably try to shoot me with a radar missile. The best way to survive in a Tornado is by flying low. You can easily fly at 100 feet or lower, and, even if other fighters can fly fairly low, they generally can't see you long enough to lock on you with a missile. They may have a lock on you, but then you vanish behind the trees or a ridge line. Also, the proximity fuse of the missile can be activated by the trees. At the Maple Flag exercises last year, no low-flying German Tornado was "shot down". The missile has a range of 8 miles or more, but if you see a Tornado that low at a half-mile distance, it's already too late. And no aircraft flies low as well as the Tornado. Our engines are optimized for low level. The F-15E Strike Eagle and the F-16—if they fly below 200 feet, they become unstable because of the configuration of their wings and tails, so they don't like to go that low.

"So, how do we get an F-16, for example? It's how we fly. We fly in pairs about 6000 to 12,000 feet apart, and twenty or thirty seconds ahead of another pair of Tornados. We also fly in a box or an offset. We are totally flexible and can mix these patterns so the fighter doesn't know where our formation starts or where it ends. For example, he sees four Tornados, but he doesn't know if they are the first four, the last four or, for that matter, the *only* four. He wonders which one of us he should take out. He might think that the last two he sees are, in fact, the *last* two. He drops in on us but isn't aware of the other two Tornados following thirty seconds behind. One of us sees him, lifts the nose and shoots the missile. That's how we get him. Usually, that's our only chance to shoot him... when he makes that mistake. If he is stupid enough to keep fighting, the next Tornado just recommits and shoots him."

A primary concern of the low-flying Tornado crews is the constant possibility of a mid-air collision. Stephan Stritter: "We make our own flight plans. When we fly VFR [Visual Flight Rules] I am responsible for collision avoidance—nobody else. If we fly instrument rules or instrument approaches, normally the radar controller is responsible. However, if something happens, the first one to be blamed is the pilot.

"There is a lot of sky to watch. If someone has planned a route that conflicts with mine, I can't know about it. I just look out there and see... hopefully. The military traffic isn't normally a problem because you know that they are looking outside too. But there are lots of pilots, private pilots, weekend pilots, many with not much flying experience, and they are looking at their maps or at the ground, 'Oh, God, where am I?' and quite often they are flying down around 1000 feet where we do our low flying. You see them pretty late because they tend to be painted white, and the sky may be white. Worse are the sailplanes or gliders, because they are white and very thin. So, we fly big circles around glider airfields because we see them so late. Then, of course, you also have helicopter traffic. You have to watch out. You have to look out all the time. In the Tornado we have two pairs of eyes. The pilot looks out front and the navigator looks to the left and right."

Wing Commander Baker was a tall, fairhaired, handsome character with a typical flowing RAF wartime moustache and the appropriate call sign of "Lochinvar". He had a happy-go-lucky personality, full of animated anecdotes and generous use of clichés using a plethora of words for ostentation to give splendour to his and our commonplace line shoots. Ww nicknamed him "Young Lochinvar"; a brave and glamorous knight amongst us. We all loved his flamboyant personal force and delightful character. His influence inspired laughter, enthusiasm and confidence and did much to facilitate a very high standard of morale throughout the whole of the operational unit, for both air and ground personnel.

How we missed him and his leadership, [his] formidable presence, and his jolly, infectious convivial company in the bar in the evenings. He went missing, presumed killed soon after D-Day. It is reported he dived to his death reporting in a calm, confident voice for the Wing to turn 180 degrees out of the intense flak. Using the Wing call sign, he called "port 180– Lochinvar out".
—from *Typhoon Tale* by James Kyle, formerly with No. 197 Squadron, RAF

LITTLE WILLIE was the name painted just below the left canopy rail of the Hawker Hurricane of RAF Pilot-Officer Alan Geoffrey Page. Before the outbreak of World War II, Page joined the University Air Squadron of London University, and completed his training at Cranwell. He was flying as a member of No. 56 Squadron from Rochford on 12th August 1940, at the height of the Battle of Britain. In his excellent book, *Tale of a Guinea Pig*, and his conversations with me, he remembered vividly the events of that day: "One moment the sky between me and the thirty Dornier 215s was clear; the next it was criss-crossed with streams of white tracer from cannon shells converging on our Hurricanes.

"The first bang came as a shock. For an instant, I couldn't believe I'd been hit. Two more bangs followed in quick succession, and as if by magic a gaping hole suddenly appeared in my starboard wing.

"Surprise quickly changed to fear, and as the instinct of self-preservation began to take over, the gas tank behind the engine blew up, and my cockpit became an inferno. Fear became blind terror, then agonized horror as the bare skin of my hands gripping the throttle and control column shrivelled up like burnt parchment under the intensity of the blast-furnace temperature. Screaming at the top of my voice, I threw my head back to keep it away from the searing flames. Instinctively, the tortured right hand groped for the release pin securing the restraining Sutton harness.

" 'Dear God, save me... save me, dear God,' I cried imploringly. Then as suddenly as terror had overtaken me, it vanished with the knowledge that death was no longer to be feared. My fingers kept up their blind and bloody groping. Some large, mechanical, dark object disappeared between my legs and cool, relieving fresh air suddenly flowed across my burning face. I tumbled. Sky, sea, sky, over and over as a clearing brain issued instructions to outflung limbs. 'Pull the ripcord—

right hand to the ripcord.' Watering eyes focused on an arm flung out in space with some strange meaty object attached at its end.

"More tumbling—more sky and sea, but with a blue-clad arm forming a focal point in the foreground. 'Pull the ripcord, hand,' the brain again commanded. Slowly but obediently the elbow bent and the hand came across the body to rest on the chromium ring but bounced away quickly with the agony of contact.

"More tumbling, but at a slower rate now. The weight of the head was beginning to tell.

"Realizing that pain or no pain, the ripcord had to be pulled, the brain overcame the reaction of the raw nerve endings and forced the mutilated fingers to grasp the ring and pull firmly.

"It acted immediately. With a jerk the silken canopy billowed in the clear summer sky.

"Quickly I looked up to see if the dreaded flames had done their work, and it was with relief that I saw that the shining material was unburned. Another fear rapidly followed. I heard the murmur of fading engines and firing guns, but it was the sun glinting on two pairs of wings that struck a chill through my heart. Stories of pilots being machine-gunned as they parachuted down came flashing through my mind, and again I prayed for salvation. The two fighters straightened out and revealed themselves to be Hurricanes before turning away to continue the chase.

"It was then that I noticed the smell. The odour of my burnt flesh was so loathsome that I wanted to vomit. But there was too much to attend to even for that small luxury.

"Self-preservation was my first concern, and my chance for it looked slim. The coastline at Margate was just discernible 6 to 10 miles away; 10,000 feet below me lay the deserted sea. Not a ship or a seagull crossed its blank, grey surface.

"Still looking down I began to laugh. The force of the exploding gas tank had blown every vestige of clothing off from my thighs downwards, including

SOMETIMES YOU LOSE

It was not like your great and gracious ways! / Do you, that have nought other to lament, Never, my Love repent / Of how, that July afternoon, You went, / With sudden, unintelligible phrase, / And frightened eye, / Upon your journey of so many days, Without a single kiss, or a good-bye?
—from *Departure* by Coventry Patmore

Left: The wreck of an Me 109 shot down over England during the Battle of Britain.

One bright morning I was standing on the edge of the airfield when two white Very lights (the signal for "Scramble") hurtled skywards. I automatically turned to look at the Readiness Typhoons, their engines always warm so they would soon be away. I was surprised to see no "Tiffies" in their usual spot at the end of the East-West runway, but a loud roaring of engines from the direction of 257 Dispersal signified action somewhere. Quickly two Typhoons were tearing across the grass using a short runway more or less West-East. Caught with their pants down the two pilots were "Scrambling" down-wind, in echelon port formation and not seeing a small Royal Naval aircraft approaching to land from the other direction. Too late, the control tower banged off a red warning signal and the next seconds were mayhem. The leading Typhoon, attempting to avoid the incoming aircraft, lifted off early and tried to turn to starboard and towards me. Without enough flying speed for such a manoeuvre the right wing stalled, hit the ground and the Typhoon cartwheeled over and over again. I started to run towards the tumbling aircraft as I saw the pilot thrown clear and tossed like a cork a hundred feet *continued*

one shoe. Carefully I eased off the remaining shoe with the toes of the other foot and watched the tumbling footwear in the hope of seeing it strike the water far beneath. Now came the bad time.

"The shock of my violent injuries was starting to take hold, and this, combined with the cold air at the high altitude, brought on a shivering attack that was quite uncomfortable. With that the parachute began to sway, setting up a violent oscillating movement with my torso acting as a human pendulum. Besides its swinging movement it began a gentle turn, and shortly afterwards the friendly shoreline disappeared behind my back. This brought with it an *idée fixe* that, if survival were to be achieved, then the coast must be kept in sight. A combination of agonized curses and bleeding hands pulling on the shrouds finally brought about the desired effect, and I settled back to the pleasures of closing eyes and burnt flesh.

"Looking down again, I was surprised to find that the water had come up to meet me very rapidly since last I had taken stock of the situation. This called for some fairly swift action if the parachute were to be discarded a second or two before entering the water. The procedure itself was quite simple. Lying over my stomach was a small metal release box that clasped the four ends of the parachute harness after they had passed down over the shoulders and up from the groin. On this box was a circular metal disc that had to be turned through 90 degrees, banged and presto! the occupant was released from the 'chute. All of this was extremely simple except in the case of fingers that refused to turn the little disc.

"The struggle was still in progress when I plunged feet first into the water. Despite the beauties of the summer and the wealth of warm days that had occurred, the sea felt icy cold to my badly shocked body. Kicking madly, I came to the surface to find my arms entangled with the multiple shrouds holding me in an octopus-like grip. The battle with the metal disc still had to be

My Goodness—My GUINNESS

IT WON'T MEAN A THING.. IF YOU DON'T PULL THE STRING

226

won, or else the water-logged parachute would eventually drag me down to a watery grave. Spluttering with mouthfuls of salt water, I struggled grimly with the vital release mechanism. Pieces of flesh flaked off and blood poured from the raw tissues.

"Desperation, egged on by near panic, forced the decision, and with a sob of relief I found that the disc had surrendered the battle.

"Kicking away blindly at the tentacles that still entwined arms and legs, I fought free and swam fiercely away from the nightmare surroundings of the parachute. Wild fear died away and the simple rules of procedure for continued existence exerted themselves again. 'Get rid of the 'chute, and then inflate your Mae West, and float about until rescued.'

" 'That's all very well,' I thought, 'but unless I get near to the coast under my own steam, there's not much chance of being picked up.' With that I trod water and extricated the long rubber tube with which to blow up the jacket. Unscrewing the valves between my teeth, I searched my panting lungs for extra air. The only result after several minutes of exertion was a feeling of dizziness and a string of bubbles from the bottom of the jacket. The fire had burnt a large hole through the rubber bladder.

"Dismay was soon replaced by fatalism. There was the distant shore, unseen but positioned by reference to the sun, and only one method of getting there, so it appeared. Turning on my stomach I set out at a measured stroke. Ten minutes of acute misery passed by as the salt dried about my face injuries and the contracting strap of the flying helmet cut into the raw surface of my chin. Buckle and leather had welded into one solid mass, preventing removal of the headgear.

"Dumb despair then suddenly gave way to shining hope. The brandy flask, of course. This was it—the emergency for which it was kept. But the problem of undoing the tunic remained, not to mention that the tight-fitting Mae West covered the pocket as another formidable barrier. Hope and joy were running too high to be deterred by such mundane problems, and so, turning with my face to the sky, I set about the task of getting slightly tipsy on neat brandy. Inch by inch my ultrasensitive fingers worked their way under the Mae West towards the breast pocket. Every movement brought with it indescribable agony, but the goal was too great to allow for weakness. At last the restraining copper button was reached—a deep breath to cope with the pain—and it was undone. Automatically my legs kept up their propulsive efforts while my hand had a rest from its labours. Then gingerly the flask was eased out of its home and brought to the surface of the water. Pain became conqueror for a while and the flask was transferred to a position between my wrists. Placing the screw stopper between my teeth, I undid it with a series of head-twists and finally the great moment arrived—the life-warming liquid was waiting to be drunk. Raising it to my mouth, I pursed my lips to drink. The flask slipped from between wet wrists and disappeared from sight. Genuine tears of rage followed this newest form of torture, which in turn gave place to a furious determination to swim to safety.

"After the first few angry strokes despair returned in full force, ably assisted by growing fatigue, cold and pain. Time went by unregistered. Was it minutes, hours or days since my flaming Hurricane disappeared between my legs? Was it getting dark or were my eyes closing up? How could I steer towards the shore if I couldn't see the sun? How could I see the sun if that rising pall of smoke obscured it from sight?

"That rising pall of smoke... that rising pall of smoke. No, it couldn't be. I yelled, I splashed the water with my arms and legs until the pain brought me to a sobbing halt. Yes, the smoke was coming from a funnel—but supposing it passed without seeing me? Agony of mind was greater than agony of body and the shouting and splashing

into the air. I was running so fast that the pilot hit the ground seconds before I reached him. His safety straps had broken and in his parachute harness he lay in a crumpled heap, bloody and broken in every limb. I knelt down, drew my sheath knife from my flying boot, and started to cut into the harness. His lips moved and his limbs twitched. I was horrified, but I had to do something. Bits of aircraft strewn about were smouldering and I felt so inadequate. I was grateful when the ambulance arrived and relieved me of the responsibility. My good friend F/Lt Dusty Miller mercifully died before arriving in hospital.
—Pilot-Officer Nick Berryman, formerly with No. 276 Squadron, RAF

For what are the triumphs of war, planned by ambition, executed by violence, and consummated by devastation? The means are the sacrifice of many, the end, the bloated aggrandizement of the few.
—from *Lacon* by Charles Caleb Colton

recommenced. Looking again, almost expecting that smoke and funnel had been a hallucination, I gave a fervent gasp of thanks to see that, whatever ship it was, it had hove to.

"All of the problems were fast disappearing and only one remained. It was one of keeping afloat for just another minute or two before all energy failed. Then I heard it—the unmistakable chug-chug of a small motorboat growing steadily louder. Soon it came into sight with a small bow pouring away to each side. In it sat two men in the strange garb peculiar to sailors of the British Merchant Service. The high revving note of the engine died to a steady throb as the man astride the engine throttled back. Slowly the boat circled without attempting to pick me up. A rough voice carried over the intervening water. 'What are you? A Jerry or one of ours?'

"My weak reply was gagged by a mouthful of water. The other man tried as the boat came full circle for the second time. 'Are you a Jerry, mate?'

"Anger flooded through me. Anger, not at these sailors who had every reason to let a German pilot drown, but anger at the steady chain of events since the explosion that had reduced my tortured mind and body to its present state of near-collapse. And anger brought with it temporary energy. 'You stupid pair of fucking bastards, pull me out!'

"The boat altered course and drew alongside. Strong arms leaned down and dragged my limp body over the side and into the bottom of the boat. 'The minute you swore, mate,' one of them explained, 'we knew you was an RAF Officer.'

"The sodden dripping bundle was deposited on a wooden seat athwart ships. A voice mumbled from an almost lifeless body as the charred helmet was removed. One of the sailors leaned down to catch the words. 'What did you say, chum?' 'Take me to the side. I want to be sick.'

"The other man answered in a friendly voice, 'You do it in the bottom of the boat, and we'll

clean it up afterwards.'

"But habit died hard and pride wouldn't permit it, so, keeping my head down between my knees, I was able to control the sensation of nausea. Allowing me a moment or two to feel better, the first sailor produced a large clamp knife. 'Better get this wet stuff off you, mate. You don't want to catch your death of cold.'

"The absurdity of death from a chill struck me as funny and I chuckled for the first time in a long while. To prove the sailor's point the teeth chattering recommenced. Without further ado the man with the knife set to work and deftly removed pieces of my life jacket and tunic with the skill of a surgeon. Then my naked body was wrapped up in a blanket produced from the seat locker.

"One of them went forward to the engine and seconds later the little boat was churning her way back to the mother ship. The other sailor sat down beside me in silence, anxious to help but not knowing what to do next. I sensed the kindness of his attitude and felt that it was up to me to somehow offer him a lead. The feeling of sickness was still there from the revolting smell of burnt flesh, but I managed to gulp out, 'Been a lovely... summer, hasn't it?' "

"We took our losses. My best friend... I lost him. I went down to the flight line till the sun was down, still in hopes he would get in there. He didn't make it. But you accept it. The old crutch... it's gonna happen to somebody else; it's not gonna happen to me... this is a great piece of faith. You're wrong! But this is what you believe."
—Captain William O'Brien, USAF (Ret), formerly with the 357th Fighter Group, 8 USAAF

Hornchurch airfield was home on 31st August 1940 to No. 54 Squadron, RAF, and to Spitfire pilot Al Deere. He recalled: "The morning was strangely and ominously quiet in the Hornchurch Sector, particularly in view of the good weather,

and it was not until about mid-day that the squadron received the order to scramble. We had just taxied into position for take-off, and were all lined up ready to go, when a counter order was passed over the R/T. No sooner were we again parked in dispersal with engines stopped than a wildly gesticulating telephone orderly indicated that we were to start up again. In a matter of seconds all twelve aircraft were again taxiing to the take-off end, urged on by the Controller's now near-hysterical voice shouting over the R/T, 'Hornet aircraft get airborne as quickly as you can, enemy in the immediate vicinity.'

"Hurriedly, desperately, for I had no wish to be caught taking off, I swung my aircraft into wind to find my take-off run blocked by a Spitfire, the pilot of which was looking vaguely around for his position in the formation. 'Get to hell out of the way, Red Two,' I bellowed, recognizing my number two from the letters on his aircraft. It was a second or two before he made up his mind to move; immediately he did so I opened the throttle and careered across the airfield in pursuit of the squadron, which had by now cleared the far hedge and, with wheels retracting, was turning and climbing away from the airfield.

"I was not quite airborne when a bomb burst on the airfield, ahead of me and to my left. 'Good, I've made it,' I thought. To this day I am not clear exactly what happened next; all I can remember is that a tremendous blast of air, carrying showers of earth, struck me in the face, and that the next moment I was thinking vaguely that I was upside-down. What I do remember is the impact with the ground and a terrifying period of ploughing along the airfield upside down, still firmly strapped in the cockpit. Stones and dirt were thrown into my face and my helmet was torn by the stony ground against which my head was firmly pressed.

"Finally the aircraft stopped its mad, upside-down dash, leaving me trapped in the cockpit, in almost total darkness and breathing petrol fumes,

Far left: Lieutenant Paul Riley of the 335th Fighter Squadron, 4th Fighter Group, 8 USAAF. Riley, flying a P-51 Mustang, suffered a mid-air collision with an Fw 190 in April 1944. Left bottom: An RAF Air-Sea Rescue Squadron Walrus amphibian plucking a British pilot from the North Sea as a Lysander in the background assists by acting as a spotter.

Remember me when I am gone away, / Gone far away into the silent land; / When you can no more hold me by the hand, / Nor I half turn to go yet turning stay. Remember me when no more day by day / You tell me of our future that you planned: Only remember me; you understand / It will be late to counsel then or pray. / Yet if you should forget me for a while / And afterwards remember, do not grieve: For if the darkness and corruption leave / A vestige of the thoughts that once I had, Better by far you should forget and smile / Than that you should remember and be sad.
—from *Remember* by Christina Georgina Rossetti

Above: The wallet of a 78th Fighter Group pilot who was killed in the crash of his P-47 in England during World War II. Right: The grave of Pilot-Officer Billy Fiske, the first American airman to die in the Battle of Britain.

the smell of which was overpowering. Bombs were still exploding outside, but this was not as frightening as the thought of fire from the petrol now seeping into the ground around my head. One spark and I would have been engulfed in flames."

Generalleutnant a.D. Günther Rall, German Air Force (Ret), recalls a day in May 1944 during the Defence of the Reich: "After nearly three years in Russia, my last action was at Cape Chersones, to the west of Sebastopol. Here combat troops concentrated in the Crimean Peninsula and defended 8 kilometres of land, before the chaos of the retreat over 400 kilometres of open sea to Romania began. Here the order came by radio for my reassignment as commander of the II/JG to the defence forces of the Reich. I left Russia with mixed feelings.

"12th May 1944, 5.00 a.m. Telephone call from the Division Commander: listening in on the enemy radio communications—we are expecting mammoth air strikes by the Eighth US Air Force. In reaction to this, two big air defence squadrons were readied—altogether fifty Fw 190s. My group of twenty-five Me 109Gs as 'top cover'—against the long-range fighter escorts. Take-off when US advance fighters are over the Zuider Zee. Rendezvous with our own heavy groups over Steinhuder Sea. *En route* climb up to 8000 metres, my group 3000 metres overhead. The contrails come in sight—we climb higher (no pressurization, no air conditioning in the cockpit). We are above the contrails—about 11,000 metres high. Order: Battle Formation! Orders to me from the 7th Air Division: Take over the whole formation, no radio communication exists to the formation leader of the heavy groups. At 8000 metres I make contact with a P-47 formation and attack with my group. I come within firing range of the leading element, a P-47 in my sight. I fire—a huge flame and explosion, the P-47 goes down, the second follows after a short fire exchange—

the leader goes down after hectic defensive manoeuvres. At this moment I am being attacked from above and behind me by the second element (four P-47s). My wingman announces engine failure and bails out. Now I am being hunted by four P-47s, who are flying in line abreast behind me, and are within firing range. Against all rules, I crash dive, although I know that the Thunderbolts are faster in the dive and structurally stable—but I have no other option. While diving, the first hits burst into my Me 109, into the body, engine, radiator, and suddenly a hit and an explosion—the thumb of my left hand is shot away while holding the throttle. My windshield ices up. I cannot see how high up I am. I clutch the stick between my legs and scrape the ice from the windshield with my still usable hand. At tree-top level I pull up my Me 109 so steeply, it reaches the stalling point. The machine is on its back. I blow off the cockpit roof and try to jump out—difficult—the force from the upside-down plane pushes me into the cockpit. Instinctively, my reflex movements come into play and I manage to free myself. I begin tumbling, and it is impossible to reach my parachute handle. After a seemingly endless free fall, I stabilize myself... I finally reach the handle, I pull it, and the parachute opens! What a feeling! But now the pain from the wound of the missing thumb hits me. I glide about another 500 metres into a forest and I get hung up on trees. Thank God for that. It could have been very dangerous to land on my back after a previous injury involving three broken vertebrae. The danger is not over. After the quick release from the parachute, I tumble head-over-heels into a ravine—but I survived—and somehow I feel lucky.

Many years later an Air Force historian identified my opponents as Hub Zemke's 'Wolf Pack'. My group suffered heavy losses in this action. We always fought against heavy odds, always realizing the certainty that every second pilot wasn't coming back. Why did we keep on fighting? Nobody believed in victory any more. It was simply the unwritten law... to save what could be saved and keep the German cities from destruction. In the end, no one thought even that was going to happen.

"Later on, I became friends with Hub Zemke. We understood each other."

"I remember seeing a new pilot on his first mission crash on take-off and burst into flames after turning over and skidding through a fence. I flew right over the black smoke coming from the wreckage as I took off and thought, 'What a pity, a nice young man of nineteen on his first mission.' Our Group Flight Surgeon was always at the end of the runway in his jeep which was loaded with all kinds of emergency equipment: axe, hatchet, fire extinguisher, medical supplies, etc. He rushed to the burning plane, knocked out the glass in the canopy, dug down into the ground, and pulled the dazed pilot from the wreckage, then dragged him away from the plane, which shortly afterwards blew up. He got the Soldier's Medal for his heroism.

When I got back from the mission, I reported to Squadron Intelligence for debriefing and, much to my shock and amazement, there stood this young fighter pilot, grinning from ear to ear, and saying, 'How did it go today, fellas?' I nearly fell over. What a happy ending to a tragic accident. He suffered only a small cut on the little finger of his left hand."
—Colonel Bert McDowell, Junior, USAF (Ret), formerly with the 55th Fighter Group, 8 USAAF

"I had lined up behind an Me 109 over France, while flying a Spitfire. I had the enemy aircraft in the centre of my gunsight, and I was ready to press my thumb on the firing button... but to no avail. I was dumbfounded and furious. I couldn't press the firing button. My thumb was frozen.

"That was a lesson in defeat for me because I lost a positive kill.

"I never did like to fly with gloves on my hands during the war, so I paid for it that day. However, our Flight Surgeon did all he could to revive my frost-bitten thumb.

The doc directed that I use my gloves whenever I flew after that, and I did. But when I arrived at the combat zone, I had to take the gloves off because they made me feel uncomfortable. Of course, on the way back to our airfield in England, I put them on again... just in case the Flight Surgeon should be at the dispersal waiting to check on me."

—Colonel Steve Pisanos, USAF (Ret), formerly with the 4th Fighter Group, 8 USAAF

A fighter pilot came down in the drink the other day and, though comparatively near land, he floated round for fifty-seven hours without being picked up. A small thing like a dinghy is difficult to see; indeed bailed-out crew have had the experience of actually being nearly run down by ships without being seen or heard in spite of their shouts. This fighter pilot might well have floated round much longer than fifty-seven hours but for one little thing—his whistle. He was not seen, but his whistle was heard. So always make certain before going out on ops that you have your whistle—and your floating torch as well. You are entitled to be issued with these and your Equipment Officer will give them to you if you ask.

—from *Tee Emm*, July 1942

A mid-air collision can ruin one's day. For 1st Lieutenant Paul Riley of the 335th Fighter Squadron, 4th Fighter Group, that day was 24th April 1944. It began inauspiciously when Riley's P-51B Mustang shed its right wing tank on take-off, forcing him to abort the mission. He quickly told his wingman to take over his position, and continued down the Debden runway to his revetment where his wing tank was replaced and the new tank filled. In ten minutes he was airborne and, by pushing the fighter hard, was able to catch up with his squadron.

The Mustangs were climbing to 25,000 feet when his CO reported up to eighteen Fw 190s slightly below and directly ahead of the American formation. Riley focused on two Fws ahead of him and rapidly closed on one, firing a four-second burst into the German machine. The Focke-Wulf nosed over and started lazily down. Riley looked around and, seeing no friendly aircraft, decided to follow his "kill" down from their 18,000 feet altitude to confirm the crash on gun-camera film. For a confirmed credit, a pilot needed either witnesses to the downing, or combat film of the enemy plane on fire, crashing, or of the enemy pilot bailing out.

On the way down, Riley saw tracers passing over his left wing and quickly pulled up hard and to the left. Almost immediately his left wing collided with another Fw 190 and the propeller of the enemy fighter sliced off about 25 per cent of the wing, causing the Mustang to tumble end over end. In the collision, the lieutenant's left leg was broken.

Dazed, but recovering from the shock of what had just happened, Riley managed to keep the Mustang flying by using full power, and tried to set a course westward towards France. Soon, though, he encountered some flak and his plane was hit, setting his left wing on fire. He prepared to bail out but, in his haste to leave the burning aircraft, he neglected to disconnect his radio-telephone plug and found himself caught half-way in and out of the cockpit.

Finally freed of the R/T connection, he was falling through space, where he pulled the D-ring of his parachute and found that he was only taking up slack in the cable. Struggling now at low altitude, he at last felt his shoulders yanked backwards and almost instantly impacted on the soft, dark earth of a newly ploughed German potato field.

He crawled through the furrows, dragging his badly injured leg, and noticed that his Mustang had crashed just to the rear of a German passenger train. At that moment, the flak crew that had shot him down arrived and one of them, a young kid, greeted Riley with the traditional "for you the war is over". Paul Riley spent the next thirteen months in a German prisoner of war camp.

"In the evening of Sunday, 11th March 1945, the US Navy aircraft carrier *Randolf*, anchored in the Ulithi Lagoon, was hit by a Japanese kamikaze twin-engine Frances bomber, blowing a huge hole in the starboard quarter of the ship and putting her out of action for nearly a month. I was working in our squadron office just beneath the flight deck and about 250 feet from where the kamikaze hit. When the tremendous explosion occurred, the shock bounced us out of our chairs. I ran up to the flight deck and saw the entire aft end of the carrier ablaze with huge clouds of black smoke boiling up. I then went down to the hangar deck where the aft end was also blazing. There were bodies about the deck, some badly mangled. I went forward to the bows to get away from the fire and smoke. The ship's firefighters were able to get the blaze under control in a remarkably short time, but the extent of the damage was staggering. A 40 x 40 x 40 foot section of the starboard quarter was missing from just below the hangar deck on up through the flight deck, and the flight deck area around the hole was twisted upwards. Soon a repair ship, the *Jason*, came alongside and in about three weeks the *Randolf* was repaired."
—Commander Hamilton McWhorter, USN (Ret), formerly with VF12

A relief boat of the Margate Lifeboat organization was sent in response to a report of an RAF pilot down in the sea off Kent on 3rd September 1940. The boat crew searched without result for two hours and had given up hope of finding the airman. They were about to turn for shore when a crewman spotted the pilot amid his billowing parachute in the water. They didn't realize the extent of the pilot's injuries when they threw a rope to him. His hands were too badly burnt for him to be able to grab and hold the rope. As they approached, they saw the awful severity of his burns and they were able to gently free him of the parachute and bring him aboard the life boat. Then they cut off his leather flying jacket and rigged a blanket over him to shield him from the intense sun. In 45 minutes they brought him to shore and he was taken to the Margate Hospital. The pilot was Richard Hillary, who was, during his recovery in the East Grinstead burn ward, to write one of the great books of that or any war, *The Last Enemy*.

"IT'S JUST LIKE being in a knife fight in a dirt-floor bar. If you want to fix a fella, the best way to do it is to get behind him and stick him in the back. It's the same in an air fight. If you want to kill that guy, the best thing to do is get around behind him where he can't see you... and shoot him."
—Captain William O'Brien, formerly with the 357th Fighter Group, 8 USAAF

"There are two things a fighter pilot must have to do his work in combat and that he can't really acquire anywhere else except in combat: confidence in his ability to kill and confidence in his ability to get away when in trouble.

"If you feel you can kill and feel they can't kill you, then you'll have the offensive spirit. Without that offensive spirit—the ability to lunge instantaneously and automatically like a fighting cock at the enemy the moment you spot him—you are lost. You either 'go along for the ride', as we call it when a fellow hangs back and doesn't make kills, or eventually you get shot down.

"I know, because it took me quite a long time to build up confidence in myself, which I had thought I had when I left home, and there was quite a long time when I went along just for the ride."
—Major Don S. Gentile, formerly with the 4th Fighter Group, 8 USAAF

"To be a good fighter pilot, there is one prime requisite—think fast, and act faster."
—Major John T. Godfrey, formerly with the 4th Fighter Group, 8 USAAF

"I think that the most important features of a fighter pilot are aggressiveness and professionalism. They are both needed to achieve the fighter pilot's goal: the highest score within the shortest time, with the least risk to himself and his wingman."
—Gidi Livni, formerly an F-16 pilot and Colonel in the Israeli Air Force

"An air victory certainly gave you a great satisfaction. You, as a pilot, saw primarily the airplane as your target and not so much its pilot. Only when you got a chance to see the debris and the dead pilot on the ground [did] you get a mixed feeling and sympathy. We, the German fighter pilots, saw many losses of our own in the air. I, personally, was shot down eight times, three of them with serious injuries, but we had to fly again."
—Generalleutnant a. D. Günther Rall, German Air Force (Ret)

"I am not an ace. I believe I am credited with three and a half victories. I had many inconclusive dogfights. When in a dogfight, one is giving it 150 per cent attention. You are pulling G and trying to look behind you with your neck on a swivel (why do you suppose fighter pilots wear scarves?) So often, on both sides, aircraft were shot down without the pilots knowing what hit them. On one occasion our squadron over the Netherlands was bounced; one section didn't get the message to break and three Spitfires went down with no defensive action whatever. At the same time, we would often see enemy aircraft below. The CO and his section would dive down and knock down two or three before the enemy aircraft realized they were being attacked.

"Most pilots wanted to stay on operations. It was a feeling you got on a good squadron—a sense of being one with your fellow pilots, and a determination to do your utmost to deserve their respect and friendship. I firmly believe that pilots often flew when their medical condition should have required treatment, but they did not want to let the squadron down.

"Every pilot, or serviceman, no doubt has their own way of dealing with fear. For my brother and me the waiting after briefing was the most worrisome time. You knew that there was a certain element of danger involved, and you could think about it. However, once you started your engine

"Let's fight till six, and then have dinner," said Tweedledum.

It was a quaint aspect of R.A.F. philosophy, upon which I was often to ponder, that a pilot whether he was training or on a squadron, must never by the smallest hint be given any sort of praise or encouragement. On the contrary he must at all times carry the burden of knowledge that he was a ham-fisted, stupid and dangerous fool in the air. I quite saw that praise, if it was ever earned, must be granted sparingly during training for fear of instilling over-confidence. There was never any danger of this. I wondered sometimes how many wretched half-trained pilots had killed themselves, overcome by panic in cloud and spinning in, or miscalculating fatally in landing or taking off from lack of self-confidence. This unsparing denigration of pupil pilots' ability certainly accounted for some of the truly ferocious number of casualties at the advanced training stage.
—from *One Boy's War* by Richard Hough

and began to taxi you were so busy taking care of what you had to do that you didn't think about the danger. In the air you had so much going on that required your attention and action there was no time to be afraid."
—Flight-Lieutenant Douglas "Duke" Warren, RCAF (Ret), formerly with No. 66 and No. 165 Squadrons, RAF

"The squadron was doing well in Huns. [Captain Albert] Ball came back every day with a bag of one or more. Besides his SE 5 he had a Nieuport scout, the machine in which he had done so well the previous year. He had a roving commission, and, with two machines, was four hours a day in the air. Of the great fighting pilots his tactics were the least cunning. Absolutely fearless, the odds made no difference to him. He would always attack, single out his man, and close. On several occasions he almost rammed the enemy, and often came back with his machine shot to pieces.

"One morning, before the rest of us had gone out on patrol, we saw him coming in rather clumsily to land. He was not a stunt pilot, but flew very safely and accurately, so that, watching him, we could not understand his awkward floating landing. But when he taxied up to the sheds we saw his elevators were flapping loose—controls had been completely shot away! He had flown back from the lines and made his landing entirely by winding his adjustable tail up and down! It was incredible he had not crashed. His oil tank had been riddled, and his face and the whole nose of the machine were running with black castor oil. He was so angry at being shot up like this that he walked straight to the sheds, wiped the oil off his shoulders and face with a rag, ordered out his Nieuport, and within two hours was back with yet another Hun to his credit!

"Ball was a quiet, simple little man. His one relaxation was the violin, and his favourite after dinner amusement to light a red magnesium flare

outside his hut and walk round it in his pyjamas fiddling! He was meticulous in the care of his machines, guns, and in the examination of his ammunition. He never flew for amusement. The only trips he took, apart from offensive patrols, were the minimum requisite to test his engines or fire at the ground target [when] sighting his guns. He never boasted or criticized, but his example was tremendous."
—from *Sagittarius Rising* by Cecil Lewis, formerly of No. 56 Squadron, RFC

"I joined [No.] 127 Squadron in July, 1944, on a strip (Funtingdon) in southern England—prior to going to B.16 near Caen. I joined with a kid by the name of Pete Attwooll. At first, we were forced together, because we arrived together. Later, we became very good friends. Pete was an orphan, as was his eighteen-year-old sister. He talked about her—often. She had never had a date, he told me. He and I had a terrible falling out in December— when a joke or jape that he began ended with me wrestling him to the mud—he, in his newly laundered white aircrew sweater. I went on Christmas leave. I saw Pete at a briefing when I got back to base, B.79, Woensdrecht. He looked at me, our eyes met, no words. Then he was on the next 'show' an hour later. The boys landed—and were talking about Pete having to pancake—as he was shot up—and out of glycol. They said he would be coming back on a truck. One hour later—the adjutant came into the hut. 'I am sorry, gentlemen—but word just came in. Flight S'arnt Attwooll didn't make it. He may have forgotten to cut the switches. He landed—and his aircraft became a flamer. The army were right there—they couldn't get him out. I'm sorry.' I was asked by the new CO if I would go to Breda, to bury Pete on the first day of January. The funeral was a ghastly disaster. I buried Pete from a stretcher that was covered with his blood—black ashes fell out of the feet end of his burial blanket—(it was crudely

On the third day of the campaign, May 12, 1940, I managed to score my first kill. It is true to say that the first kill can influence the whole future career of a fighter pilot. Many to whom the first victory over the opponent has been long denied either by unfortunate circumstances or by bad luck can suffer from frustration or develop complexes they may never rid themselves of again. I was lucky. My first kill was child's play. I took all this quite naturally, as a matter of course. There was nothing special about it. I had not felt any excitement and I was not even particularly elated by my success. That only came much later, when we had to deal with much tougher adversaries, when each relentless aerial combat was a question of "you or me." On that particular day I had something approaching a twinge of conscience. The congratulations of my superiors and my comrades left an odd taste in my mouth. An excellent weapon and luck had been on my side. To be successful the best fighter pilot needs both.
—from *The First and The Last* by Adolf Galland

sewn with string) and the Dutch onlookers were appalled. I sobbed my heart out. I gave a report to my fellow pilots. They were broken up, too. I was asked to write a report for the group-captain in charge of 132 Wing. I did so. I was called in to see the group-captain. He told me that he was sorry—said something about my courage—and something about his decision that no pilot would ever go to the funeral of another.

I took pictures with our sergeant photographer [of the grave]. I took them home on leave—and then to Pete's young sister. (I had borrowed wreaths from well-kept graves to put before Pete's wooden cross.) She said how nice the grave looked. I died inside at her courage. I never saw her again—and that is, perhaps, my shame. I have never got over my shame at the stupid argument Pete and I had—or the sadness and horror of the funeral. Eighteen months later—I wrote a short story, 'A Brevet For Breda', simply to get over the grief—and the nightmares I was having. The story was rejected a number of times. Almost fifty years later—it was published as a chapter of *Spitfire Diary*. I changed but a word, from my yellowed copy of 'Brevet'."
—Flying-Officer E. A.W. Smith, formerly with No. 127 Squadron, RAF, author of *Spitfire Diary*

General Johannes Steinhoff, formerly with JGVII, GAF: "I have always wondered whether it was man's aggressive disposition to hunt that triggered one's reflexes so swiftly and immediately or whether it was the experience gained in a hundred dogfights that prompted one to make the right decisions in a fraction of a second—whether in defence or in attack. Undoubtedly the state of extreme tension was partly responsible for that reflex reaction, as well as the fact that years of practice at sneaking up on the enemy, dodging out of his way, and hiding in the infinity of the sky had developed new and unknown instincts in the few who had survived."

"I think the most significant properties of a good combat fighter pilot are attitude and opportunity. He must have a desire to close with the enemy and destroy him, and he must possess or create the chance to engage his opponent. All the other components—marksmanship, eyesight, airmanship etc—will flow from attitude and opportunity."
—Captain William O'Brien, USAF (Ret), formerly with the 357th Fighter Group, 8 USAAF

"Certainly in all three services, in every country involved in the war, there was serious drinking. The reasons for drinking are probably as numerous as the men who drank. A lot of drinking occurred because it was the thing to do. Your friends went to the pub and you went with them. Duke and I went to museums and historical sites. We saw old buildings and churches, and found all of them very interesting. We did go to pubs if there was a special party, and enjoyed being there. Our drink was a 'shandy', which seemed to be a mixture of beer and a soft drink. In the RAF Officers' Mess one signed for drinks and was billed at the end of the month. Some Commanding Officers kept a watchful eye on the amount of liquor charged on a young officer's account and would caution the officer if they thought it excessive."
—Flight-Lieutenant Douglas "Duke" Warren, RCAF (Ret), formerly with No. 66 and No. 165 Squadrons, RAF

Major Jonathan Holdaway, USAF, has been an exchange officer with the RAF on No. 43 Squadron, flying F3 Tornado aircraft from RAF Leuchars in Scotland. "The exchange is normally about a three-year tour. I have extended for six months. I leave this summer [1998] to go back to the States. We have exchanges with numerous air forces around the world. It's a two-year tour following completion of whatever training those nations put us through. When pilots or aircrew come over to the UK on exchange with the RAF, we go through ten to twelve months of training before they send us to whatever squadron we will be assigned to, and then, once you show up on the squadron, it's normally for two years. I actually started out flying the Hawk at Valley, Wales, which is a trainer. They do that because the flying system and the rules and regulations that the RAF have are quite different from the USAF, so they put us through a short course in the Hawk that lasts about three months, purely to familiarize us with the way the airspace regulations are set up here in the UK—to get us used to their way of doing business. Then they send us to whatever training course we're going to go through. For me, it was the Tornado F3. We have other guys on the Tornado GR1, the Jaguar, some guys on the Harrier, some on C130s. There's generally at least one exchange officer in each of type of plane the RAF flies."

"I sort of divided luck, or pilotage I guess you'd say, into several categories. The first thing you've got to do is get an airplane and make sure it's ready to go. If you're very careful about that, you eliminate an awful lot of the bad luck. But you could still use good luck. Every once in a while a part would break or something... while you were flying. I always used to know where I was going to land in case of an emergency. You're always picking out places to land. So, if you had it happen in the air, and you had any control over the plane, the luck [requirement]was cut down, way down... but you could always use a little. When you're in combat, if you trained properly and planned your missions properly, you could eliminate a lot of the luck requirement. If a pilot said that luck was worth maybe 50 per cent of your survival overall, I'd say that, by doing those things, you'd cut it down to maybe 10 per cent. I didn't drink in those days. I didn't run around to the pubs with the guys on the time off. I always did my studying of airplanes, targets and how to attack them. I never lost a guy that flew with me on a mission. We always planned the mission properly, as well as we could. I went out and spent a lot of time attacking English gun posts, gun emplacements, going over and visiting with people and becoming familiar with their weapons, and I soon found out where they had blank spaces on their predictors, and all the rest of it. So, all I needed was intelligence reconnaissance pictures of a given airfield, for instance, or a town or whatever—wherever they had emplacements—and I could look at 'em and tell you where you could attack them without

Below: USAF fighter pilots at their Saudi Arabian base during the Gulf War in 1991.

The fastest I ever went in the Phantom was 2.0 mach at 48,000 feet. It's a very impressive ride. I did that ride on no external tanks and you use quite a lot of gas accelerating. It was nice to see such an old airplane have no problem in getting to twice the speed of sound. The only problem that you have is to reduce the power very, very slowly. Otherwise there would be so much suction in the back of the engines that all of the nozzles would be squeezed and you could do a lot of damage to the engines. Actually, the decelerating nearly took longer than the accelerating.
—Hauptmann Peter Grosserhode, 1/AG51, German Air Force

...they shall mount up with wings as eagles;
—Isaiah 40:31

getting shot at. That's where I did the attacking, and the hell with getting shot at when you didn't have to. And there were little things—things you could do—if you did 'em that way all the time, you had a good chance of not getting shot down. So, I would say that part of it was hard work, nose-to-the-grindstone kind of thing, and planning, and a lot of practice.

"I had good eyesight and I was serious. I'd been flyin' longer than most... had more hours than most. I certainly did more missions than anybody else.

"I figured things out when they weren't figuring them out, and I never did just blindly follow somebody's plan that they'd figured out. In other words, I always figured out a mission myself even when I wasn't leading. It's using your head, all your faculties... and flying ability, too. I'm not saying I was the best ever. You've got to have a knack about you, about doing the right thing at the right time... making decisions when you know damned well everything else is wrong, or sounds wrong anyway, and you've got to have the guts not only to make the decision, but to do it."
—Major General Carroll W. McColpin, USAF (Ret.)

"Emergencies are just an occupational hazard for air crew, so routine that we almost get blasé about them. We will be sitting around in the crew room, when the tannoy blares out: 'State Two. Tornado, ten miles, engine vibration.'

"We know that the crew will have an amber caption showing on their emergency warning panel. They will already have dumped fuel and will be dealing with the emergency as calmly as they can. Unless it is a jet from our own squadron, the normal reaction is simply to carry on drinking our coffee and struggling with the *Telegraph* crossword. Somebody is working hard, in a potentially dangerous situation, but we expect them to sort it out and land safely. There may be a good tale to tell afterwards, but it is an everyday occurrence; we have all had emergencies, we all expect to have more, and none of us ever expects the worst.

"It is very different when the worst actually happens. In training, none of us ever really believed our instructors when they told us how many mates they had lost, but by the time you have joined a squadron, you quickly become used to death. We never really get hardened to it, we simply get accustomed to the idea, and we all have an unstated, but unshakeable belief, summed up in six words. 'It will never happen to me.' You could not do the job otherwise."
—from *Team Tornado* by RAF Flight-Lieutenants John Peters and John Nichol

Japanese ace Saburo Sakai and eight of his fellow Imperial Navy pilots of the Tainan Wing flew their Zero fighters from Rabaul to their new field at Lae, New Guinea, on 8th April 1942. They had been told that the move was in preparation for the complete occupation of New Guinea by Japanese forces. At Lae they found a tiny runway not more than 3000 feet long, no control tower, no hangars and no maintenance facilities. The field was tightly enclosed by mountains on three sides and, as he began his approach, the prospect of operating from it made Sakai cringe. The arriving airmen were greeted by the other twenty-one pilots of the Wing, who had flown in several days earlier, and were given the grand tour.

In the next four months Sakai and the members of the new Lae Wing fell into a dull, unvarying routine. Mechanics began their labours at 2.30 each morning. The pilots were roused at 3.30 and took exactly the same breakfast—a dish of rice, soybean-paste soup with dried vegetables and pickles—each day. Sakai remembers the fare at Lae as 'pitifully inadequate'.

With breakfast finished, an alert flight of six Zeros, whose engines had already been warmed-up, sat primed for immediate take-off to intercept any

enemy aircraft in the area. The pilots waited by the fighters, which had been positioned at the end of the runway. They could be airborne in seconds.

The other pilots of the Wing tended to hang around the Command Post awaiting orders. They played chess and checkers to pass the time.

A patrol formation was launched every morning at eight. If a bomber escort effort was ordered, the Zeros flew a south-easterly course down the Papuan coast, joining with the bombers at Buna. The Lae pilots were normally back at the field by noon for the usual uninspired lunch of rice and canned fish or meat. Between meals, Sakai recalls, all the pilots were given fruit juice and candy to help make up for the vitamin deficiency of their diets.

The routine continued at five each evening with all pilots gathering for compulsory callisthenics, followed by supper, bathing and letter-writing or reading. They were usually in bed by eight or nine.

At their Lae base there was little recreation or amusement, and there were no women. The only entertainment occurred when a few of the pilots produced a harmonica, guitar or ukulele. Yet Sakai remembers that their morale was high and that there were few complaints. They were fighter pilots, there to engage the enemy in combat. They wanted to fight.

Peter Townsend was one of the most famous and highest-achieving fighter pilots of World War II. He recalls the day war broke out, 3rd September 1939, when he was with No. 43 Squadron at RAF Tangmere, Sussex: "At that moment on the grass at Tangmere airfield I was lying beside my Hurricane watching flaky white clouds drift across a blue sky, while hovering larks shrilled and voices came to me from pilots and ground crew also lying beside their dispersed aircraft. Never in my life had I experienced so peaceful a scene.

"At 11 a.m. Squadron Adjutant John Simpson walked into the hangar and said to Warrant Officer Chitty, 'The balloon goes up at eleven fifteen.

That's official.'

"We all foregathered in the mess, where we had listened to Hitler's shrieking voice just a year ago. Our station commander, Fred Sowrey, looked grave. But the presence of this veteran was reassuring for us who did not know war. Twenty-three years earlier to the very day, Fred Sowrey had been on patrol with Lieutenant Leefe Robinson when Robinson sent a Zeppelin crashing in flames near London. Then Zeppelin L32 had fallen to Sowrey's guns, and in May 1918 he was in at the kill of the last German raider to crash on English soil. This veteran of the first generation of airmen was about to see the horror of a second attempt by the Germans to reduce England to her knees by bombing. He steadied us in our ardour to 'get at the Hun'. He told us, 'Don't think a fighter pilot's life is one of endless flying and glory. You will spend nine-tenths of your time sitting on your backsides waiting.' "

"The fighter pilot has extensive training; he is familiar with his airplane, he has confidence in his skills as a pilot, he has been briefed on all aspects of combat flying, he has camaraderie with his flight and squadron buddies, and he has the youth to embrace excitement and adventure. No fear—only that nagging thought that he can go down in flames, just as he has seen others go down, but he allows this thought only a fleeting moment in the certain knowledge that such things happen to other people, not to him.

"Consider personality and character. The quiet type [who] simply goes about his pilot job with skill and courage... the fighter who breaks rank and discipline to chase anything that moves in the air or on the ground, anything that will give him an excuse to pull the trigger... the cautious type who doesn't make a move in the air until he has assessed the situation... the aggressive type who seeks out the enemy, employing skill and a knowledge of his aircraft to bring maximum

damage to the enemy—he is the most effective of them all... and finally, the apathetic type, who looks forward to completing his tour."
—Lieutenant Robert Strobell, formerly with the 353rd Fighter Group, 8 USAAF

"I've been in the RAF seven years now. I like my job very much. Whilst I'm called a navigator, that's not really what we do in the F3. I'm more of a weapons system operator, as the Americans would call it. You work the radar and sort of build the air picture and run the battle in the air. You're an airborne battle manager, as well as a navigator. The front and back seater relationship is very important. It's all down to experience, really. If you have an experienced pilot flying with an experienced navigator, you can get a lot out of the aircraft. If you have a very experienced pilot flying with quite a new navigator, the pilot will be doing a lot more of the workload, and vice versa. The workload in each cockpit can move around, depending on the experience there. But you tend to work well together and get the most out of the jet. We do have specific jobs that we do and you also monitor the other person's jobs in the cockpit. You do need to be able to get on. You can't have a character clash within the cockpit. There aren't any pilots on the squadron I'd clash with, certainly. And I totally trust flying with all of the pilots on the squadron. You trust that they're not going to fly you into the ground, for instance. So, I can get on with my job and trust what my pilot's doing."
—Flight-Lieutenant Mark Pearce, No. 43 Squadron, RAF

"The fighter pilots were another breed of cat. On their personal skill and aggressiveness depended not only their lives and the lives of their teammates, but the lives of the bomber crews and the success of the air war."
—Colonel Budd J. Peaslee, formerly with the 384th Bomb Group (H), 8 USAAF

Bobby Richards was Johnny Godfrey's room-mate at Debden. They had been friends for two years. On Saturday, 4th March 1944, Lieutenant Richards died when his P-51B Mustang crashed 800 yards south-west of Durban's Farm near the small Suffolk town of Framlingham, England.

The 4th Fighter Group had had very little experience with their new Mustangs, having transitioned to them from P-47s just a few days before the escort mission on which Richards was killed. The group had taken their Mustangs into combat just twice before 4th March. In his book, *The Look of Eagles,* Godfrey recalled: "Rumors had been flying hot and heavy that we were being transferred from P-47s to P-51s. We had heard a lot of talk about this amazing plane. By cutting the fire power to four machine guns and using a new type of carburetor, it was capable of 1800-mile flights with its two belly tanks. Our P-47s had only one belly tank which was slung underneath the fuselage. The 51s had them slung underneath each wing, with two more permanent tanks in the wing and another tank just to the rear of the cockpit.

"On 22nd February, the rumors became a fact; one P-51 landed and we were all (sixty pilots) ordered to fly it in preparation for the change-over. It was a beautiful airplane; it reminded me of the Spitfire with its huge in-line engine. And, like the Spitfire, it, too, was glycol-cooled. We queued up on the plane like housewives at a bargain sale. The time in the air was spread very thin, forty minutes was all the time I had in the air in a '51 when on the morning of the 28th the group flew to Steeple Morden Base in their P-47s and traded them for P-51s. The planes didn't have their auxiliary tanks on, but they were full of fuel and the machine guns were loaded. Our briefing was held on the ground among our '51s. No flying back to Debden for us, but off on a fighter sweep to France. We were familiarizing ourselves with this plane the hard way.

"The Air Force had made no mistake when they

Below: Captain Alan F. Bunte of the 4th Fighter Group, crashed his P-51B into a lake near Potsdam, Germany on 5th April 1944 after hitting a high-tension wire while on a ground attack mission. He too, became a prisoner of the Germans.

243

Above: Flight-Lieutenant R. Reynell of No.43 Squadron, RAF, was wounded in an air battle with Bf 109s over London on 7th September 1940. He bailed out and was dead when he landed.

made their purchase of Mustangs from the North American Aviation Company. They were the hottest planes in the skies. From zero to 30,000 feet they were able to match anything the German Air Force put into the air. If the fighting spirit of the group was high before the advent of the 51', it was now at fever pitch.

"But horrible little bugs were plaguing the '51s—motor trouble, gas trouble, radio trouble—and the worst bug of all, besides our windows frosting up, was in our machine guns. At high altitudes they froze up on us; moreover, in a dogfight they were often jammed by the force of gravity in a turn. That meant straightening out before firing, a feat that was practically impossible under the circumstances. Technicians were rushed to the base to iron out our problems. The war was still going on and the great air offensive against Germany was now in full swing, so we had to fly them, bugs and all.

"4th March: Bob was flying on my wing over the Channel. He called me, 'Hello, Shirt Blue Red Leader, this is Red Two. My motor's acting up, am returning to base.'

'Roger, Red Two.' I didn't know it then, but those were the last words I was to hear from Bob. "Motor difficulty was common [in] those days, and over the radio I could hear other boys reporting trouble. On approaching the Dutch coast my own engine started coughing and spitting. It was my turn now.

Of the sixteen planes that took off that morning, only three from our squadron were able to meet the bombers over Berlin. Those three returned safely to the base. The three missing boys were from the other two squadrons. Weather was very bad over England. I started to let down through the clouds, but when ice formed on my wings, I turned back toward the Channel.

"Emerging from the clouds I flew south, letting down gradually until 500 feet above the Channel, then I turned back to England and flew at 600 feet just below the cloud base.

"Bob was not at Debden when I landed, but I didn't worry, and in fact gave no thought to it even an hour later when I still had no word. Probably he had landed at Martlesham Heath to see J.J. (our buddy, Joseph Jack), and just forgot to call the base. I was still sitting in the dispersal hut when the phone in the intelligence room rang. I heard low talking but the words were indistinct. Mac, the intelligence officer, approached me with a bottle and a glass. At the end of every mission a glass of whiskey was always given to the pilot, if he wished it, to settle his nerves.

" 'Here, Johnny, this is a bonus day. Have another drink.' I gladly accepted the offer of the free drink, but was suspicious of Mac, who didn't look into my eyes as he usually did when he handed a drink to me. His presence suddenly made me uncomfortable.

" 'Somebody's got to tell you, Johnny, and I guess I'm the one. A call just came through from the RAF. Bob's plane crashed at Framlingham. He was still in the cockpit. He'd dead, Johnny.'

"His words hit me like a lightning bolt. It just didn't seem possible—not Bob, my war buddy. After living together for two years, our comradeship had strengthened into a love which for me was even greater than the feeling I had for my own brothers. We had shared everything, clothes, money, and, yes, even girls. I knew his faults and merits just as he knew mine. I cried inwardly, but I didn't break down."

"In my view, the single most important aspect of being a fighter pilot was to want to do it; to be the first to engage, and then to follow with determination. After all, this was like hunting the lion, only this time the lion could shoot back. Still, there was no greater thrill than aerial combat."
—Colonel Walker M. Mahurin, USAF (Ret), formerly with the 56th Fighter Group, 8 USAAF

"In the Royal Air Force we are called 'navigator', but really, we navigate the Tornado between us. I mean, I'm not there with a map... we have a display and my job is more in the tactical environment, working the radar and trying to work out the best way that we're going to kill the enemy guy. I really do everything as part of a team, although both of us can put chaff and flares out if we need to; both of us can decide on which way to turn."
—Flight Lieutenant Martin Harris, No. 43 Squadron, RAF

"Right now [1998]the US Air Force is on the back end of the pendulum swing. They're facing a big crunch over the next couple of years. They cut way back after the end of the Cold War and, with the rest of the down-sizing, the Air Force cut back pilot training and a lot of our squadron strength. Now that the airlines are on a big hiring boom and the economy in the States is going very well, a lot of guys are leaving the Air Force for a variety of reasons. The ops tempo that they have to deal with is one of them. The Air Force is losing more guys than they can produce through their stripped-down pilot training now, so, as a result, they are trying to beef up pilot training. The only way to do that is to get more instructors and the only place to get them is from the front lines, which are already undermanned. It's a vicious circle, with the Air Force trying to cope with the loss of more pilots than they can produce in the short term— the next two or three years. It'll be interesting to see the kind of decisions that the upper echelons, especially the personnel sections, are going to make."
—Major Jonathan Holdaway, USAF, No. 43 Squadron, RAF

During the Korean War, Jack Bolt, a US Marine Corps fighter pilot, wangled an exchange tour with the US Air Force, culminating in a stint with the Oregon National Guard flying F-86s. Initially,

however, he served in Korea with VMF-115. "I got out there about May of '52, flying the F9F-4. I flew ninety-four missions: air-to-ground, interdictions, close-air support, etc. We were down at Po Hang Do. The airfield was called K-3. That tour was coming to an end and, on taking R&R, I made contact with an Air Force squadron commander named George I. Ruddell. He was commanding the 39th Fighter Interceptor Squadron. I showed him I had a hundred hours, not only in the F-86 but also in the F-86F. His was the only squadron of Fs on the field, so I had experience he really needed. Ruddell was friendly towards me and let me fly his birds. I just took some familiarization flights with a few guys.

"I did a second R&R trip that Christmas of '52 and, at the time, Joe McConnell, one of the leading aces in Korea with eight or nine victories, had just been grounded. Ruddell sent McConnell up to teach me some tactics. So I flew two or three flights with him, and he was good. They were just fam hops; he'd had some flight infraction, and Ruddell was punishing him by grounding him. But McConnell was allowed to take test hops and teach me. I made friends with McConnell and he really taught me lots of things. He became the leading ace of the Korean War and was very deserving of the fame that he had. He was killed soon after the war on a test flight at Edwards Air Force Base.

"I put in for an Air Force exchange tour, so the Air Force General sent a wire to the Marine General saying, 'We're willing to have your pilots, but they come up here having never flown the plane, and they present a training burden on our people. But now we have a rare instance of having a pilot who's shown enough initiative to come up here and get checked out, and he's ready to go. Would you mind appointing John Bolt?'

"Well, there was nothing the Group could do; it came down from the Wing. They put me in Ruddell's squadron.

"McConnell became the top ace, and I was flying

Above: German World War II Hauptmann Heinrich Sturm, who shot down 158 aircraft on the Russian Front. Sturm, of IV/JG52, died in a take-off accident on 22nd December 1944 at Czor, Hungary when his landing gear struck a truck. The aircraft turned over, crashed and caught fire.

Right: Lieutenant Colonel James Clark, briefs Mustang pilots of the 4th Fighter Group at Debden in April 1944. Below: Captain Donald Emerson of the 336th Fighter Squadron, 4th Fighter Group, escorting an Eighth Air Force B-17 bomber. Below right: Emerson's girlfriend, Elinor Lindemann. Far right: Captain Emerson, and other 4th Fighter Group pilots, were escorting B-24s to a target near Kassel, Germany on 25th December 1944. His plane was hit by ground fire and was seen to crash-land near the Dutch border with Belgium. He was found dead at the crash site. Far right below: The Donald Duck design for Emerson's P-51 Mustang fighter.

WESTERN UNION   FJ-A
32 Govt   Washington DC
1010pm   Jan 12

Mrs Mabel Emerson
Pembina N Dak

The Secretary of War desires
me to express his deepest
regrets that your son Captain
Donald Emerson was killed in
action on twenty five
December in European area
confirming letter follows

Dunlop Acting the Adjutant
General

Below: Major John F. Bolt
was the only US Marine
Corps fighter ace of the
Korean War. Flying an F-86
Sabre, Bolt shot down six
MiG 15s in three months
while temporarily attached
to the US Air Force. He had
downed twelve Japanese
Zekes in World War II.

on his wing when I first got up there. I was in his flight—Dog Flight—and Ruddell was really nice to me, although he was a very tough guy. He had four or five victories, but the MiGs had quit coming south of the Yalu River, and we weren't supposed to go north. If you went north of the river, it was at the risk of your professional career if you got caught. The Chinese were yelling and screaming about the 'pirates' that were coming over there, but that's where the action was. When McConnell left, I took over the command of Dog Flight, a quarter of the squadron with about twelve pilots.

"On a river-crossing flight, we would take off and go full bore. We'd put those planes at 100 per cent power setting until we got out of combat. They drew 100 per cent all the time, engine life was planned for 800 hours, and we were getting about 550 or so. Turbine blade cracks were developing. Also, we were running them at maximum temperature. You could put these little constrictors in the tailpipe—we called them 'rats'— and you could 'rat 'em up' until they ran at maximum temperature, so they were really hot rods. You'd run your drop tanks dry just about the time you got up there, and if you didn't have a contact, you weren't supposed to drop your tanks. We skinned 'em every time. By the end of the flight, on at least two occasions, I had been to over 50,000 feet in that bird. When it got empty and you still hadn't pulled power back (you were still at 100 per cent), you could really get up there. The MiG-15 could get up there too, to 50,000 feet.

"The 'kill rules' were, if you got seven hits on one (enemy aircraft), they would give you a kill. They didn't torch off at high altitude. They simply would not burn because of the air density. So they would count the incendiary hits on them (we had good gun cameras). They figured that if you got seven hits in the fuselage, the odds were it was dead, and they'd give you a kill. They could count the incendiary hits, and they knew that every third one was an incendiary so, in effect, if you got

three incendiary hits in the gun camera, they would say that it was a dead MiG.

"The salvation of the F-86 was that it had good transonic controls, and the MiG's controls were subsonic. You could cruise at about .84 Mach readily in the F-86. The MiG had to go into its uncontrollable range to attack you, and its stick forces were unmanageable. The kill ratio between the F-86 and the MiG was, to my recollection, eight to one. It was due almost exclusively to the F-86's flying tail, although there were other superior features (the gun package, for example). The MiG's gun package was meant to shoot down B-50 bombers; a 37mm and two 23mm cannons. It was overkill and not very good against fighters. Although the F-86 package was essentially the same as a World War II machine gun, the rate of fire was doubled, and it was a good gun for shooting down fighters.

"Down low, where you were out of that transonic superiority range, we had a G-suit and they didn't. You can fight defensively when you are blacked out, but you can't fight offensively. If you had enough speed to pull into a good 6G turn, you'd go black in 20 to 30 degrees of turn, and they couldn't follow you, blacked out themselves. You've lost your vision—you're still conscious, though you have three to five seconds of vision loss. When you thought you'd gone about as far as you could carry that, you could then pop the stick forward and you'd immediately regain your vision. You'd already started your roll, and they were right there in front of you, every time, because they'd eased off in their turn (they didn't have a G-suit and your G tolerance was twice theirs). So they were right there—they probably overshot you."

"It seemed to me that the best fighter pilots, and those who enjoyed the greater degree of success, were the ones who were quick on the uptake and had a good grasp of the tactical situation as it was developing. They were able to improvise in such

way as to gain the advantage on the enemy or, as my old boss used to say, 'turn a disadvantage into an advantage'. There are, of course, a number of other qualities that go into the matrix to make a good fighter pilot, not the least of which is luck. You can't fulfil the purpose of the fighter pilot, ie. shoot down enemy planes, unless you are in the right place at the right time. Some of the other qualities which, from my observation, were possessed by the better fighter pilots were keen vision, an unselfishness that permitted the individual to be a good team player, an inner calmness, a cool head and a steady hand. But perhaps the most critical of all was self-confidence. If you were to ask all the pilots in a squadron to name the five best pilots in the unit they would all identify the same five guys, but each would include his own name in the top five. I always thought I was one of the top two or three of the forty-five pilots in our outfit."
—Commander William E. Copeland, USN (Ret), formerly with VF-19

Twenty-eight-year-old Flight-Lieutenant Helen Gardiner is currently [1998] the only female front-line fighter pilot in the Royal Air Force. She flies the Tornado F3, with sixteen other pilots and about sixteen navigators of No. 43 Squadron at RAF Leuchars near St Andrews, Scotland.

Others may be coming along in the system, and a few women fly some of the other aircraft in the RAF inventory, such as the Jaguar. But for now Gardiner is unique. Yet, in an occupation where all who practise it are special, she is probably no more—or less—unique than any of the other pilots she flies with on 43.

She was born in Nottingham and came to the RAF through the University Air Squadron [UAS] at Newton. Other women were on the UAS with her in those days, and since then the Air Force has had time to adjust to the idea of women flying fast jets—and flying them in combat.

"When I was at university on the UAS, there were probably a few of the older instructors who were a little bit 'Ooo, never in my day!' sort of attitude, but once people [female pilots] arrived and started going through the system, and these instructors actually saw that we could fly just as well as the next guy, they stopped getting upset about it. There was always the question about fast jets, front line, etc., but I think it's a case of, if you get to this stage you're obviously good enough to fly the jet or you wouldn't have got here in the first place. If you don't accept that this is the job that you do, and [that] you might be sent here, there and everywhere tomorrow at the drop of a hat—then you shouldn't be here, and you probably wouldn't enjoy it anyway. I think people just accept it now quite happily.

"[When I joined 43 Squadron] it was a little bit daunting at first. I can't say it wasn't. But I've been through the training system and been in the RAF long enough to know what the crew room atmosphere is like. By the time I came through the system, the instructors had seen two or three [other female pilots in training]. It was simply a case of 'you-don't-get-through-unless-you're-good-enough'. When I first arrived on the squadron, I don't think I had any opposition whatsoever. Nobody came up saying 'I don't want you to be here'. There were probably some people who were a little bit wary and interested to see how I'd get on, but there were a few guys here who were instructors of mine going back through training, so they knew whether I was good enough or not. The fact that they were here, and obviously passed it on that 'she wouldn't be here unless she was good enough', is a nice way to arrive."

At Leuchars, 43 Squadron maintains two Tornado F3s and two crews on continuous Quick Reaction Alert [QRA] status, an aspect of Cold War policy. All the pilots and navigators are scheduled in a rotation for a regular twenty-four-hour QRA shift. When on QRA, the crews 'live' out on the aircraft

Below: Commander William E. Copeland, USN (Ret), became and ace on 24th October 1944 when, flying an F6F Hellcat fighter, he shot down three Japanese bombers, a Nell, a Betty and a Lily during the Battle of Leyte Gulf, Philippines in World War II. His confirmed score—6 victories.

Right: F3 Tornado pilot Flight-Lieutenant Helen Gardiner of No. 43 Squadron, RAF Leuchars, Scotland. Right centre: Gulf War US Air Force F-16 pilots discussing the last mission at their Saudi Arabia air base. Below: A No. 43 Squadron Tornado F3 in its "HAS" or hardened aircraft shelter at RAF Leuchars. Until the Eurofighter becomes operational early in the next century, the F3 remains the primary front-line fast jet fighter of the Royal Air Force.

Left: US Air Force F-15C Eagles during Operation Desert Storm in 1991. This pair shows their three long-range external fuel tanks as well as AIM-7M and AIM-9M missiles. 120 Eagles, Cs and Ds, participated in Gulf War operations. The Eagle was the premier air-to-air combat fighter of the War and was extremely efficient in its assigned job of gaining and holding air supremacy. Below: USAF fighter pilots head for their aircraft on a Saudi air base during the Gulf War.

To be alone, to have your life in your own hands, to use your own skill, single-handed, against the enemy.

It was like the lists of the Middle Ages, the only sphere in modern warfare where a man saw his adversary and faced him in mortal combatr, the only sphere where there was still chivalry and honour. If you won, it was your own bravery and skill; if you lost, it was because you had met a better man. You did not sit in a muddy trench while someone you had no personal enmity against loosed off a gun, five miles away, and blew you to smithereens—and did not know he had done it! That was not fighting; it was murder. Senseless, brutal, ignoble. We were spared of that. As long as man has limbs and passions he will fight. Sport, after all, is only sublimated fighting, and in such fighting, if you don't "love" your enemy in the conventional sense of the term, you honour and respect him. Besides, there is, as everybody who has fought knows, a strong magnetic attraction between two men who are matched against one another. I have felt this magnetism, engaging an enemy scout three miles above the earth. I have wheeled and circled, watching how he flew, taking in the power and speed of his machine, seen him, fifty yards away,

dispersal area in quarters that provide basic comforts. At each end of the building sits a HAS, or hardened aircraft shelter, containing a flight-ready F3 jet, which is connected by an electric umbilical to a power source. The aircraft and crew are required to be airborne within a maximum of fifteen minutes when ordered up. Gardiner describes a QRA assignment: "If any Russian aircraft decide to come round into UK airspace, we would go out and effectively escort them outside—which used to happen quite often. Now, it happens very rarely, but we're still here [on QRA] in case anything else happens where we are required. The last time we saw any Russian aircraft come round was eighteen months ago, when I actually got scrambled to go up and intercept them. We had been up a couple of days before and had been turned away at the boundary. It tends to be when there is a big naval exercise going on, and it is usually their maritime patrol aircraft that come round to have a look. Obviously, with the cutbacks that they've got over there, it doesn't happen that often. The second time we got airborne, they kept coming and ended up just to the north of Shetland. We actually launched both of our Q aircraft. We went up, tanked just off the North Sea, headed all the way and intercepted them. There were two Mays (maritime patrol aircraft) and we followed them down to low level and shadowed them from behind, just keeping an eye on them. We had an E3 airborne at the time—just by chance—and we were talking to them about what the [Russian] aircraft were doing. We followed the Russians for about a quarter of an hour. Then our other aircraft turned up, along with our tanker which is based at Brize Norton near Oxford. We went to the tanker as we were getting short on fuel, and the other jet took over the shadowing until the Russians actually went back out of UK airspace. It was nice to be there and do a launch for real."

Asked if she wants to remain in the Air Force as a

fighter pilot for the duration, she replied: "Yes. At the moment I'm having a great time. I love the job, and the plane, to me, is great. I really do enjoy flying it, but the thought of Eurofighter [the coming replacement for the Tornado] is something completely different. Obviously, you're going to single-seat at that point, but it's more of a fighter than the F3, and I would love to fly it."

Would she like to fly a Spitfire or one of the other great old fighters sometime? "Oh yeah. A lot of it back then was purely flying ability, and actually a very raw machine that you had to throw around the sky trying to get into a position to be able to fire the weapon against the enemy. Now it's all wizardry, computers, and things that go on that I don't know how they work. It's a completely different animal from what it was forty, fifty years ago. You're more of an operator, as far as actually working the kit, especially for the navigator in the back."

"The changes men have seen in this last century are hardly to be believed. It seems we exult in handing over every aspect of our lives to the idols we have created. Computers book in our arrival and programme our departure, pass our news, govern our business, and titillate our leisure. Loudspeakers shout a sermon from our pulpits:
'I believe in atomic fission, breaker of heaven and earth!' And as for aircraft, which in my youth trembled like living things, if they trembled today, [they] would be sent back to servicing for overhaul.

"We shrug and say: It can't be helped; but what captain of a transport aircraft, hedged in with courses, corridors, controls, does not long to send them all to the devil, vault into the cockpit, flip a switch and take off, bareheaded, into the wind? Perhaps not, perhaps the breed has changed—but I know which I would choose!"

When Cecil Lewis, fighter pilot and gifted writer of the Great War, wrote those words, he reflected the view of many—if not most fliers—who yearn for a simpler time and a purer flying experience.

Picture Credits The photographs by Philip Kaplan are credited: PK. Photographs from the author's collections are credited: AC. Jacket front: US National Archives; jacket back: John McQuarrie. Jacket back flap: Margaret Kaplan. PP2-3: PK, PP4-5: USAF Museum, P6: PK, P7: USAF Academy Library, P8: San Diego Aero-Space Museum, P9: AC, P10: Imperial War Museum, P11: AC, P12; left (both): USAF Academy Library, P12; top: San Diego Aero-Space Museum, P13; both: San Diego Aero-Space Museum, P14; both: AC, P15; left: Imperial War Museum, P15; right: PK, PP16-17: San Diego Aero-Space Museum, P18; left: AC, P18; right: Imperial War Museum, P19; top: PK, P19; bottom: San Diego Aero-Space Museum, P19; top right: Jagdstaffel 712 'Richthofen', German Air Force, P19; centre right: Mike Herrling, PP20-21: Robert Dance, P21: AC, P22-23: AC, P25, top left: courtesy John F. Bolt, P25; top right: courtesy E.R. Hanks, P25; bottom: courtesy Michael O'Leary, PP26-27: Frank Wootton, P28; top: courtesy Elvin Lindsay, P28; bottom: AC, P30; both: PK (goggles courtesy Keith Braybrooke), P31: PK, P32; top: courtesy William Hess, P32; bottom: courtesy Urban Drew, P34; left: courtesy William Hess, P34; right: PK, P35: AC, P36; top: AC, P36, bottom: courtesy Antonin Vendl, P37: Mark Brown-USAF Academy Library, P38: Courtesy Oscar Boesch, P39: AC, P40: AC, P41: AC, P42, US National Archives, P43: PK, P44: courtesy Michael O'Leary, P46; top: courtesy Gidi Livni, P46; bottom: John McQuarrie, P49: RAF Museum, P50; all: PK, P52; top: courtesy Horst Petzschler, P52; bottom: courtesy John Strane, P55; top" courtesy Jack Ilfrey, P55; bottom: US National Archives, P56: British Film Institute, P58; top left: AC, P58; top right: Imperial War Museum, P58; bottom: AC, P59: PK, P60: courtesy William Sharpe and John Phegley, P63; top left: AC, P63; top right and bottom: USAF Academy Library, P64: AC, P66: PK, P67: PK, P68; top left: AC, P68; top right: courtesy Dennis Wrynn, P68; bottom: courtesy Michael O'Leary, P69: AC, P70; top: PK (plate courtesy M. O'Leary), P70; bottom: Cliff Knox, P71: AC, P73: AC P75: Cliff Knox, PP76-77: Vickers, P78:AC, P79; top: PK, P79; bottom: AC, P80; top left and right: courtesy Stanley Vejtasa, P80; bottom: AC, PP82-83: John McQuarrie, P84: Courtesy Merle Olmsted, P86: Courtesy Tom Harris, P87: courtesy Stanley Vejtasa, P88: Merle Olmsted, P89: AC, P90: PK, PP92-93: courtesy Michael O'Leary, P93: AC, P94: PK, P95: courtesy Iven Kincheloe and Warren Thompson, PP96-97: courtesy Dennis Wrynn, PP98-99: Cliff Knox, P100: PK, P101: AC, PP102: courtesy Merle Olmsted, P103: James Frary, P104: courtesy Merle Olmsted, P105: centre-courtesy William O'Brien, P105: right through 112; all: courtesy Merle Olmsted, P113: Toni Frissell-Library of Congress, P114: courtesy Michael O'Leary, PP114-115: PK, P116: courtesy Merle Olmsted, P118: courtesy Oscar Boesch, PP118-119: Robert Bailey, P121: AC, P122; both: USAF Academy Library, P123: PK, P124: Michael O'Leary, P125: courtesy Edward Wendorf, P126: AC, P127: PK, PP128-129: AC, PP130-131: PK, P132: AC, P134; top: USAF Academy Library, P134; bottom: PK, P135; top: courtesy Hans-Joachim Jabs, P136: AC, PP138-139: John McQuarrie, P139; right: PK, PP140-141: San Diego Aero-Space Museum, P142; both: courtesy Frantisek Perina, P143: courtesy Michael O'Leary, P144; top left: courtesy Walter Konantz, P144; top right: courtesy Michael O'Leary, PP144-145: courtesy John Cunnick, P146: AC, P147: courtesy William Hess, PP148-149: AC, P150; left: PK, P150; right: Imperial War Museum, P151: PK, PP152-153: courtesy Gidi Livni, P154: courtesy Frank Hearell, P155: Toni Frissell-Library of Congress, P156; top: courtesy Frantisek Fajtl, P156; bottom: courtesy Günther Rall, P158; left: courtesy Bruce Porter, PP158-159: USAF Academy Library, P161: Cuthbert Orde, P162: US National Archives, P164: AC, P166; top: courtesy Kath Preston, P166; bottom: PK, P167; both: courtesy Michael O'Leary, P169; top: courtesy Robert F. Cooper, P169; bottom: AC, P170; both: USAF Academy Library, P171: courtesy Michael O'Leary, PP172-174: AC, PP176-178: Mark Brown-USAF Academy Library, PP179-180: AC, P182; top: PK, P182; bottom: L. Moon-courtesy William Hess, P183-AC, P184; top: courtesy Robert Strobell, P184; bottom: courtesy Walter Konantz, P186: AC, P187; all: USAF Academy Library, P188: Mark Brown-USAF Academy Library, P190; top: PK, P190; bottom: courtesy Harvey Mace, P191: AC, P193: courtesy Carlton Smith, P194: PK, PP195-197; all: courtesy Douglas Warren, P198; top: PK, PP198; bottom-200: courtesy Douglas Warren, PP202-203; all: PK, P204 and P207: courtesy Douglas Warren, P206: AC, PP208-209: courtesy Jack Ilfrey, P210: Mark Brown-USAF Academy Library, P211: John McQuarrie, P213; top: courtesy William Laubner, P213, bottom: courtesy Tunis J. Lyon, P214; top: AC, P214; bottom: courtesy Jack Ilfrey, P215; both: PK, P217: AC, PP218-220; all: AC, P222; both: PK, P224: AC, P226; both: AC, P228; top: courtesy Paul Riley, P228; bottom: AC, PP230-231; both PK, P232: courtesy Merle Olmsted, P234: John McQuarrie, P235: AC, P237: AC, P239: USAF Academy Library, P240: AC, P241; top left: courtesy Wayne Rosenoff, P241; top right: AC, P241; bottom: courtesy Art Roscoe, P242: AC, P243: AC, P244: AC, P245: courtesy Gitte Sturm, P246; top: AC, P246; bottom left: courtesy Malcolm Bates, P246; bottom right: courtesy Sandra Merrill, P247: AC, PP248: courtesy John F. Bolt, P249: courtesy William E. Copeland P250; top left: PK, top right: USAF Academy Library, bottom: PK, P251; both: USAF Academy Library, P254: PK.

Acknowledgements I am particularly grateful to the following people for their generous help in the development of this book: Robert Bailey, Malcolm Bates, Nick Berryman, Oscar Boesch, Eric Brown, Robert Floyd Cooper, John Cunnick, Randy Cunningham, Hargi Danko, Al Deere, Dale Donovan, James H. Doolittle, Gary Dunlop, Lou Fleming, Betty Frey, Royal Frey, Helen Gardiner, Stephen Grey, Peter Grosserhode, Roger Hall, Mark Hanna, Ray Hanna, Mike Herrling, Bill Hess, Jonathan Holdaway, Jack Ilfrey, Markus Isphording, Yasuho Izawa, Neal Kaplan, Margaret Kaplan, Cliff Knox, Walter Konantz, Edith Kup, John Lamb, Charles Lawson, Alan Leahy, Gidi Livni, Grant Lucas, Harvey Mace, Walker M. 'Bud' Mahurin, Judy McCutcheon, Rick McCutcheon, Bert McDowell, John McQuarrie, Tony Mead, Sandra Merrill, John Nesbitt-Dufort, William O'Brien, Michael O'Leary, Merle Olmsted, William Overstreet, Geoffrey Page, Horst Petzschler, John Phegley, Steve Pisanos, Günther Rall, Duane Reed, Robert L. Scott, Eudora Seyfer, William Sharpe, E.A.W. Smith, Stephan Stritter, Robert Strobell, Peter Townsend, Bill Vincent, Ray Wagner, Douglas Warren, Frank Wootton, Dennis Wrynn, Jan Zdiarsky and Hub Zemke.

I greatly appreciate the kind help and inspiration of: Paddy Barthropp, George Behling, Robert Best, D-Reg Bhasin, Donald Blakeslee, John Bolt, Keith Braybrooke, Bob Brown, Mark Brown, Kazimierz Budzik, Piers Burnett, Shimon Camiel, John Carroll, James Cain, George Chandler, Kim Chetwyn, Albert P. Clark, Evelyn Clarke, Pat Collier, Richard Collier, Ed Copeland, Edward Crew, Don Cummings, Kate and Jack Currie, Glenn Duncan, Dewey Dumford, Frantisek Fajtl, Francis Fleming, Paul Fletcher, Sir Christopher and Lady Foxley-Norris, Ella and Oz Freire, Adolf Galland, Peter Gallante, William Ganz, Ed Giller, Geoffrey Goodman, James Goodson, Jim Gray, Grover C. Hall, E.R. Hanks, Martin Harris, R.C. Harris, Tom Harris, Frank Hearell, George Hollowell, Hans-Joachim Jabs, Jack Jenkins, George N. Jensen, Herta Krull, James Kyle, Hasso Kortge, William Laubner, Furio Lauri, Lionel Leventhal, Elvin Lindsay, Robert Littlefield, Tunis Lyon, Roy Macintyre, Richard May, Carroll W. McColpin, Tilly and James McMaster, Hamilton McWhorter, Thomas Moore, H. Moranville, Ray Mull, Mary Lou Neale, John Nichol, Doug Nicholson, Robert Nishiyama, Leo Nomis, Mark Pearce, Frantisek Perina, John Peters, Dan Rehm, Paul Riley, Art Roscoe, Wayne Rosenoff, David Soper, Lloyd Stovall, John Strane, Louis Sturdivan, Gitte Sturm, Jack Taylor, Ann Turley-George, Dickie Turley-George, Franklin Troup, Stanley Vejtasa, Antonin Vendl, David Wade, A.S. Walker, Dirk Weigmann, Edward Wendorf and Denis Wissler. Special thanks to the following for permission to use their texts: Nick Berryman, John Bolt, Tony Mead, H.B. Moranville, Merle Olmsted, William Overstreet, Günther Rall, E.A.W. Smith, Robert Strobell, Peter Townsend, Bill Vincent and Douglas Warren.

eyeing me, calculating, watching for an opening, each of us wary, keyed up to the last pitch of skill and endeavour. And if at last he went down, a falling rocket of smoke and flame, what a glorious and heroic death! What a brave man! It might just as well have been me. For what have I been spared? To die, diseased, in a bed! Sometimes it seems a pity.

—from *Sagittarius Rising* by Cecil Lewis

What are the emotions of a fighter pilot during combat? Obviously each individual is different but in some respects there are similarities. Winston Churchill said, "Nothing in life is so exhilarating as to be shot at without result." This was especially true of the World War II air war for the fighter pilot. At times, he could almost be mesmerized by the slow motion effect of the "white or red golf balls" going by in a pyrotechnic display of personal deadliness, coming from a camouflaged gun emplacement. The sight of one's own gunfire making flashing strikes, raining destruction on an enemy plane or a locomotive below. Seeing the target and the ground about it being torn asunder by one's own gunfire creates a high that no drug can equal.

—from *Double Nickel-Double Trouble* by R.M. Littlefield

"There's one coming down in flames—there, somebody's hit a German—and he's coming down completely out of control—a long streak of smoke— ah, the man's baled out by parachute— he's a Junkers 87 and he's going slap into the sea...and there he goes... s-s-smash...Oh boy, I've never seen anything so good as this—The RAF fighters have really got these boys taped.
—Charles Gardner reporting for the BBC at Dover, 10th July 1940

below: The British 1939-45 European Campaign star with Battle of Britain clasp.

Grateful acknowledgment is made to the following for permission to reprint previously published material:
ERIC BROWN: Excerpts from *Wings of the Luftwaffe* and *Wings of the Navy*, published by Airlife Publishing Ltd.. Reprinted by permission.
HARPER COLLINS: Excerpt from *One of the Few*, by J.A. Kent.
RANDY CUNNINGHAM: Excerpt from *Fox Two*, published by Warner Books. Reprinted by permission.
JAMES H. FARMER: Excerpts from *Celluloid Wings*, by James H. Farmer, published by Tab Books.
GREENHILL BOOKS: Excerpts from *Sagittarius Rising*, by Cecil Lewis. Reprinted by permission of Greenhill Books on behalf of Fanny Lewis.
ROGER HALL: Excerpt from *Clouds of Fear*, published by Coronet Books.
ROBERT M. LITTLEFIELD: Excerpts from *Double Nickel-Double Trouble*, by Robert M. Littlefield, published by R. M. Littlefield. Reprinted by permssion.
MACMILLAN GENERAL BOOKS: Excerpts from *The Last Enemy*, by Richard Hillary. Reprinted by permission.
WALKER M. MAHURIN: Excerpts from *Honest John*, by Walker M. Mahurin, published by G. P. Putnam's Sons.. Reprinted by permission.
SANDRA MERRILL: Excerpts from *Donald's Story*, by Sandra D. Merrill, published by Tebidine. Reprinted by permission.
JOHN NESBITT-DUFORT: Excerpt from *Scramble*, by John Nesbitt-Dufort, published by Speed and Sports Publications Ltd.
W.W. NORTON & COMPANY: Excerpts from *Serenade To The Big Bird*, by Bert Stiles.
GEOFFREY PAGE: Excerpt from *Tale of a Guinea Pig*, by Geoffrey Page, published by Corgi. Reprinted by permission.
PENGUIN BOOKS LTD: Excerpts from Team Tornado by John Peters and John Nichol, Copyright (c) 1994 by the authors.
RANDOM HOUSE: Excerpts from *The Look of Eagles*, by John T. Godfrey, Copyright (c) 1958 by Random House, Inc. Copyright renewed 1986 by Robert E. Godfrey and John T. Godfrey. Reprinted by permssion of Random House, Inc.
EUDORA SEYFER: For *Remembering Raydon*, by Eudora Seyfer, published by Mature Outlook magazine.
VINTAGE-RANDOM HOUSE: Excerpt from *The Fatal Englishman*, by Sebastian Faulks. Reprinted by permission.
WIND CANYON PUBLISHING, INC: For *Dogfight Over Paris*, by Henry C. Woodrum. Reprinted by permission.
All reasonable efforts have been made to contact those believed to hold copyright for previously published material reprinted in *Fighter Pilot*. We apologize for any inconvenience caused to copyright holders whom we have been unable to contact.

Bibliography
American Fighter Aces Association, *American Fighter Aces Album*, 1978.
Barker, A. J. *The Yom Kippur War*, Ballantine Books, 1974.
Bekker, Cajus, *The Luftwaffe War Diaries*, Doubleday & Co., Inc.., 1968.
Brown, Eric, *Wings of the Luftwaffe*, Airlife Publishing Ltd., 1993.
Brown, Eric, *Wings of the Navy*, Airlife Publishing Ltd., 1987.
Beedle, J., *43 Squadron, A History of the Fighting Cocks*, 1916-1984, Beaumont Aviation Literature, 1966.
Bishop, Edward, *The Battle of Britain*, George Allen and Unwin Ltd. 1960.
Campbell, Christopher, *Aces and Aircraft of World War 1*, Treasure Press, 1981.
Clancy, Tom, *Fighter Wing*, Berkley Books, 1995.
Collier, Richard, *Eagle Day*, Pan Books, 1968.
Costello, John, *Love Sex & War*, Collins, 1985.
Craven, Wesley F. and Cate, James L., *The Army Air Forces in World War II, Volume Six-Men and Planes*, The University of Chicago Press, 1955.
Deere, Alan, *Nine Lives*, Hodder & Stoughton, 1959.
Deighton, Len, *Fighter*, Ballantine Books, 1977.
Emde, Heiner, *Conquerers of the Air*, The Viking Press, 1968.
Farmer, James H., *Celluloid Wings*, Tab Books, 1984.
Faulks, Sebastian, *The Fatal Englishman*, Vintage, 1997.
Freeman, Roger A., *Mighty Eighth War Diary*, Jane's, 1981.
Galland, Adolf, *The First and the Last*, Ballentine Books, 1954.
Gallico, Paul, *The Hurricane Story*, Four Square Books, 1967.
Gardner, Brian, *The Terrible Rain*, Methuen, 1966.
Gelb, Norman, *Scramble*, Michael Joseph, 1986.
Gilbert, James, *The Great Planes*, Ridge Press, 1970.
Gunston, Bill, *Fighter!*, Parragon, 1997.
Gurney, Gene, *Five Down and Glory*, Ballantine Books, 1958.
Hall, Grover C., Jr., *1000 Destroyed*, Putnam, 1946.
Hall, Roger, *Clouds of Fear*, Coronet Books, 1975.
Haugland, Vern, *The Eagle Squadrons*, Ziff-Davis Flying Books, 1979.
Hess, William and Ivie, Thomas G., *Fighters of the Mighty Eighth*, Motorbooks International, 1990.
Hillary, Richard, *The Last Enemy*, Macmillan & Co., Ltd., 1950.
Ilfrey, Jack, with Reynolds, Max, *Happy Jack's Go-Buggy*, Exposition Press, 1979.
Infield, Glenn, *Big Week!*, Pinnacle Books, 1974.
Johnson, J. E., *The Story of Air Fighting*, Arrow Books, 1985.
Johnson, J. E., *Wing Leader*, Ballantine Books, 1957.
Kelly, Orr, *Hornet*, Airlife Publishing Ltd., 1990.
Kent, J. A., *One of the Few*, Corgi, 1975.
Laming, Tim, *RAF Fighter Pilot*, W H Allen, 1991.
Lee, Asher, *Goering-Air Leader*, Hippocrene Books, 1972.
Lewis, Cecil, *Sagittarius Rising*, Greenhill Books, 1993.
Littlefield, Robert M., *Double Nickel-Double Trouble*, R.M. Littlefield, 1993.
Lloyd, Ian, *Rolls-Royce-The Merlin at War*, Macmillan Press Ltd., 1978.
Mahurin, Walker M., *Honest John*, G. P. Putnam's Sons, 1962.
Mason, F. K., *Battle Over Britain*, Alban Books.
McManners, Hugh, *Top Guns*, Network Books, 1996.
McQuarrie, John, *Canadian Fighter Pilot*, McGraw-Hill Ryerson, 1992.
Merrill, Sandra D., *Donald's Story*, Tebidine, 1996.
Morris, Danny, *Aces & Wingmen, Vol. 1*, Aviation Usk, 1989.
Morse, Stan, *Gulf Air War Debrief*, Aerospace Publishing, 1991.
O'Leary, Michael, *Mustang, A Living Legend*, Osprey, 1987.
O'Leary, Michael, *United States Naval Fighters of World War II*, Blandford Press, 1980.
O'Leary, Michael, *USAAF Fighters of World War Two*, Blandford Press, 1986.
Olmsted, Merle, *The 357th Over Europe*, Phalanx, 1994.
Olmsted, Merle, *The Yoxford Boys*, Aero Publishers, Inc., 1971.
Page, Geoffrey, *Tale of a Guinea Pig*, Wingham Press, 1991.
Peters, John and Nichol, John, *Team Tornado*, Penguin Group, 1994.
Quill, Jeffrey, *Spitfire*, Arrow Books, 1985.
Robinson, Derek, *Piece of Cake*, Alfred A. Knopf, 1984.
Sakai, Saburo, with Caidin, Martin and Saito, Fred, *Samurai*, Four Square Books, 1966.
Scutts, Jerry, *Fighter Operations*, Patrick Stephens Limited, 1992.
Speer, Frank, *Wingman*, Frank Speer, 1993.
Toliver, Raymond F., and Constable, Trevor J., *Fighter Aces*, The Macmillan Company, 1965.
Townsend, Peter, *Duel of Eagles*, Simon and Schuster, 1970.
Townsend, Peter, *The Odds Against Us*, William Morrow and Co., 1987.
Turner, Richard E., *Mustang Pilot*, New English Library, 1975.
Wagner, Ray, *Mustang Designer*, Orion Books, 1990.
Wagner, Ray, *The North American Sabre*, Doubleday and Company, 1963.
Wagner, William, *Ryan the Aviator*, McGraw-Hill, 1971.
Williams, Peter, and Harrison, Ted, *McIndoe's Army*, Pelham Books, 1979.
Willis, John, *Churchill's Few*, Michael Joseph, 1985.
Yeager, Chuck, and Janos, Leo, *Yeager*, Bantam Books, 1985.
Zemke, Hub, with Freeman, Roger A., *Zemke's Wolf Pack*, Orion Books, 1988.